D0934778

PLAYS OF CONFESSION AND THERAPY

THE WASHINGTON STRINDBERG
Translations and Introductions by Walter Johnson

4495317\5918532

PT
9812
T5
E5
1979

Plays of

Confession and Therapy

TO DAMASCUS, I
TO DAMASCUS, II
TO DAMASCUS, III

by AUGUST STRINDBERG

Translations and Introductions
by Walter Johnson

· DISCARDED

University of Washington Press
Seattle and London

FE 22 '82

Copyright © 1979 by the University of Washington Press
Printed in the United States of America

All rights reserved. No part of this publication may be reproduced or transmitted in any form or by any means, electronic
or mechanical, including photocopy, recording, or any information storage or retrieval system, without permission in writing from the publisher.

No performance or dramatic reading of the contents of this
book may be given without the written permission of the publisher. Inquiries should be addressed to the University of Washington Press, Seattle, Washington 98105.

Library of Congress Cataloging in Publication Data
Strindberg, August, 1849–1912.
  Plays of confession and therapy.

  (The Washington Strindberg)
  Includes bibliographical references.
  CONTENTS: To Damascus, I.—To Damascus, II.—
To Damascus, III.
  I. Johnson, Walter Gilbert, 1905–   II. Title.
PT9812.T5E5 1978   839.7'2'6   78–20962
ISBN 0–295–95567–8

Contents

Illustrations

Erland Josephsson of the Royal Dramatic Theater and Nils-Gustaf Hildeman of the Swedish Institute have generously supplied these illustrations.

PLAYS OF CONFESSION AND THERAPY

Preface

A QUARTER OF a century ago a colleague and I prepared a rough translation of the Damascus trilogy, each of us doing alternating scenes. For reasons both academic and personal, nothing was done to put that translation into publishable form, and it has rested untouched in a carton since then. The translation here published is entirely new. It is the product of one hand, and has been done in keeping with the principles applied in earlier volumes of the Washington Strindberg: to present an American version, faithful to the original and expressed in language as idiomatic and natural as the original Swedish.

The plays are among the most important of Strindberg's works. They are as autobiographical as *The Son of a Servant* (1886–87), that fabulous four-volume study of the development of one human being from a realistic or Strindbergian naturalistic point of view. Even dry-as-dust supposedly objective autobiographies cannot escape subjectivity, and *The Son of a Servant*—theoretically an objective case study of the author himself in terms of heredity, environment, time, and chance—is, like practically everything Strindberg wrote, much more subjective than these. Strindberg dealt with both external and inner factors in reporting on his development. In so doing, he tried to abide by the basic principles of case reporting, and, by making far greater use of subjectivity, even in *The Son of a Servant* produced a more subtly naturalistic study of himself than Strindberg scholars have been willing to acknowledge. Perhaps "supernaturalistic" is the term one should use for *The Son of a Servant.*

At the end of his Inferno period (1894–97), Strindberg did not have to be disturbed by the theoretical demands of realism-naturalism. The autobiographical volumes, *Inferno* (1897) and *Legends*

3

(1897–98), are admittedly autobiographical and unabashedly subjective in keeping with the changes that had taken place in the 1890s in both theory and practice. While these autobiographical volumes are primarily concerned with inner experiences, they do not neglect experiences involving "outer" matters that can be taken in by the five senses and that have to do with heredity, environment, time, and chance. It is this remarkable combination of objectivity and subjectivity which probably helps account for the great interest that psychologists, psychiatrists, and others who are fascinated by human nature and the human condition have taken in Strindberg's works from the time they first appeared.

The Damascus trilogy is Strindberg's deliberate attempt to put into dramatic and essentially poetic form his Inferno experiences, which led him from what might now be called agnosticism and would-be atheism through conversion to faith in what probably should be called Strindbergian Christianity. But even though his emphasis had shifted to subjectivity his conditioning to the demands of realism-naturalism never permitted him to neglect external and objective factors.

It is by means of this remarkable combination that Strindberg created what he called his dream plays and in so doing changed the course of development of both modern drama and modern theater. One way of saying this is that he dared to disregard the popular insistence on at least superficial verisimilitude in serious stage productions by insisting on what he believed to be a far more important verisimilitude—the inner life with its failures to abide by the rules and regulations of, say, external reality. In the Damascus plays, Strindberg put into dramatic form for stage presentation the kind of material that has concerned lyric poets throughout the history of humankind.

I have called this volume *Plays of Confession and Therapy* because that is precisely what they were supposed to be and what they are. Strindberg passed through harrowing experiences in the 1890s which led to his personal conviction of sin and attempts at coming to terms not only with what he calls the Powers and the Invisible One but also with his fellow human beings. His attainment of an appreciably stable faith which, in spite of recurring doubt and backsliding, permitted him to put up with himself and other human beings for the rest of his days, also enabled him, in his final years, to make an amazingly extensive and influential contribution to literature, theater, and his world in general.

The Damascus plays are confessional in the sense that Strindberg presents detailed testimony about his own life and personality, his own record as a rebel, and his ultimate conversion and reluctant submission. As every Strindberg scholar knows, Strindberg was fascinated by himself and what happened to him, externally and inwardly. He probably deliberately extended his areas of experience through such faculties as his imagination in order to have material to exploit in his creative writing, and there is no question that he used his writing for therapeutic purposes. The world is the richer for his doing just that.

WALTER JOHNSON

The Damascus Trilogy

FOR SOMEONE AS familiar with the Bible and as conscious of self as Strindberg, it was not surprising that he saw himself as a modern parallel to St. Paul. As he says in his autobiographical volumes, he had been exposed from childhood on to the teachings of both the high-church national Church of Sweden his father preferred and the low-church pietists his mother and his stepmother favored, and he found the Christian emphasis on such matters as the sinfulness of the individual, God's constant awareness of each human being, and the existence of individuals chosen for very special missions fascinating and appropriate for himself.

For anyone not familiar with Strindberg as a modern Saul/Paul converted on the way to his Damascus, careful reading of *The Son of a Servant, Married* (or, as one translator puts it, *Getting Married*, 1884, 1886), *A Madman's Defense* (1887), and *Inferno* should serve to remedy that ignorance. In the process, the reader will discover the nature of Strindberg's conversion from atheism or, as a later generation might say, agnosticism to syncretism or Strindbergian Christianity. The reader will discover, too, the combination of neurotic states, developing from his early childhood and culminating in his Inferno period (1894–97), which were based on such factors as these: (1) Strindberg's conviction that he had had an unusually unhappy childhood, adolescence, and teen-age period, an early life marked by fears, feelings of insecurity, lack of affection and understanding, and conviction of personal worth, even superiority; (2) the pietistic conditioning of his early years (conviction of sin, guilt feelings, ambivalent faith—a religion of black and white, either damnation or sanctification in a life beyond this, ideas supported in the Bible and not denied by the Church of Sweden, into which

7

he was confirmed in early adolescence); (3) the direct conflict of
that conditioning with the intellectual discipline of his teens and
early manhood: Naturalism with its rejection of blind faith, holding
up doubt and questioning as the supreme virtues in the only life
we know and can have. Among the many conflicts these last two
factors led to was his attitude toward human sexuality, which disturbed Strindberg, fascinated, and, on occasion, repelled him: on
the one hand, the Pauline ideal of repression, sublimation, and
strict control, on the other, "healthy" expression of one's sexuality;
or, in other words, essential rejection of one's body versus frank
and delighted acceptance of it.

Reading everything Strindberg wrote before *Inferno,* one would
probably conclude that Strindberg's concept of his role as a writer
was not unlike that of Saint Paul as a religious writer. Just as Paul
had ready answers for his fellowmen's problems, Strindberg thought
of himself as the rebel, the prophet of truth, whose task was (1)
to analyze the individual, the relationship of the individual with
other individuals, the individual in the community, and the individual and the universe; and (2) to present his findings so that society
could be remade and the world set right for man in terms of Truth,
Work, and Love.

Read *Master Olof* (1872) and discover how very idealistic the
rebel and the prophet of truth is. Read *The Red Room* (1879) and
discover that the rebel and the prophet of truth can look at his
world and present its flaws in horrifying detail. Read *Married*(*Getting
Married,* 1884, 1886), and *A Madman's Defense* (1887) and discover
that the human institution which Strindberg considered primary
in importance was usually, perhaps always, as flawed and imperfect
as any women's liberation extremist would insist it is. These few
works and *The Son of a Servant* should make it clear that Strindberg
had an appreciable measure of faith in the idea that society and
man could be improved, if not perfected, and that he had a definite
role in bringing about that improvement.

The reward for Strindberg's efforts was neither general approval
nor general appreciation but humiliating rejection, condemnation,
and even ridicule. That an individual conditioned to extreme scru-
tiny, analysis, and judgment, even condemnation, of himself could

undergo agony as a result of the usually unfavorable reception of what he wrote is probable and believable, and no other dramatist has succeeded more brilliantly in putting that agony into a form remarkably well suited for the modern theater that had developed in our century. The concern for both outer and inner experience, and careful selection of detail, the close attention to effective arrangement and presentation, and the techniques that Strindberg's expressionist disciples were to exploit are all there.

Students of modern drama and modern theater cannot afford to disregard the Damascus trilogy. Out of these plays came not only the pattern for such dramas as Strindberg's *A Dream Play* and the chamber plays but also the inspiration for some of the finest plays other dramatists have created in this century.

In this volume each of the three plays will be considered individually, partly because each can stand by itself and partly because Strindberg did not initially plan to write a trilogy. *To Damascus, I* was composed in less than two months in early 1898, apparently without any thought of writing a companion play. But within a few months, realizing that he had still more about his conversion and its development to exploit in dramatic form, Strindberg wrote *To Damascus, II*, which deals with many things still weighing on his conscience: his concern for his children, his second divorce, his failure as a goldmaker, and his inability to avoid doubt and backsliding. By early 1901 he knew only too well that he had not succeeded in forsaking the world; he had yielded to the temptation of entering into a third marriage and was quickly to find that this, too, was imperfect. Perhaps that fact above all others led to Strindberg's conclusion, in moments of meditation, that complete withdrawal from the world might well be his final answer. That, at any rate, is the final statement of *To Damascus, III*, which he apparently completed in the late summer of 1901.

Introduction to
'To Damascus, I'

IT MAY BE that all human beings have road-to-Damascus experiences somehow reminiscent of those recorded in chapter 9 of Acts. Certainly Strindberg believed that he had as much right as Saul/Paul to consider his conversion from atheism (or agnosticism) to Strindbergian Christianity (his own brand of providentialism and syncretism) the result of definite intervention and pressure from God (the Eternal One). During his Inferno Period (1894–97), he had kept careful account of his experiences, real and imagined, in his daybook, and after the period was pretty well over, he had selected and arranged the material recorded in his daybook and his memory in *Inferno, Legends,* and *Jacob Resists,* autobiographical reports on those experiences, with emphasis placed on what had taken place as changed in his mind, his thought, and his imagination, and complemented by recollections of his pre-Inferno years (1849–93) as recorded in his thoroughly human and therefore imperfect memory.

In early 1898, and probably late in 1897 when he returned to the writing of drama for the stage, Strindberg knew he had extremely rich material to exploit, and, apparently, he had no hesitation about adopting a form different from those used by any of his predecessors or contemporaries in the theater. In the explanatory note prefaced to *A Dream Play* (1901), he gave this definition of his own term for the new drama, "dream play":

> In this DREAM PLAY as in his earlier dream plays *To Damascus,* the author has tried to imitate the disconnected but apparently logical form of a dream. Everything can happen; everything is possible and likely. Time and space do not exist; on an insignificant basis of reality

the imagination spins and weaves new patterns: a blending of memories, experiences, free inventions, absurdities, and improvisations.

Strindberg frequently commented on the difficulty of separating waking and dreaming, knew every kind of dream experience, and made use of every one of them in his thinking and his writing. In *To Damascus, I,* it is as if all his life had taken on qualities of genuine nightmare when he deliberately or unintentionally recalled, unconsciously or consciously distorted, and artistically presented his childhood, youth, manhood, and particularly his suffering in the middle 1890s.

What we get in the Damascus plays is a series of images, more rather than less connected with the nuances of experience rejected by the Unconscious in favor of distilled and distorted matters out of what from a naturalistic point of view may seem false—reverie or daydreaming, flashes of insight or vision, delusions, hallucinations, or deliberate extension through speculation and imagination. Perhaps the revelation of the workings of hidden forces within a human being in their intricate and apparently inseparable connections may, as Strindberg thought in 1898, give a truer and more accurate representation of life than the realism and naturalism of the 1880s had been able to do.

While Strindberg does not imitate the dream proper in *To Damascus, I* or its two companion plays, he does exploit possibilities of laying hold on the strange intimations of truth to be got at before self-control and logical thinking take over. Hence the unexpected connections and fantastic implications that combine with the reporting of actuality to make the Damascus trilogy and many later Strindberg plays, as Eric Bently observes in *Playwright as Thinker* (New York: Reynal & Hitchcock, 1946), p. 221, maintain an interplay between the outer and inner, objective and subjective, naturalistic and nonnaturalistic. Certainly the Damascus plays are a fusion of "reality" and dream states.

Carl E. W. L. Dahlström, who saw in many of the post-Inferno plays from *To Damascus, I* to *The Great Highway* (1909) the source, in both form and substance, of expressionistic drama, provides a set of characteristics that are useful in gaining an understanding and appreciation of these plays. As you read or reread *To Damascus,* it would be well to keep in mind these characteristics: the out-and-out subjectivity, the deliberate effort to give an expression of the inner man, the search for the elemental and spiritual, the use of lyricism and musical counterpoint, the search for divinity, and the unqualified insistence on the dignity of human beings.

What Strindberg himself had to say is highly important. On March 8, 1898, he wrote to his then friend and literary adviser, Gustaf af Geijerstam:

> Here is a play, about whose value I haven't the slightest idea.
> If you think it is good, have the theater people take a look at it.
> If you think it's impossible, put it away in Gernandt's safe.
> But the manuscript remains my property.
> It's my only savings account.

Five days later:

> Only a few changes may be made in the play. Its plan must not be touched, for that provides the symbol of "the pilgrimage"!

On March 17:

> You're the first person to have read it, and your comment pleased me. Yes, it's certainly a poem with a terrifying half reality back of it. The art lies in its composition, which symbolizes *"Gentagelsen"* [the repetition] Kierkegaard talks about; the action goes forward to the Asylum; there it collides with "the pricks" and is kicked back, the pilgrimage, the repetition, the humiliations; so it begins again at the same place; the game ends where it began. Perhaps you haven't noticed how the scenes unfold in reverse from the Asylum which is the backbone of the play and which winds up and encloses the action. Or like a snake which bites itself in the tail.

To Damascus, I does indeed tell a story, but it tells it in a way far more reminiscent of the medieval *Everyman* than of Strindberg's own stories of marital hell in, for example, *The Father* (1887) or *Creditors* (1888). The story is that of a pilgrimage of a sinful Rebel from Arrogance, Pride, and Selfish Ambition to a measure of Humility, from Doubt and Lack of Faith to Faith in the Eternal One and the Powers. It is a passion play in that it tells a story of personal suffering, and a morality play in that it can be considered a rather unusual object lesson for those who would lead a Christ-like life. But, perhaps above all, it should be considered a drama that deals primarily with inner reality, and only secondarily with that outer reality our senses can appreciably take in and apprehend. From a religious point of view, it surely presents a valid reality.

For projecting inner reality into visible outer forms, Strindberg chose a modified version of Christ's progress to the cross, that is, seven instead of fourteen stations. The following diagram illustrates his pattern:

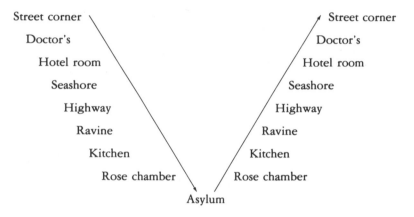

The Stranger's *via dolorosa* consists of his progress from station to station of humiliation as he, defiantly proud, undergoes torments and anguish while he considers himself justified in his suspicions and resentments—until, that is, he reaches the asylum, "The Good Help," where, beside himself and for a time pretty well stripped of his egotism, he begins to experience what is generally called conversion: that state of depression and self-reproach called self-conviction of sin followed by self-condemnation and testimony and at least tentative acceptance of faith in the Creator and other higher Powers.

The reversal of stations or scenes is one of the finest illustrations of Strindberg's conviction that everything repeats itself *(Allt går igen)* and may be said to illustrate Strindberg's genuine insight into human beings whose nature prevents absolute and sustained faith but brings forth doubt and backsliding and at best led Strindberg (and perhaps Everyman) to the verge of Resignation and Humility. The return to the street corner, the point of departure for the pilgrimage, is, as it were, a result of chastening by the Eternal Ones and the Powers. It is a curiously effective use of the *via dolorosa*, as anyone who has been fortunate enough to see a production of *To Damascus, I* can testify: not least impressive is that his progress to his cross deserves dignified treatment even though he may be exposed to jeering, belittling, and ridicule just as Christ was on His way to Calvary.

Before we turn to a detailed examination of the play, it might be well to note that the "characters" are not the characterless characters, the dynamic and complex human beings, that Strindberg had discussed at some length in the Preface to *Lady Julie* (1888) and created in most of his pre-Inferno and certainly in his historical dramas. The "characters" in *To Damascus* and his other dream plays are closer to the types he mentions in the Preface to *Lady Julie* than to the characterless characters; they are reminiscent of the personifications in, say, *Everyman*. They are synthetically rather than analytically presented aspects of human beings seen in one role or from one point of view. The names suggest and emphasize that fact.

The Stranger *(Den okände,* the unknown, the one who is not known), for example, is not only unknown by others but does not really know himself. Surely, too, the Beggar, the Confessor, and the Tempter are nothing more or less than other aspects of the central "character" as exposed to humiliation through having to accept charity from others in order to survive, as exposed through self-conviction of sins to crushing moral demands and humiliating self-condemnation, and as led into doubt and intellectual speculation challenging the Creator and His Powers.

The very vagueness and shadowiness of all these figures and the other "characters" in *To Damascus* suggest that Strindberg was not only implying the difficulties of taking hold of any one human being but also presenting his view that all human beings are essentially alike, though each may insist on his own measure of individuality. Thus, the Lady perceived by the Stranger, the Beggar, the Confessor, and the Tempter is not, for example, Frida Uhl Strindberg, but the embodiments as it were of each one's apprehension of that one woman or that one person.

Strindberg had attempted to give full reports on individual dynamic and complex characters in such pre-Inferno plays as *The Father, Lady Julie,* and *Creditors* by "looking" at each of them from various points of view, both "at rest" and in action. He had insisted that human beings are not static and simple but "characterless," that is, extremely difficult to analyze in depth, understand fully, and characterize definitely. In a curious way what he does with his "characters" in *To Damascus* is not a contradiction of what he had said about human beings in the Preface to *Lady Julie* but rather a shift in approach and emphasis. In *To Damascus* the approach is synthetic "insight," not analytic penetration, and the emphasis is on impression at a given point in time, under certain circumstances, and in certain states, not on cold logical judgment of what the senses report. It is as if human beings, including himself, were seen by the Stranger through a glass darkly.

The extremes in this approach and presentation are probably best illustrated in the opening scene on the street corner and the Asylum scene. In the former, the man and the woman do have a reality that could be that of, say, *The Father;* they are there in flesh and blood, ready as it were to be examined and analyzed through the reports of the senses. In the asylum scene, however, Strindberg's opening stage directions must be kept in mind: these figures who resemble the Lady, the Doctor, and so forth but are not the Lady, the Doctor, and so forth nevertheless have a "terrifying reality":

> STRANGER: . . . But that crowd over there—what do they look like? Are they real?
>
> ABBESS: If you mean actual, they have a terrifying reality: that you see them in a strange way probably depends on your still being feverish or . . . on something else.
>
> STRANGER: But I seem to know them, the whole lot! And I see them as if in a mirror; and they only pretend to eat. . . . Is it a play that's being put on? . . . There's a couple resembling my parents, but only slightly.

In varying degrees every "character in *To Damascus* takes on actuality as conceived in the mind of the Stranger. The dream plays present "reports" that are strikingly different from the reports presented in a play like *The Father.* And the former may be even more terrifyingly real than the latter.

The Stranger "sees" himself in strange ways just as the others "see" him, themselves, and each other. In nightmarish fashion the Stranger splits into the religious moralist, the Confessor, who presents demands and threats rather than comfort and compassion; the Beggar, who presents claims of cultural achievement even while he is engaged in humiliating activity; Caesar, who is considered mad even though he may be the one who is sane and who in humiliating fashion serves as a reminder of early error and present misjudgment; the Tempter, who in diabolic and fascinating fashion exercises the gifts of doubt and brutally frank articulation; and the "unknown self," who searches for answers beyond rebellion.

One may justifiably say that there are two key scenes: the Asylum scene, which Strindberg himself called the backbone of the play, and the second Kitchen scene, which clarifies the religious basis of the play. While the Asylum scene has a realistic enough setting, the dining room of a religious institution with its very "natural" equipment, the primary emphasis is placed on matters that are not primarily perceived by the senses. The Stranger has been delirious and, when beside himself, has condemned himself and "seen" his victims. But the Stranger is now "awake" and highly disturbed by what he "sees" and "hears." In his stage directions Strindberg states that the veiled figures with their waxen yellow and corpselike faces are not what they seem; they are ghostlike in appearance and gestures; they are, one might say, projections of the sources of the Stranger's guilt feelings (the people he has "corrupted" through his writings, his neglect of his parents, his cruelty to his sister, his desertion of his first wife, his failure to support his children, and so forth). Whether one considers the Confessor another human being or the Stranger's moral self making ethical demands and passing judgment, the effect is the same: the Stranger has been exposed to a harsh moral standard and has been found deplorably wanting. No other scene in *To Damascus, I* is so emphatically "dreamlike."

The very combination of outer reality and inner reality has made the production of *To Damascus, I,* and its two companion plays, challenging for Swedish and foreign directors from its first première at the Royal Dramatic Theater in November 1900 through Ingmar Bergman's production in 1974. As the modern theater has acquired technical resources not available at the turn of the century, it has been possible to exploit more and more effectively the magic nuances of *To Damascus,* for example, through the contemporary use of stage lighting to bring out the shadowy, the suggestive, and the imaginative elements.

What has fascinated students of Strindberg as well as Swedes in general perhaps as much as the rich stage possibilities and the universal implications of the journey to Damascus is the fact that every part of the play rests firmly on Strindberg's own experiences, actual, imagined, or deliberately induced. A close comparison of the details of his autobiography as revealed in *The Son of a Servant, A Madman's Defense, Inferno, Legends,* and *Jacob Resists,* or as interpreted in biographies such as Martin Lamm's, demonstrates Strindberg's deliberate use of personal matter, selected, changed, and arranged for creative use and, consciously or unconsciously, for self-therapy. Interesting as all this must be for any student, a more important fact is that, in writing *To Damascus, I,* Strindberg created a play that has universal human application.

To Damascus, I[1]

Characters [2]

THE STRANGER
THE LADY
THE BEGGAR
THE DOCTOR
THE [DOCTOR'S] SISTER
THE OLD MAN
THE MOTHER
THE ABBESS
THE CONFESSOR
MINOR CHARACTERS *and* SHADOWS

Settings

ACT I: *The street corner. At the Doctor's.*
ACT II: *A hotel room. By the sea. On the highway. In the ravine. In the kitchen.*
ACT III: *In the Rose Chamber. The asylum. The Rose Chamber. The kitchen.*
ACT IV: *In the ravine. The highway. By the sea. The hotel room.*
ACT V: *At the Doctor's. The street corner.*

ACT I

THE STREET CORNER

A street corner with a bench under a tree. The side doors of a small Gothic church can be seen as well as a post office and a café with chairs outside. The post office and the café are closed.

The notes of a funeral march³ can be heard approaching and then fading away.

The STRANGER *[literally, the Unknown]⁴ stands on the edge of the sidewalk apparently wondering which direction he should take. The clock in a church tower strikes: first four times for the quarter hours in a higher note, then three for the hour in a lower.*

The LADY *enters, greets the* STRANGER, *wants to pass him but stops.*

STRANGER: There you are! I almost knew you'd come.

LADY: So you did call me—well, I felt you did.—But why are you standing here on the street corner?

STRANGER: I don't know—I suppose I have to stand somewhere while I'm waiting.

LADY: What are you waiting for?

STRANGER: If I only could put it into words.—For forty years I've been waiting for something—I think it's called happiness—maybe it's only the end of unhappiness.—Listen to that terrible music! Listen! Don't go, I beg you, don't go, for I'm terrified when you go!

LADY: My friend! We met for the first time yesterday; we talked for four hours all by ourselves. You aroused my sympathy, but you mustn't take advantage of my kindness because of that.

STRANGER: That's true, I shouldn't. But I beg you: Don't leave me alone. I'm in a strange city, haven't a friend, and the few people I know seem worse than strangers—I'd like to say enemies.

21

LADY: Enemies everywhere! Everywhere alone! Why did you leave your wife and children?

STRANGER: If I only knew!—If I even knew why I exist, why I'm standing here, where I'm going, what I should do.—Do you think some people are damned even here on earth?

LADY: No, I don't.

STRANGER: Look at me!

LADY: Haven't you ever had any joy in life?

STRANGER: No, and when I've seemed to have some, it was only a trap for tricking me into going on with the misery of living. When I did catch the golden fruit occasionally, it was poisoned or rotten.

LADY: What's your religion?—Forgive me for asking.

STRANGER: This: when it gets unbearable, I'll go my way.

LADY: Where?

STRANGER: To extinction. The fact I have—death in my hand gives me an unbelievable sense of power . . .

LADY: Good heavens, you're playing with death!

STRANGER: As I play with life—I was a writer, you know. In spite of my innate seriousness I've never been able to take anything really seriously, not even my own great misfortunes—and there are moments when I doubt life has more reality than my poems. *(The funeral procession can be heard, psalm melodies: De profundis.)* 5 Now they're back again! I don't know why they should be marching around here on the streets!

LADY: Are they the ones that terrify you?

STRANGER: No, but they irritate me . . . it's as if things were bewitched . . .—It's not death, but loneliness that terrifies me, for in loneliness one *meets* somebody. I don't know if it's someone else or myself I sense, but in loneliness one isn't alone. The air gets closer, the air sprouts, and beings start developing, beings who are invisible but are sensed and have life.

LADY: You've noticed that?

STRANGER: Yes, I've noticed everything for quite a while. I didn't use to, though, when I observed only things and happenings, forms and colors, but now I see thoughts and meanings. Life, which used to be nothing but nonsense, has taken on meaning,

and I detect a purpose where I used to see only a chance.—So
when I met you yesterday, I got the idea you were sent either
to save me or destroy me.

LADY: Why should I destroy you?

STRANGER: Because that was your assignment.

LADY: I haven't any thoughts like that . . . and since you arouse
my sympathy most of all—yes, I've never seen another human
being, whose very appearance makes me ready to weep . . .
What do you have on your conscience? Have you committed
some terrible crime that hasn't been discovered or punished?

STRANGER: You may well ask! Not that I have more crimes on
my conscience than others who are still at liberty————yes, one:
I wasn't willing to be fooled by life!

LADY: One has to let himself be fooled more or less to be able
to live.

STRANGER: That seems almost a duty, and as I wanted to avoid
that . . . or there may be another secret in my life that I don't
know about . . . you know, there's a story in my family that
I'm a changeling. 6

LADY: What's that?

STRANGER: It's a child the elves 7 have exchanged for a newborn
human being.

LADY: Do you believe that?

STRANGER: No, but I think there's something to it, figuratively.—
When I was a child, I cried all the time and didn't seem to
feel at home in life. I hated my parents as they hated me; I
couldn't stand discipline or convention or rules; the only thing
I longed for was to get out to the forest and the sea.

LADY: Have you ever had visions?

STRANGER: Never! But I've often seemed to notice that two kinds
of beings control my destiny: the one gives me everything
I want, but the other stands alongside throwing dirt on the
gift so it's worthless and I don't want it. It's really true I've
got everything I've wanted in life—but all of it's been worthless.

LADY: So you've got everything and are dissatisfied anyway.

STRANGER: That's what I call the curse . . .

LADY: Don't curse!—But why haven't you extended your wishes beyond this life, to a place where there isn't any dirt?

STRANGER: Because I've doubted there is anything beyond this life.

LADY: What about the elves then?

STRANGER: Why, that's only a story!—But why don't we sit down on the bench over there?

LADY: All right, but what are you waiting for?

STRANGER: For the post office to open, really—there's a letter for me that's been forwarded time and again without reaching me. *(They sit down)* Tell me something about yourself! (*The* LADY *crochets*)

LADY: There's nothing to tell.

STRANGER: Strange—I'd prefer to think of you as impersonal and nameless—why, I don't know your full name—I'd like to give you a name—let me think what it's to be! Yes, your name's to be Eve. 8—*(Gestures towards the wings)* Fanfares. *(The funeral march can be heard)* There's the funeral march again!—Now I'll give you an age, for I don't know how old you are . . . From now on you're thirty-four and born in 1864.—Now your character, for I don't know that either. You'll get a very good one, for your voice sounds like my dead mother's—by mother I mean an abstract idea mother, pronounced "mother," for my mom never caressed me, but I remember she beat me. Yes, you see, I was brought up in hate. Hate! Hard against hard! An eye for an eye! Look at the scar here on my forehead. That's from an axe my brother wielded—I had knocked out a front tooth of his with a stone. I didn't attend my father's funeral, because he had me thrown out when my sister got married. I was born illegitimate 9 in the midst of bankruptcy, while the family was in mourning for an uncle who had committed suicide. Now you know my family. That kind of tree, this kind of fruit! In all I've barely escaped from fourteen years of hard labor in prison. So I have reason to be grateful to if not exactly happy about . . . the elves.

LADY: I like to hear you talk, but don't touch the elves—that hurts me very, very much!

STRANGER: Frankly speaking, I don't believe in them, but just the same they show up every time. Aren't the elves damned spirits who haven't been saved? Well! Then I, too, am a troll child. I thought once I was close to salvation—through a woman, but I've never been more mistaken, for that began the seventh hell.

LADY: How you talk! Yes, you're one of the damned, but you're not going to remain one.

STRANGER: You mean the tolling of bells and holy water would give me peace . . . I've tried that, but it only got worse. What happened to me then is what happens to the devil when he sees the sign of the cross. Let's talk about you!

LADY: There's no need!—Has anyone ever accused you of misusing your gifts?

STRANGER: They've accused me of everything. No one else in my city was as hated as I, no one so despised. I had to come and go—alone! If I entered a public place, people moved five feet away from me. If I wanted to rent a room, it was already taken. Ministers condemned me in the pulpit, teachers in the classroom, and parents in the homes. Once the church council wanted to take my children from me.[10] Then I lost my head and raised my fist against heaven.

LADY: Why are you hated so?

STRANGER: I don't know! Well, I couldn't stand seeing people suffer—so I said, and wrote: Set yourselves free—I'll help. And I said to the poor: Don't let the rich bleed you white! and to woman: Don't let man suppress you! And—what was worst of all probably—I said to the children: Don't obey your parents when they're unjust. The results: well, they're absolutely incomprehensible—both the rich and the poor, men and women, parents and children all turned against me. And there followed illness with poverty, begging with dishonor, divorce, court trials, exile, isolation, and now last of all—Do you think I'm insane? [11]

LADY: No, I don't!

STRANGER: Then you're certainly the only one who doesn't! But I appreciate that all the more!

LADY (gets up): Now, I have to leave you . . .

STRANGER: You, too!

LADY: But you mustn't stay here.

STRANGER: Where shall I go?

LADY: Go home and work.

STRANGER: I'm no worker, I'm a writer.

LADY: I didn't want to hurt you, and you're right: Writing is a gift which is given but which can be taken away. Don't let yourself lose it!

STRANGER: Where are you going?

LADY: On an errand only . . .

STRANGER: Are you religious?

LADY: I'm nothing.

STRANGER: All the better—then you're going to be something. I wish I were your blind old father that you led about at fairs to sing,[12] but the unfortunate thing is I can't get old—that's how it is with the children of elves—they don't grow, just get a large head and scream . . . I wish I were someone's dog so I could follow him and never be alone—get a little food occasionally, a kick now and then, a pat once and blows of the whip twice—

LADY: Now I have to go! Good bye!

STRANGER *(absentmindedly):* Good bye!

(He remains sitting on the bench, takes off his hat, wipes his forehead. Then he sketches with his cane in front of him [in the sand]).

(*The* BEGGAR *enters. Extremely strange appearance; picking up things in the gutter.*)

STRANGER: What are you picking up, Beggar? [13]

BEGGAR: In the first place: what do you mean? And I'm no beggar—have I asked for anything?

STRANGER: I beg your pardon—it's rather hard to judge people by their appearance.

BEGGAR: Yes, I'm sure it is. For example: Can you guess who I am?

STRANGER: No, I neither can nor want to. In a word: I'm not interested.

BEGGAR: Who can be sure of things like that ahead of time? The interest generally comes later—when it's too late. *Virtus post nummos!*

STRANGER: What! You know Latin, Beggar?

BEGGAR: See—you're getting interested. *Omne tulit punctum qui miscuit utile dulci.* I'm the one who has succeeded in everything I've undertaken, for the reason I've never done anything. I'd like to call myself Polykrates [14]—the fellow with the ring. You know, I've always got everything I've wanted out of life? But I've never wanted anything, so tired of success I threw away the ring. Now that I'm getting on in years, I'm sorry I did, so I'm looking for it in gutters, but as the search may take a long time, I don't sneer—for want of the gold ring—at some discarded cigar butts.

STRANGER: I don't know if you're being sarcastic or if you're not all there.

BEGGAR: Well, I don't know that either.

STRANGER: But you know who I am?

BEGGAR: Not in the least, and I'm not interested.

STRANGER: The interest generally comes later . . . Well, listen to that: you're fooling me into repeating what you said. Why, that's just like searching for other people's cigar butts! Ugh!

BEGGAR *(lifts his hat):* And you don't want to smoke my butt?

STRANGER: What sort of scar's that on your forehead?

BEGGAR: A close relative gave me that.

STRANGER: No, now I'm getting frightened. May I touch you to see if you're real? (*He feels the* BEGGAR*'s arm*) Yes, you're real!— Won't you stoop to accepting a small monetary gift in return for your promise to look for Polykrates' ring in another part of town? *(Hands him a coin) Post nummos virtus* . . . No, now I'm repeating what you said again. Go! Go!

BEGGAR: I'll go, but this is entirely too much. Look! I'll give you three-fourths back—then we won't owe each other anything but a gift between friends!

STRANGER: A friendly gift! Am I your friend?

BEGGAR: At least I'm yours—when you're alone in the world, you shouldn't be too choosy.

STRANGER: By way of parting let me toss "mind your manners" at you.

BEGGAR: Fine, fine; but when we meet again, I'll have something just as good to toss at you. *(Goes)*

STRANGER *(sits down; sketches [in the sand] with his cane):* It's Sunday afternoon! The long, gray, dull Sunday afternoon when families have eaten sauerkraut and roast beef with boiled potatoes. And the old people are taking a nap; the young playing chess and smoking; the servants have gone to evening services; and the stores are shut. Oh this long deadly afternoon, the day of rest, when the mind stops functioning, when it's just as impossible to run across a person you know as to get into a tavern . . .

(*The* LADY *returns; has a flower on her bosom.*)

STRANGER: There! It's strange I can't open my mouth without being contradicted right away.

LADY: You're still sitting here?

STRANGER: Sitting sketching in the sand here or somewhere else seems to be all the same, just so I write in the sand.

LADY: What are you writing? Let me see!

STRANGER: Eve, 1864, I think . . . No, don't step on it . . .

LADY: What would happen if I did?

STRANGER: A misfortune for you, and for me.

LADY: And you know that?

STRANGER: Yes! And I know the Christmas rose you are wearing is a mandrake.[15] As a symbol it means malice and slander, but in medicine it was used in the old days to cure insanity.

LADY (*hesitates*): As medicine?

STRANGER: Naturally!—Have you read the books I've written?

LADY: You know I've read them, that I'm grateful to you for setting me free, for making me believe in human rights and human dignity!

STRANGER: Then you haven't read the latest books!

LADY: No, and if they're like the earlier ones, I don't want to know anything about them!

STRANGER: That's good! And promise me you'll never look into any book I write.[16]

LADY: Let me think that over first!—Yes, I promise!

STRANGER: Good! But don't break this promise! Remember Bluebeard's wife, when curiosity fooled her into opening the forbidden room . . .

LADY: Do you notice how your demands are already like Bluebeard's?[17] And how you've long since forgotten I'm married, that my husband's a doctor, and that he admires you, so his home is open to you whenever you wish to come?

STRANGER: I've done everything I could to forget all that and have succeeded so well it isn't real for me any more.

LADY: Well then, do you want to go home with me tonight?

STRANGER: No! But do you want to go with me?

LADY: Where?

STRANGER: Out into the world, anywhere at all. I don't have any home, just a suitcase; I sometimes do have money, but rarely— it's the only thing life is stubborn about giving me, probably because I haven't really insisted on it.

LADY: Hm!

STRANGER: Well, what are you thinking about?

LADY: I'm amazed I'm not insulted by your joke.

STRANGER: Joke or not—it's all the same to me.———There! The organ's playing; then the tavern will soon be opened.

LADY: It's true you drink?

STRANGER: A lot! Wine makes my soul leave my body; I fly out into space, see what no one has sensed; and hear what no one has heard . . .

LADY: And the next day?

STRANGER: I have beautiful pangs of conscience; experience the saving feeling of guilt and regret; enjoy my physical suffering while my soul hovers like smoke about my forehead; it's like being between life and death when my spirit feels it has lifted its wings and can take flight if it wants to.

LADY: Come to church with me, only for a little while; you won't have to listen to any sermon, only the beautiful music of vespers.

STRANGER: No, not to church! It disturbs me, makes me feel I don't belong there, that I'm damned, and that I can't ever get in any more than I can get to be a child again.

LADY: You know all that already?

STRANGER: I've come that far; it seems to me as if I'm lying chopped to pieces in Medea's kettle [18] simmering: Either I'll end up in the soap factory or rise up rejuvenated out of my own soup. It all depends on Medea's skill.

LADY: That sounds like an oracle. We'll see if you can't become a child again!

STRANGER: Then it would have to begin by the cradle—and the right child come back!

LADY: Precisely!—But wait for me here while I go into St. Elizabeth's Chapel. If the café were open, I'd ask you nicely: Don't drink! But fortunately it's closed.

(*The* STRANGER *sits down again; sketches in the sand.*)

(*Six brown-clad funeral pallbearers and guests come on stage. One carries a flag with the insignia of the carpenters and a brown mourning veil on it; another one a large broadaxe with evergreen twigs wound about it; a third is carrying a pillow with a speaker's gavel on it. They stop in front of the café and wait.*)

STRANGER: May I ask who the dead man was?

GUEST I: He was a carpenter! (*He makes a sound like a watch*)

STRANGER: A real carpenter or one of those who sit in wooden walls ticking away? [19]

GUEST II: Both, but usually one of those sitting in walls ticking away—What's their name?

STRANGER (*to himself*): Rascal! Now he wants to fool me into saying "death watch," but I'll answer something else to annoy him. Do you mean a goldsmith?

GUEST II: No, I don't! (*The ticking of the watch can be heard again*)

STRANGER: Are you trying to frighten me or is the dead man performing miracles? If that is it, may I tell you I'm neither frightened nor do I believe in miracles. All the same I do find it strange you're mourning in brown. Why not in black? It's inexpensive, attractive, and practical!

GUEST III: In our simplicity it's black to us, but if your grace says so it's brown to you.

STRANGER: I can't deny you're a mighty strange crowd, and I feel an uneasiness I'd prefer to blame on drinking too much Moselle yesterday. But if I say that's evergreen twigs on the axe, you'll tell me it's—well, what is it?

GUEST I: It's a grapevine.

STRANGER: I suspected it wouldn't be evergreen twigs. There! They're opening the tavern—at last!

(*The café is opened. The* STRANGER *sits down at a table and is served wine. The funeral guests sit down at the other tables.*)

STRANGER: The dead man was a happy man, I see—the mourners get drunk after the sacred act.

GUEST I: Well, he was a useless person who couldn't take life seriously.

STRANGER: And who most likely misused strong drink, too?

GUEST II: Yes, he did.

GUEST III: And he let others support his wife and children.

STRANGER: That was badly done. I suspect that's why he's getting such a fine tribute from his friends.—Please don't bump into my table while I'm drinking.

GUEST I: When I'm drinking, it's right . . .

STRANGER: When I do, yes, for there's a big difference between you and me.

(GUESTS *murmur.*)

(*The* BEGGAR *enters.*)

STRANGER: There's the Beggar who picks up things again!

BEGGAR (*sits down at a table and orders wine*): Wine!—Moselle!

PROPRIETOR (*comes out with a bulletin board*): Please leave! You won't be served anything, since you haven't paid your taxes. Yes indeed—here's the court's decision and your name and your age and your description.

BEGGAR: *Omnia serviliter pro dominatione!* I'm a free man with academic training—I didn't pay my taxes since I didn't *want* to become a representative.—Moselle!

PROPRIETOR: And you'll get a free trip home to the municipal poor house if you don't leave—at once!

STRANGER: Couldn't you men settle the matter elsewhere? You're disturbing the customers!

PROPRIETOR: Yes, but you're to witness I've gone about this properly . . .

STRANGER: Well, I think the whole thing's extremely painful, and even if a man doesn't pay his taxes—hm—he certainly has the right to enjoy the little pleasures of life.

PROPRIETOR: So . . . you're one of those going about setting scoundrels free of their responsibilities!

STRANGER: No, now this has gone too far! Don't you know I'm a famous man?

(PROPRIETOR *and* GUESTS *laugh.*)

PROPRIETOR: Infamous maybe! Listen, if the details on this notice don't jibe: thirty-eight years old, brown hair, moustache, blue eyes; no regular job; unknown income; married, but has deserted his wife and children; known for subversive views about political questions; and gives the impression he is not in full control of his senses . . . That fits!

STRANGER *(gets up, pale and crushed):* What is this?

PROPRIETOR: My soul, I think it did fit!

BEGGAR: Maybe it's he, not I!

PROPRIETOR: It looks like it! I think you fellows could take each other by the arm and be off!

BEGGAR (*to the* STRANGER): Come on—let's go!

STRANGER: You and I!—This is beginning to look like a plot!

(The bell in the church tower rings; the sun comes out and lights up the rose window above the entrance, which opens, revealing the interior of the church; organ music and the hymn "Ave Maris Stella" are heard.) [20]

LADY *(comes out of the church):* Where are you? What are you doing? Why did you call me again? Like a child clinging to a woman's skirts!

STRANGER: Now I am afraid. Things are happening that can't be explained naturally.

LADY: Why, you weren't afraid of anything, not even death.

STRANGER: No, not of death, but of the—other thing! The unknown!

LADY: My dear, give me your hand and I'll lead you to the doctor! You are sick! Come!

STRANGER: Maybe so. But tell me one thing first. Is this a carnival or is it real?

LADY: They're undoubtedly real in their way . . .

STRANGER: But that beggar! He's surely a nasty person. Does he really resemble me?

LADY: Yes, if you keep on drinking, you'll be like him. But go into the post office and get your letter. Then you're to come with me.

STRANGER: No, I won't go to the post office. The letter contains only documents about the trial,[21] I suspect.

LADY: But if it didn't?

STRANGER: Then there'd be only bits of malice.

LADY: Do as you wish. No one avoids his fate. Just now I feel as if higher powers [22] had held a hearing about us and had come to a decision.

STRANGER: You, too! Just now I heard the gavel fall, the chairs shoved back from the table, and the servants sent out . . . oh, this anguish . . . No, I won't come with you.

LADY: What have you done to me . . . I couldn't feel reverent in the chapel; a candle on the altar went out; and a cold wind brushed my face just when I heard you calling me.

STRANGER: I didn't call; I just longed for you . . .

LADY: You're not the weak child you pretend to be; your powers are unbelievably great—I'm afraid of you . . .

STRANGER: When I'm alone, I'm as weak as a paralytic, but when I get hold of another human being, I become strong! Now I want to be strong—so I'll go with you!

LADY: Do, and you'll probably be able to set me free from the werewolf! [23]

STRANGER: Is he a werewolf?

LADY: That's what I call him . . .

STRANGER: Good! Then I'm with you: to fight with trolls, free princesses, slay werewolves—that's living!

LADY: Come, my liberator!

(She pulls her veil down over her face, kisses him hastily on his mouth, and hurries out.)

(The STRANGER stands amazed and silenced—for a moment.)

(A loud chord in several parts of women's voices approaching screams can be heard from within the church. The lighted rose window turns dark quickly; the tree above the bench shakes; the funeral guests get up from their places and stare up at the sky as if they were seeing something unusual and terrifying.)

(The STRANGER hurries out after the LADY.)

[CURTAIN]

AT THE DOCTOR'S

A yard, enclosed by three row houses, all of them wooden houses with tile roofs. Small windows in all these houses. To the right glass doors and a porch. To the left outside the windows a rose hedge and beehives. In the middle of the yard a woodpile in the form of an oriental cupola; next to it a well. Above the middle row, protrudes the top of a walnut tree. In the right corner a gate to the orchard.

Next to the well a large turtle. To the right stairs down to the entrance to the wine cellar. An ice box and a garbage can. Outside the porch tables and chairs.

SISTER *(comes from the porch with a telegram):* Now misfortune has struck your house, Brother!

DOCTOR: When hasn't it?

SISTER: But this time—Ingeborg is coming home, bringing—guess who!

DOCTOR: Wait a minute! I know, I've sensed it for a long time, and have longed for it. I've admired that author, learned from him, and have wanted to know him. Now he's coming, you say! Where did Ingeborg get hold of him?

SISTER: In town, apparently; in the literary circle most likely.

DOCTOR: I've often wondered if that man's my schoolmate with a similar name. I wish he weren't, for there was something fatal about that youngster—he ought to have been able to develop his fatal talents unbelievably in a generation's time.

SISTER: Don't let him come into your house. Go away—prevent a visit with him.

DOCTOR: No, one can't escape one's destiny . . .

SISTER: You, who've never bowed down before anything, are crawling before the foolish notion you call fate.

DOCTOR: Life has taught me that—I've wasted time and energy struggling against what can't be avoided.

SISTER: But why do you let your wife run about compromising herself and you?

DOCTOR: You know why. When I released her from her engagement, I offered her a life of freedom from the prison she had been in. Besides I couldn't love her if she obeyed me or if I could order her about.

SISTER: And so you're your enemy's friend.

DOCTOR: There, there!

SISTER: And you let her drag home the man who's going to destroy you. If you knew how infinitely I hate that man!

DOCTOR: I know, I know! His latest book [24] is despicable, but it shows he's not quite balanced mentally.

SISTER: That's why they should have put him away in an insane asylum . . .

DOCTOR: Several people have said that, but I can't see he has crossed the line . . .

SISTER: Because you're eccentric yourself and have a wife who's absolutely crazy.

DOCTOR: I can't deny maniacs have always interested me very much, and what's queer is at least not ordinary . . . *(A steamboat whistle blows)* What was that? Someone screamed!

SISTER: You're nervous—it was only the steamboat. . . . But I beg you: Go away!

DOCTOR: I think I'd like to, but it's as if I were nailed down . . . when I stand here, I can see his portrait in my study . . . The sunlight throws a shadow on it distorting his whole figure so he looks like . . . That was nasty. Do you see whom he looks like?

SISTER: He's like the devil!—Run away!

DOCTOR: I can't!

SISTER: But defend yourself at least . . .

DOCTOR: I used to! But this time it feels as if a storm were approaching. How many times I've wanted to move but haven't been able to! It's as if the ground were iron and I a magnetic needle . . . and if misfortune comes, I won't have chosen it myself . . . Now they came in through the gate!

SISTER: I didn't hear anything!

DOCTOR: But I, I can hear! And see, too, now! It *is* my childhood companion. He pulled a trick in school . . . I got the blame and was punished. But he got the nickname Caesar—I don't know why!

SISTER: And this man . . .

DOCTOR: Yes, life's like that!—Caesar!

LADY *(enters):* Hello, dear! I have a precious guest with me.

DOCTOR: That's what I heard. He's welcome!

LADY: He's in the guest room tidying up.

DOCTOR: Are you satisfied with your conquest?

LADY: I think he's the unhappiest person I've ever seen!

DOCTOR: That's saying a lot!

LADY: Yes, enough and more for everyone.

DOCTOR: That's certain. But, Sister, won't you show him in? *(She goes)*

DOCTOR: You've had an interesting trip?

LADY: Yes, I've met a lot of strange people . . . Have you had any patients?

DOCTOR: No, my reception room was empty all morning. It looks as if I'll lose my practice.

LADY *(in a friendly way):* You poor man . . . Listen, aren't you going to have the woodpile taken in soon? It'll get damp!

DOCTOR *(without any hint of reproach):* Yes, of course it should be; and the bees ought to be taken care of and the fruit in the orchard picked, but I don't get around to anything . . .

LADY: You're tired, dear!

DOCTOR: Tired of everything.

LADY *(without bitterness):* And you have a bad wife who's of no help to you!

DOCTOR *(gently):* Don't say that when I don't think it!

LADY *(turned toward the porch):* Now!

   (*The* STRANGER, *dressed so that he looks younger than in the first scene, comes out from the porch with a forced ease; apparently recognizes the* DOCTOR; *almost collapses; stumbles forward; but recovers his self-control.*)

DOCTOR: Welcome!

STRANGER: Thank you, Doctor!

DOCTOR: You bring beautiful weather. We can use it—it's been raining here for six weeks . . .

STRANGER: Not seven! It usually rains for seven weeks after the rain on Seven Sleepers' Day [25] . . . but that's true it's not July 27 yet—stupid of me!

DOCTOR: For a man used to the pleasures of city life, this simple village life will probably seem monotonous.

STRANGER: Oh no—I'm just as little at home there as here . . .
Excuse me for asking a question that's not pertinent: Haven't
we met before—when we were young?

DOCTOR: Never!

(*The* LADY *has sat down at the table and is crocheting.*)

STRANGER: Are you sure?

DOCTOR: Absolutely! I've followed your literary career from the
beginning, as I'm sure my wife has told you, with the greatest
interest. So if we had known each other before, I'd have remem-
bered—at least your name.—*But* here you see how a country
doctor lives.

STRANGER: If you could imagine how a so-called liberator lives,
you wouldn't envy him.

DOCTOR: I can imagine, I think—I've seen how people love their
chains. Maybe that's how it's supposed to be!

STRANGER *(listening intently to something offstage):* That's strange!
Who's playing next door?

DOCTOR: I don't know. Do you, Ingeborg?

LADY: No!

STRANGER: It's Mendelssohn's funeral march which pursues me.
I don't know if I'm actually hearing it played or . . .

DOCTOR: Have you ever had hearing delusions?

STRANGER: No, not delusions, but actual ordinary events seem
to be pursuing me time and again . . . Don't you hear the music,
too?

DOCTOR AND LADY: Yes! someone's playing . . .

LADY: And it's Mendelssohn . . .

DOCTOR: But that piece is popular just now . . .

STRANGER: I know, but that it's played at the right place at the
right moment . . . *(Gets up)*

DOCTOR: To calm you I'll ask my sister . . . *(Goes in on the
porch)*

STRANGER (*to the* LADY): I'm suffocating here! And I won't sleep
one night under this roof. Your husband does look like a werewolf, and it's as if you were changed to a pillar of salt [26] in his
presence. Murders have been committed here; ghosts are about;
I'll flee as soon as I get a good excuse.

DOCTOR *(comes out):* Well, it's the woman at the post office who's playing the piano . . .

STRANGER *(nervously):* Good! Then it's all right!—You have an unusual home, Doctor; everything's unusual. That woodpile, for example . . .

DOCTOR: Yes, lightning has struck it twice . . .

STRANGER: That's nasty! But you still keep it?

DOCTOR: Yes, for that very reason; I've made it two yards higher—and it gives me shade in the summer. That's my pumpkin . . . when fall comes, it's put away in the woodshed . . .

STRANGER *(looks about):* And here you have Christmas roses . . . where did you get them? . . . that bloom in the summer . . . why, everything's reversed here . . .

DOCTOR: Oh, those . . . Well, I have a patient staying here who's a little mentally unbalanced . . .

STRANGER: Here in your home?

DOCTOR: Yes, but he's a quiet soul who just speculates about the pointlessness of nature, and, since he thinks it's stupid that the Christmas roses are to freeze in the snow, he puts them in the cellar and then sets them out in spring.

STRANGER: Do you have a madman in your house? That's most unpleasant!

DOCTOR: Yes, but he's very peaceful.

STRANGER: How did he go insane?

DOCTOR: Well, who can say? He's ill mentally, not physically.

STRANGER: One thing: Is he here—nearby?

DOCTOR: The madman? Yes, he's out in the orchard rearranging creation, but, if his presence bothers you, we'll lock him up in the cellar.

STRANGER: Why don't they put poor devils like that to death?

DOCTOR: Well, one can't tell if they're ready . . .

STRANGER: For what?

DOCTOR: For the next life!

STRANGER: But there isn't any! *(Pause)*

DOCTOR: Who knows!

STRANGER: I don't know why but it's horrible here. Do you have dead bodies, too?

DOCTOR: Yes, indeed! I have a few pieces in the icebox here that

I'm going to send up to the medical board . . . *(Takes out an arm and a leg)* See!

STRANGER: Heavens, this is like Bluebeard's place.

DOCTOR *(sharply):* What do you mean by that? (*Gives the* LADY *a sharp look*) Do you think I murder my wives?

STRANGER: Good heavens, no; it's clear you don't.—But I suppose the house is haunted?

DOCTOR: If it's haunted! Ask my wife!

(*The* DOCTOR *has withdrawn back of the woodpile so the* LADY *and the* STRANGER *cannot see him.*)

LADY (*to the* STRANGER): You can speak up—my husband's hearing isn't very good, but he does read lips.

STRANGER: Then I'll take the opportunity to say I've never lived through a more painful half hour. Here we stand talking the most stupid nonsense just because no one has the courage to say what he thinks. I suffered so a bit ago I thought of taking my knife and opening my veins to cool off a bit. But right now I'd like to speak bluntly to him and blow him up into the air. Shall we tell him to his face we're planning to run away and that we've had enough of his stupidity?

LADY: If you talk like that, I'll hate you. Under all circumstances, we must behave decently.

STRANGER: You *are* well brought up!

(*The* DOCTOR *coming—can be seen by the two others who continue their conversation.*)

STRANGER: Will you go away with me—today?

LADY: You . . .

STRANGER: Why did you kiss me yesterday . . .

LADY: You . . .

STRANGER: Imagine if he could hear what we're saying. . . . He looks so hypocritical . . .

DOCTOR: What shall we do to entertain our guest?

LADY: He doesn't ask for much entertainment—his life hasn't been very pleasant . . .

(*The* DOCTOR *blows a whistle.*)

(*The madman appears in the garden; he has a laurel* [27] *wreath about his head and is oddly dressed.*)

DOCTOR: Caesar! Come here!

STRANGER *(unpleasantly affected):* Is his name Caesar?

DOCTOR: No, that's a nickname I gave him as a reminder of a schoolmate . . .

STRANGER *(uneasy):* What?

DOCTOR: Well, it was an unusual case, but I got the blame.

LADY (*to the* STRANGER): Have you ever heard of a child's being so depraved?

STRANGER *(tortured).*

CAESAR *(enters.)*

DOCTOR: Come and bow to the great author, Caesar.

CAESAR: Is that the great man?

LADY (*to the* DOCTOR): Why did you call him in when you see it tortures our guest?

DOCTOR: Don't be impolite, Caesar, or you'll feel the whip.

CAESAR: Why, he's Caesar, but he isn't great! He doesn't even know which was first, the chicken or the egg.—But I know!

STRANGER (*to* LADY): I'll be on my way! Have you ambushed me? What am I to believe? In a minute he'll let out the bees to entertain me, I suppose.

LADY: Have full confidence in me no matter how bad it looks . . . and don't talk so loudly . . .

STRANGER: But he'll never leave us—that werewolf! Never!

DOCTOR *(looks at his watch):* If you'll excuse me—I have to make a call—I'll be gone for an hour. I hope you won't find the waiting too long.

STRANGER: I'm used to waiting for what never comes . . .

DOCTOR (*to* CAESAR): Caesar, you rascal, come here so I can lock you up in the cellar! (*Goes out with* CAESAR)

STRANGER (*to the* LADY): What is this? Who's persecuting me? You assure me your husband is friendly toward me. I believe you, but all the same he can't open his mouth without hurting me. Every one of his words cut me . . . and now the funeral march is being played; it's really being played . . . and there's the Christmas rose again.—Why does everything repeat itself . . . dead bodies and beggars and madmen and human destinies and childhood memories . . . Come away from here. Let me be your liberator from this hell!

LADY: That's why I brought you here—*and* so no one could say you had stolen another man's wife. But I must ask you one question: Can I rely on you?

STRANGER: On my feelings, you mean . . .

LADY: We won't talk about them, since we've proceeded from taking them for granted, and they'll last as long as they last . . .

STRANGER: You mean financial support! Well, I have a lot of money coming—I need only write or telegraph . . .

LADY: Then I'll rely on that!——Well then. *(Puts her crocheting in her pocket).* Go out through that gate over there—follow the lilac hedge until you come to a wooden entrance. Open it and you'll be on the main highway. I'll join you in the next village!

STRANGER: I don't like walking out like that; I'd rather have fought with him right here in the middle of the yard . . .

LADY *(makes a gesture):* Quickly!

STRANGER: Come with me!

LADY: I will! But then I'll go first! *(Turns; throws a kiss toward the porch)* Poor werewolf of mine!

[CURTAIN]

ACT II

A HOTEL ROOM [28]

STRANGER *(with a suitcase in his hand):* There isn't any other room?

PORTER: Absolutely not!

STRANGER: But I don't want to stay in this one!

LADY: Since there isn't any other, dear, and all the other hotels are full . . .

STRANGER *(to the* PORTER): That will be all! [PORTER *goes*]

(*The* LADY *sinks down into a chair without having taken off her outer garments and hat.*)

STRANGER: Do you have any wish?

LADY: Yes, one: Kill me!

STRANGER: I can understand that. Driven from the hotels because we're not married, sought by the police, we end up in this hotel, the very last one I wanted to stay in, and in this room, number eight . . . Someone is struggling against me; there is someone!

LADY: Is this number eight?

STRANGER: So you've been here before, *too?*

LADY: And you?

STRANGER: Yes!

LADY: Let's get out of here, out into the street, into the woods, anywhere at all . . .

STRANGER: Gladly! But I'm just as tired as you after this wild chase! I had a feeling we'd end up here: I struggled against it and tried to go elsewhere, but the trains were delayed, everything went wrong, and we had to come here, and into this room. It's the devil I'm calling; but we're going to have one set-to more, he and I!

LADY: I have a feeling we'll never have peace again in this life!

STRANGER: Odd, how everything's the same, here. There's the ever withering Christmas rose . . . there he is again!—And there's the picture of Hotel Breuer in Montreux—I've lived there, too . . .

LADY: Did you go to the post office?

STRANGER: I expected that question. Yes, I was there. The only answer to five letters and three telegrams was one telegram: My publisher has gone away for fourteen days.

LADY: Then we're absolutely lost.

STRANGER: Just about!

LADY: In five minutes the porter will be here to ask for our passports; then the manager will come and ask us to leave.

STRANGER: Then there's only one thing left for us . . .

LADY: Two!

STRANGER: But the second's impossible.

LADY: What's the second?

STRANGER: To go to your parents out in the country.

LADY: You're already reading my thoughts.

STRANGER: We can't have any secrets from each other any more . . .

LADY: That's why the whole dream is over . . .

STRANGER: Perhaps!

LADY: Send another telegram!

STRANGER: I ought to, but I can't move from this spot: I don't believe in the success of my efforts any more————someone has paralyzed me.

LADY: And me!—We decided not to talk about the past and we keep dragging it with us. Look at the wallpaper here: Do you see the portrait the flowers form?

STRANGER: Yes, it's he! Everywhere, everywhere! How many hundred times . . . But I see someone else in the pattern of the tablecloth . . . Is this real? No, it's delusion!—I'm expecting to hear my funeral march at any time to round it all out! *(Listens)* There it is!

LADY: I can't hear anything!

STRANGER: Then I am—on the way!

LADY: Shall we go home?

STRANGER: The last thing, the worst!—Come as adventurers, beggars, no, that's impossible.

LADY: It is really————, that's too much! With shame and disgrace bringing sorrow to the old people . . . And to see each other in a humiliating position. We'd never be able to respect each other any more!

STRANGER: True—it would be worse than death; but imagine, I feel it's becoming inevitable and I'm beginning to long for it, to get through it fast since it must be.

LADY *(takes up her crocheting)*: But I have no desire to be humiliated in your presence . . . and there has to be another way out. If we were really married . . . and that won't have to take long, for my former marriage is legally invalid—according to the laws of the country in which the ceremony took place . . . all we need to do is to go there and be married by the same clergyman who . . . but that would be humiliating for you . . .

STRANGER: It's in keeping with everything else . . . since this wedding trip's becoming either a pilgrimage or running the gauntlet . . .

LADY: You're right about that, and in five minutes the manager will be here to throw us out!—to get an end to these humiliations there's only one thing to do—swallow the last one voluntarily . . . sh, I hear footsteps . . .

STRANGER: I sense what's coming and am ready . . . I'm prepared for everything nowadays, and since I can't fight the invisible one, I'll show how long I can bear all this . . . We'll pawn your jewelry—I can redeem them when my publisher gets home, if he doesn't drown or get killed in a trainwreck. If anyone's ambitious as I am, he has to be prepared to sacrifice honor first of all!

LADY: Since we agree, don't you think it's best we voluntarily leave this room . . . Oh God! Now he's coming! The manager!

STRANGER: Let's go.————Running the gauntlet of waiters, waitresses, porters, and attendants . . . the blush of shame and the pallor of anger . . . The animals of the forest get to hide in dens, but we have to put our shame on display.—Let your veil down at least!

LADY: This is liberty!

STRANGER: And this is the liberator! *(They go)*

[CURTAIN]

BY THE SEA

A cottage on a bluff by the sea. Outside a table and chairs. The STRANGER *and the* LADY *dressed in light-colored clothes, look younger than in the preceding scene. The* LADY *is crocheting.*

STRANGER: Three days of happiness and peace by my wife's side, and my anxiety's back.

LADY: What are you afraid of?

STRANGER: That this won't last long!

LADY: Why shouldn't it?

STRANGER: I don't know—I think it has to end—quickly, terribly. There's something false about the sunshine itself and the lack of wind—I feel happiness isn't part of my destiny.

LADY: But everything's patched up: my parents are resigned, and my husband has written a friendly and understanding letter . . .

STRANGER: What good does that do, what good does that do . . . Fate's weaving its plot—I hear the gavel fall again and the chairs shoved back from the table—the judgment has been handed down, but it must have been handed down before I was born for even in my childhood I began to serve my sentence . . . There isn't one point in my life that I can look back to with pleasure . . .

LADY: And you, poor man, have received everything you wanted of life.

STRANGER: Everything, but I forgot to wish for gold, unfortunately.

LADY: So your thoughts are there again.[29]

STRANGER: Is that to be wondered at?

LADY: Sh-h!

STRANGER: What are you always crocheting? You sit there like one of the three fates [30] pulling the yarn between your fingers . . . but keep on; the most beautiful thing I know is a woman bent over her work or her child. What are you crocheting?

LADY: It isn't anything really, only a piece of needlework . . .

STRANGER: It looks like a net of nerves and knots where your thoughts have been fixed; I imagine your brain looks like that inside . . .

LADY: If I had only half the thoughts you ascribe to me! But I haven't any at all!

STRANGER: That's probably why I enjoy your company so, why I find you perfect, so that I can't think of living without you!— Now the cloud passed on! The sky's clear, the wind comfortably warm—feel how it caresses one! This is living! Yes, now I am living, just now! And I feel my self expanding, stretching out, condensing, becoming infinite: I'm everywhere, in the ocean which is my blood, in the mountains which are my skeleton, in the trees, in the flowers; and my head reaches up into the sky; I look out over the universe which is I; and I feel the creator's

full power in myself, for I am he. I'd like to take the whole
mass into my hand and reshape it into something more perfect,
more lasting, more beautiful . . . I'd like to see the whole creation
and all created beings happy: be born without pain, live without
sorrow, and die in quiet joy! Eve! Don't you want to die with
me, right now, for suffering will be over us in a minute!

LADY: No, I'm not ready to die!

STRANGER: Why not?

LADY: I have a notion I have something still left to do. Maybe I
haven't suffered enough . . .

STRANGER: So that's the meaning of life?

LADY: It looks like it!—But now I'll ask you nicely for one thing.

STRANGER: Go ahead!

LADY: Don't blaspheme Heaven as you just did and compare yourself to the Creator, for in moments like that you remind me of
Caesar back home . . .

STRANGER (*disturbed*): Of Caesar! How can you know . . . say
that.

LADY: If I said something bad, I didn't mean to! I was stupid when
I said back home . . . Forgive me!

STRANGER: Don't you mean anything but the blasphemy when
you say I resemble—Caesar?

LADY: Nothing at all!

STRANGER: Strange! I believe what you say and that you don't
want to hurt me, but all the same you do hurt me, you as well
as all the others I run across. Why???

LADY: Because you're too sensitive.

STRANGER: So you're back to that! Do you mean I have secret
sensitive spots?

LADY: No, by all that's holy, that's not what I meant!—The spirits
of disunity and suspicion have come between us! Drive them
away—in time!

STRANGER: You mustn't say I'm blaspheming when I repeat the
old well-known "Lo, we are gods!"

LADY: If we are, why can't you help yourself, help us?

STRANGER: Can't I? Just wait: We've seen only the beginning.

LADY: If the finish is to be like the start, Heaven help us!

STRANGER: I know what you're afraid of, and I had intended to wait with a happy surprise, but I don't want to torture you longer. *(Takes out a registered, unopened letter)* Look at this . . .

LADY: The money has come!

STRANGER: This morning? Who can ruin me now?

LADY: Don't say that! You surely know who can ruin us!

STRANGER: Who would that be?

LADY: The one who punishes human arrogance?

STRANGER: And courage! Especially courage! This was my Achilles' heel,[31] and I've borne everything but this fatal lack of money, which always hit me on the right spot!

LADY: Excuse me, but how much did you get?

STRANGER: I don't know—I haven't opened the letter yet, but I know approximately what I could expect! *(Opens the letter)* What's this? No money, only a statement showing I don't have any coming. Can this be right?

LADY: I'm beginning to believe it's as you say!

STRANGER: That I'm damned, yes! But I'll take the curse with two fingers and toss it back at the generous giver! . . .—*(He throws the letter upwards)*—along with my curse!

LADY: Don't! I'm afraid of you!

STRANGER: Fear me, but you're not going to despise me. Now the glove has been thrown, and we'll see a set-to between big shots!

(Opens his coat and vest and throws a threatening look upwards.) Come on! Strike me with your lightning if you dare! Frighten me with your storm if you can!

LADY: No, no! Don't!

STRANGER: Yes, just like that! Who dares disturb me in the dream of my love? Who takes the beaker from my mouth and my woman from my arms? Envious ones, gods or devils! Small middle-class gods who parry the thrust of the sword with pin pricks from in back, who won't meet one in the open, but answer with an unpaid bill, coming by way of the kitchen to humiliate the master before the hired help. No thrust, nor fair play, but spitting on, screaming . . . shame! Powers, worthies, lords, shame!

LADY: May Heaven never punish you . . .

STRANGER: The sky is just as blue and silent, the sea just as blue and stupid . . . Sh-h, I hear a poem coming . . . That's what I call it when a motif begins to develop in my brain . . . but I hear the rhythm first . . . this time it's like a horse's trot, the rattle of spurs and the rustle of weapons . . . but it's a flutter, too, as when it whips the sail: It's flags . . .

LADY: No, it's the wind you hear sighing in the tree . . .

STRANGER: Sh-h!—Now they're riding over a bridge, but it's a wooden bridge and there's no water in the river, only pebbles . . . wait! Now I hear them reciting a rosary, men and women;— the Angelus; [32] but now I see—do you know where?—on your crocheting—a large kitchen, a white one—the walls are white-washed; there are three small recessed windows with bars, and flowers; in the left corner is the stove; in the right the dining table with pine benches; and over the table in the corner is a black crucifix; a lamp is burning under it . . . but the beams are dark with soot! . . . and on the walls mistletoes are hanging, somewhat withered . . .

LADY *(frightened):* Where do you see all that? Where?

STRANGER: On your crocheting . . .

LADY: Do you see any people?

STRANGER: I see an old, very old man sitting by the kitchen table . . . bent over a hunting bag . . . but he has his hands folded in prayer . . . and on the floor an older woman is kneeling . . . and now I hear as if from out on a veranda the Angelus . . . but both of them in the kitchen look as if they were of white wax or honey . . . and there's a veil over all of it.—— —No, this is no poem! *(Comes to)* This is something else!

LADY: It's reality! That's the kitchen in my parent's home, where you've never been. [33] The old man's my grandfather, the forester, and the woman's my mother, who was praying—for us! The time is six o'clock; then the servants recite the rosary out in the entrance . . .

STRANGER: That's unpleasant! So I'm getting to see ahead, too!— But it was beautiful—what a room, snowywhite with mistletoe and flowers . . . but why are they praying for us?

LADY: Yes, why? Have we done wrong?

STRANGER: What is wrong?

LADY: I've read it doesn't exist, but all the same . . . I'm longing so for my mother, not for my father, for he rejected me just as he rejected Mother— 34

STRANGER: Why did he desert your mother?

LADY: Who knows about things like that? The children least of all. But let's go home—I'm longing so . . .

STRANGER: Lion's dens and snakepits: one more or less doesn't matter. I'll go for your sake but not as a prodigal son 35—no, you'll see I can go through fire and water for your sake . . .

LADY: You don't know that . . .

STRANGER: But I usually feel . . .

LADY: Do you also feel that the road is very difficult, for the old people live in the mountains where no cart can go?

STRANGER: That sounds like something out of a fairy tale, but I seem to have read or dreamt something like that——

LADY: Possibly! But everything you'll see is absolutely real, a little unusual perhaps, but even the people aren't ordinary——Are you ready to come with me?

STRANGER: Absolutely ready—for everything!

LADY (kisses him on his forehead and makes the sign of the cross, simply, shyly, and without pretense): Come!

[CURTAIN]

ON THE HIGHWAY

A hilly landscape; a chapel to the extreme right of a knoll. The highway bordered by fruit trees winds forward to the back; between the trees can be seen calvaries, small atonement chapels, memorial crosses over accidents. In the foreground a road sign with the notice "Begging forbidden in this district."

LADY: You're tired, poor man.

STRANGER: I won't deny that! But the fact I'm hungry because I haven't any money humiliates me. I'd never have thought this would happen to me!

LADY: It seems to me we'd better be really ready for anything—I think we're out of favor. You know my shoe has cracked—I'm ready to cry over getting there looking like beggars.

STRANGER *(points at the road sign):* And begging's forbidden here. Why should it say so just there in capital letters?

LADY: The sign has always said that as far back as I remember. Imagine: I haven't been here since I was a child. Then I thought the road was very short, the hills over there weren't so high; the trees were smaller; and birds were singing, it seems to me.

STRANGER: Birds sing the whole year through for you—child, child! Nowadays they sing only in spring—and it's almost fall now! Back in those days you danced along this endless road to Calvary [36] and picked flowers at the foot of the crosses———— *(A French horn sounds far away)* What's that?

LADY: I know—it's Grandfather coming home from hunting. The good, kind old man! Let's go on so we get there before dark.

STRANGER: Do we still have far to go?

LADY: Not far—just beyond the mountains and the river.

STRANGER: So it's the river I can hear?

LADY: Yes, the great river [37] beside which I was born and brought up. I was eighteen before I got to cross over to this shore to see what turned blue in the distance—now, I've seen it.

STRANGER: You're weeping!

LADY: The good old man! When I was stepping into the boat, he said: "There's the world, child; when you've seen enough, come back to your mountains. The mountains conceal!" Well, I've seen enough! enough!

STRANGER: Let's go on! The road is long, and it's beginning to turn dark.

(They pick up their baggage and go on)

[CURTAIN]

IN THE RAVINE

A narrow entrance to a ravine between steep mountains with a spruce forest on them.

In the foreground a shed; against its entrance is leaning a broom and on its handle hangs a buckhorn. To the left a smithy with its door open; through it a red glow can be seen. To the right a mill.

In the background the ravine with millbrook and footbridge. The jagged edges of the cliffs form profiles of giants.

When the curtain goes up, the SMITH *is standing in the smithy door and the* MILLER'S WIFE *in the mill's door. When the* LADY *enters, they gesture to each other and then disappear in separate directions. The* LADY'S *and the* STRANGER'S *clothes are tattered.*

(*The* LADY *enters; goes up to the smithy.*)

STRANGER *(enters):* They hid, most likely from us.

LADY: I don't think so!

STRANGER: How strange nature is here—it's as if everything were put together to make people uneasy. Why arc the broom and the buckhorn standing there? Probably because that's their ususal place, but just the same they make me think of a witch . . . Why's the smithy black and the mill white? Because the one's sooty and the other covered with flour, but all the same when I saw the blacksmith stand in the glow from his fire opposite the miller's wife I thought of an old poem . . . Do you see the giants up there? . . . No, this will be unbearable . . . Can't you see your werewolf that I rescued you from . . . Why, that *is* his profile . . . Look . . . there!

LADY: Yes, it is! But it's really a cliff!

STRANGER: It is a cliff, but it's he all the same!

LADY: Don't make me say why we see him!

STRANGER: You mean—conscience's awakening when we're tired and hungry, but that will pass when we've slept and eaten . . . Isn't it hellish we'll have to arrive like tramps? . . . Our clothes are tattered from our long journey among the hawthorn bushes . . . I think someone's fighting against me . . .

LADY: Why did you challenge him?

STRANGER: Because I want a fight in the open . . . I don't want to fight with unpaid bills and empty pocketbooks. But even if that's it: Here's my last penny—let the river sprite [38] take it if he exists! (*He throws a coin into the stream*)

LADY: Oh no! We should have had that for the ferry! Now we'll have to talk about money the first thing we get there . . .

STRANGER: When did we ever get to talk about anything else . . .

LADY: I suppose it's because you've treated money with contempt . . .

STRANGER: Like everything else . . .

LADY: But everything isn't contemptible; there's a lot that's good . . .

STRANGER: I've never noticed that . . .

LADY: Come with me—you'll see . . .

STRANGER: I'll come with you . . . *(Hesitates when he has to pass the smithy.)*

LADY *(who has gone ahead):* Are you afraid of the fire?

STRANGER: No, but . . .

(The French horn can be heard in the distance. He plunges by the smithy after her.)

[CURTAIN]

IN THE KITCHEN

A large kitchen with whitewashed walls; three windows in the right corner—two are at the back and one on the right wall; the windows are small with deep niches in which there are flower pots; the ceiling is brown with soot and the beams show; in the left corner a large stove with copper-, bronze-, iron-, and pewter containers as well as wooden cans. In the right corner a crucifix with a lamp. Below it an oblong table with benches along the wall.

Mistletoe hangs here and there. A door at the back. Outside can be seen the poorhouse and, through the windows at the back, the church.

By the stove a bed for dogs and the beggars' table.

The OLD MAN *is sitting at the table under the crucifix with his hands folded; in front of him the hunting bag. He is in his eighties, is powerfully built, has white hair and a full beard, and is dressed like a forester.*

The MOTHER *is kneeling in the middle of the floor; she is grayhaired going on fifty years old, and is dressed in black and white.*

From outside can be heard plainly men, women, and children reciting in unison of the Angelus: "Holy Mary, mother of God, pray for us poor sinners, now and at the moment of our death. Amen."

OLD MAN AND MOTHER: Amen!

MOTHER: Now I'll tell you, Father. People have seen two wanderers by the river; they were tattered, dirty, and wet. When they were going to pay the ferryman, they didn't have a penny. Now they're in the ferry hut drying their clothes.

OLD MAN: Let them stay there!

MOTHER: Don't deny your house to a beggar! He might be an angel!

OLD MAN: That's true!—Let them come!

MOTHER: I'll put out food here on the beggars' table if it won't upset you.

OLD MAN: Not at all!

MOTHER: Shall I give them cider?

OLD MAN: Yes.—Have a fire made in the stove, too, since they're cold.

MOTHER: It's a little late for making a fire, but if that's what you wish, Father . . .

OLD MAN *(looks out through the window):* Oh yes, do . . .

MOTHER: What are you looking at, Father?

OLD MAN: I'm looking at the river—it has risen . . . and I'm wondering what I've wondered for seventy-five years—when will I get to the sea . . .

MOTHER: You're feeling sad tonight, aren't you, Father?

OLD MAN: . . . *et introibo ad altare Dei: ad Deum qui laetificat juventutem meam.*—Yes, I'm sad . . . *Deus, Deus meus: quare tristis es anima mea, et quare conturbas me.*

MOTHER: *Spera in Deo . . .*

(*The* MAID *enters; gestures to the* MOTHER, *who goes up to her. They whisper; the* MAID *goes.*)

OLD MAN: I heard what you said!—My God, my God, even this I must bear!

MOTHER: You don't need to see them—you can go up to your room.

OLD MAN: No, I'll take it as penance.—But why do they come like this, like tramps?

MOTHER: They probably lost their way and ran into hardships . . .
Do you think that . . .

OLD MAN: But that she's bringing her————husband here! That's
shameless. . . .

MOTHER: You know how different Ingeborg is—she thinks everything she does is proper, not to say right. Have you ever seen
her ashamed of anything she's done or suffer because of correction? I never have. But still she's not shameless, rather the opposite, and everything she does no matter how tastelessly becomes
her.

OLD MAN: I've been amazed, too, that one can't get angry with
her . . . she always feels she's not to blame, never takes an insult
personally. It's as if she were selfless or were two persons, one
of whom does evil and the other absolves . . . But the man
she has brought! I've never despised anyone else as much as
him. He sees only evil everywhere, and I've never heard as much
that's bad about anyone else.

MOTHER: That's right, Father, but it's possible Ingeborg has a role
in this man's life and he in hers. Perhaps they're to torture each
other to salvation . . .

OLD MAN: That may be, but I still don't like being an assistant
in an enterprise that seems shameless to me . . . And this man
in my house! But I'll have to put up with that! As with everything
else . . . I have coming!

MOTHER: In the name of God then!

(LADY *and* STRANGER *enter.*)

MOTHER: Welcome!

LADY: Thank you, Mother! (*Goes toward the* OLD MAN)

(*The* OLD MAN *gets up and stares at the* STRANGER.)

LADY: God's peace, Grandfather! This is my husband! Give him
your hand.

OLD MAN: I want to look at him first. (*Approaches the* STRANGER,
puts his hands on his shoulders, and looks into his eyes) With what
intentions do you come into this house?

STRANGER (*simply*): Only to keep my wife company and at her
insistence!

OLD MAN: If that's true, welcome! I've had a long and stormy life—I've finally found a certain peace in solitude: I beg you don't disturb it!

STRANGER: I haven't come to ask any favor, and I won't take anything with me when I leave!

OLD MAN: That answer doesn't please me, for we all need each other, perhaps even I need you. One doesn't know things like that, young man.

LADY: Grandfather!

OLD MAN: Yes, child! I don't wish you happiness, for there isn't any, but I wish you the strength to bear your lot.—Now I'll leave you for a while! Your mother will look after you! *(Goes)*

LADY (*to* MOTHER): Have you set the table for us, Mother?

MOTHER: The beggars' table you mean? No, that was a misunderstanding, as you must know.

LADY: Well, we do look miserable after having lost our way in the mountains, and if Grandfather hadn't blown his hunting horn . . .

MOTHER: He hasn't hunted for a long time.

LADY: Then someone else blew a horn . . . but, Mother, I'll go up to the rose chamber to get it ready . . .

MOTHER: Go ahead, child; I'll come up soon . . .

(*The* LADY *wants to say something but cannot manage; goes.*)

STRANGER (*to* MOTHER): I have seen this room before . . .

MOTHER: And I've seen you before; I've almost expected you . . .

STRANGER: As one expects misfortune?

MOTHER: Why did you say that?

STRANGER: Because I generally bring destruction with me, but since I have to be somewhere and I can't change my fate, I have no scruples . . .

MOTHER: In that you're like my daughter————she never has any hesitation and never any pangs of conscience.

STRANGER: What's that?

MOTHER: You thought I meant something bad, but I surely can't stand here saying bad things about my child. I made the comparison only on the assumption you, too, knew what she's like.

STRANGER: I haven't noticed the qualities you ascribe to Eve . . .

MOTHER: Why do you call Ingeborg Eve?

STRANGER: By giving her a name I selected I made her mine just as I intend to make her over according to my wishes . . .

MOTHER: In your image! *(Smiles)* I've heard magicians out in the country used to carve a doll resembling the one they want to bewitch and give it the name of the person they intended to destroy; That's how you intend to destroy her whole family through the Eve you've created!

STRANGER (*looks at the* MOTHER *with amazement*): That was damnable! Forgive me—you're my mother-in-law, but you're religious, too! How can you have such thoughts?

MOTHER: They're yours.

STRANGER: This is getting interesting! I thought I was coming to an idylic spot in the solitary forest and I run into a witches' kitchen.

MOTHER: Not quite, but you forgot or didn't know I'm a woman that a man has insultingly deserted and that you're a man who has shamefully deserted a woman.[39]

STRANGER: That was frank—now I know where I am.

MOTHER: Now I want to know where I am: Can you support two families?

STRANGER: Yes, if everything goes well.

MOTHER: Everything doesn't go well the way one wants it, and money can be lost.

STRANGER: But my talent is capital that can't be lost . . .

MOTHER: That's strange! Haven't the greatest talents gradually or quite suddenly been lost?

STRANGER: I've never met another person who can rob one of self-confidence as you can . . .

MOTHER: Your arrogance has to be brought low! Your last book was weaker . . .

STRANGER: So you've read that one, too . . .

MOTHER: Yes, and that's why I know all your secrets. So don't try to pretend to me. If you don't, things will go well for you.— And a minor matter that reflects unfavorably on us: Why didn't you pay the ferryman?

STRANGER: My Achilles' heel!—Well, I threw my last penny away . . . But can't you talk about anything but money in this house?

MOTHER: Yes, we can, but in this house we have the habit of doing our duty before we relax. So you've come on foot because you don't have any money?

STRANGER: Yes-s-s!

MOTHER *(smiles):* And haven't had anything to eat either?

STRANGER: No-o-o!

MOTHER: Listen: why, you're a boy, a frivolous young scamp . . .

STRANGER: I've gone through a lot in my day, but I've never been in on anything like this . . .

MOTHER: I almost pity you; I'd like to laugh at your misery if I didn't know you'll have to weep and many others with you.— Now that you've had your way, stay with her who loves you, because if you desert her, I won't smile any more and you'll quickly forget what happiness is.

STRANGER: Is that a threat?

MOTHER: No, a warning;—Go ahead now—and have your dinner.

STRANGER *(nods toward the beggars' table):* At that table?

MOTHER: That's a nasty joke, but it could become serious. I've seen that happen.

STRANGER: Soon I'll believe the worst is possible—for this is the worst I've ever been in on.

MOTHER: Oh no! It can get worse! Just wait!

STRANGER *(depressed):* Yes, now I'll expect everything! *(Goes out)*

(MOTHER *alone; then the* OLD MAN *enters.)*

OLD MAN: Well? That was no angel!

MOTHER: At least none from Heaven!

OLD MAN: What's that?—You know the people here are extremely superstitious; well, when I got down to the river, I overheard them talking. One man said his horse shied away from *him;* another said his dogs got so wild he had to tie them up; the ferryman insisted his boat got lighter when *he* stepped into it. All that's superstition, of course, but . . . but . . .

MOTHER: But?

OLD MAN: Well, it's only that a magpie flew through the window, the closed window, through the glass window pane in their room. But probably I didn't see right!

MOTHER: Probably. But why does a person see wrong sometimes in the right place . . .

OLD MAN: This man's very presence makes me sick, and it's as if I were dying when he looks at me.

MOTHER: We must try to get him to leave . . . but I'm almost sure he won't be happy here very long . . .

OLD MAN: I, too, think he won't stay long. . . . You see, I got a letter tonight warning me about this man, partly because officials are looking for him . . .

MOTHER: Policemen in your house!

OLD MAN: Yes, about financial matters! But I beg you . . . The laws of hospitality, even toward beggars, toward the enemy, are sacred. Leave him in peace for a few days until he has recovered from this wild chase. You certainly see how Providence has taken hold of him, and his soul is going to be ground in the mill before he goes through the sieve.

MOTHER: I've already felt an irresistible calling to be the instrument of Providence in his case . . .

OLD MAN: But distinguish carefully between your desire for revenge and your calling . . .

MOTHER: I'll try! If it's possible!

OLD MAN: Good night then!

MOTHER: Do you think Ingeborg has read his latest book?

OLD MAN: I don't know. Most likely not, for how could she become attached to a man who has ideas like that?

MOTHER: That's right! She hasn't read it! But she's going to!

[CURTAIN]

ACT III

IN THE ROSE CHAMBER

A simply but comfortably furnished room in the OLD MAN'S *home. The walls are whitewashed a rosy tint, the curtains are rose-red colored*

thin muslin. In the small barred windows are flower pots. A writing
desk and a book shelf to the right. To the left an ottoman with rose-
colored curtains above it in the shape of a baldaquin. Chairs and table
in old German style.

A door at the back. Outside: landscape and the poorhouse—a dark
shabby building with black window openings without curtains. The
sun is shining brightly.

The LADY *is sitting crocheting in the ottoman.*

The MOTHER *is standing holding a book bound in red in her*
hand.

MOTHER: You don't want to read your husband's own book?

LADY: No, not that book—I promised him I wouldn't.

MOTHER: You don't want to know the man to whom you've en-
trusted your fate?

LADY: No! What good would that do? We have it as good as we
want.

MOTHER: You don't have great demands on life.

LADY: Why should I? They're never fulfilled anyway.

MOTHER: I don't know if you're born with all the wisdom of the
world or if you're only naïve.

LADY: I don't know anything about myself either.

MOTHER: You're content if only the sun shines and you have food
for the day!

LADY: Yes! And when the sun doesn't shine, I think that's probably
how it's supposed to be!

MOTHER: To change the subject: Do you know your husband's
in danger of getting arrested because of money matters?

LADY: Yes, I know, but then all poets are!

MOTHER: Can you tell me if your husband's a fool or a rascal?

LADY: No, I can't . . . Mother. He's probably neither. He is a
bit unusual, and it's really too bad I can't say anything he hasn't
heard before. That's why we speak very little, but he's happy
if I'm only near him. So am I!

MOTHER: There! You're already in still water—you don't have
far left to the rapids then. But don't you think you'd have something to talk about when you've read what he's written?

LADY: Perhaps! You can leave the book there . . .

MOTHER: Put it away yourself. It'll amaze him when you quote something from his masterpiece.

LADY *(puts the book in her pocket):* He's coming! It's as if he felt even at a great distance when one talks about him.

MOTHER: If he could feel, too, when other people suffer because of him—at great distances. *(Goes)*

(*The* LADY *alone for a moment, reads here and there in the book, appears amazed, hides the book in her pocket.*)

STRANGER *(enters):* Your mother was here; you talked about me, of course; I can still hear the vibrations of her evil words; I feel how they beat the air and see how they darken the rays of sunlight; I seem to make out the impression of her body in the air in this room; and she leaves a smell like that of a dead snake behind her.

LADY: My, how nervous you are today!

STRANGER: Terribly! Some bungler has stretched my nerves out of tune, and now he's playing with a horsehair bow so that it squeaks like a partridge cry . . . you don't know what that is . . . But there's someone here who's stronger than I, someone who goes about with a searchlight picking me out. Listen: Do they usually make use of magic around here?

LADY: Don't turn your back on the sunlight! Look at the beautiful landscape, and you'll feel calmer.

STRANGER: No, I can't look at the poorhouse over there—it seems to have been built for my sake alone. And there's always a crazy woman over there standing waving this way.

LADY: Do you feel people here are mistreating you?

STRANGER: In a way, no, but they stuff me with good things as if I were being fattened for slaughter—yet nothing tastes good because it's given begrudgingly, and I feel the hate like an ice-house when it radiates cold. Imagine: I feel a cold wind everywhere even though there's no wind and it's unbelievably hot. And I keep hearing that blessed mill . . .[40]

LADY: But it's not grinding now . . .

STRANGER: Oh yes, it grinds and grinds . . .

LADY: There isn't any hate—at the most sympathy . . .

STRANGER: And then something else . . . why do people cross themselves when they meet me on the highway?

LADY: They're only saying their prayers silently as they usually do!—But you did get an unpleasant letter this morning.

STRANGER: Yes, of the kind that made my hair stand on end and made me want to spit my destiny in the face. Imagine: I have money coming but can't get at it; now I'm being sued by—my children's guardian because I haven't paid child support. Have you ever seen another human being in such a humiliating situation? And still I'm not to blame. I have the means, I want to do the right thing, but I'm not allowed to. Am I to blame then? No, but I get the shame. There's something unnatural about this. It's the devil's work!

LADY: But why?

STRANGER: There! That's it! Why was I born an ignorant being, ignorant about laws, customs, conventions, which one breaks in ignorance and gets whipped for doing so? Why does one become a young fellow with ideals that one wants to realize and then why is one driven into all sorts of wretchedness that one despises? Why, why?

LADY *(who, without being detected, has been reading in the book, absent-mindedly):* It has some purpose or other, I suspect, even if we can't tell what it is.

STRANGER: If it's to make one humble as they say, it's a poor technique, for I only get prouder . . . Eve!

LADY: You may not call me that!

STRANGER *(startled):* Why not?

LADY: I don't like it any more than you would if I called you Caesar . . .

STRANGER: So we're there?

LADY: Where? What?

STRANGER: Did you have any concealed intention with that name?

LADY: Caesar? No, I hadn't, but I'm just about to find out something.

STRANGER: Fine! Let me have the honor of being felled by my own hand: I *am* Caesar, the schoolboy who was guilty of mischief for which another boy was blamed. That other boy was your husband—the werewolf! That's how fate enjoys braiding bonds for eternity. Noble joys!

(*The* LADY *hesitant; says nothing.*)

STRANGER: Say something!

LADY: I can't!

STRANGER: Say he became a werewolf because as a child he lost his faith in divine justice when he was tortured for another child's mischief. Say that and I'll say how I suffered pangs of conscience tenfold and how I came out of the religious crises that followed so chastened I've never committed another deed like it.

LADY: It's not that! That isn't it!

STRANGER: What is it then?—That you can't respect me any more.

LADY: It's not that either!

STRANGER: Then it's because I'm to feel my shame before you, and then it's over between us.

LADY: No!

STRANGER: Eve!

LADY: Don't! That awakens evil thoughts . . .

STRANGER: You've broken your promise—you have read in my book!

LADY: Yes!

STRANGER: That was wrong!

LADY: But my intention was good, only good!

STRANGER: The result of good intentions seems to be evil, too: Now I'm exploded, and I've furnished the powder myself.—Imagine: everything repeats itself, everything: boyhood pranks and big ones; reaping what one has sown is fair enough, but if I could only see one fair deed rewarded justly—but I never do! Anyone who records all small flaws and great ones gets shame; not even a human being is guilty of that, and human beings can forgive, but the gods never do.

LADY: Don't say that!—Not that! But say that you can forgive!

STRANGER: I'm not small minded as you know, but what do I have to forgive you?

LADY: Oh, that's more than I can say . . .

STRANGER: Tell me, and then we're quits perhaps!

LADY: It's this: He and I used to read the curse of Deuteronomy [41] over you . . . the man who had ruined his life.

STRANGER: What curse is that?

LADY: It's from the books of Moses which the priests used to repeat in unison at the beginning of Lent . . .[42]

STRANGER: I don't remember it, but what difference would that make? One more or less?

LADY: Well, in our family there's the tradition that the one we curse is struck . . .

STRANGER: I don't believe in that, but I don't doubt that evil comes from this house! May it come back over their heads— that's my prayer! Now—according to your national practice—I should shoot myself, but I can't as long as I haven't fulfilled my obligations . . . Imagine: I can't even die, so I've lost the last of what I called my religion . . . Beautifully calculated! I've heard man can wrestle with God [43] and not without success, but even Job couldn't struggle with Satan! Shall we talk about you now?

LADY: Not yet, but soon perhaps!—After reading in your terrible book—I've really only glanced at it, read a few lines here and there—I seem to have eaten of the fruit of the tree of knowledge: my eyes have been opened and I know what is evil and what is good!—I didn't know that before! And now I see how evil you are! Now I know why you called me Eve. But if sin came into the world through that mother, redemption came through another mother! If the curse came through the first, blessing came through the second! Through me you're not going to destroy the human race—perhaps I have another role in your life! We'll see!

STRANGER: You have eaten of the tree of knowledge! Farewell!

LADY: You intend to leave?

STRANGER: Yes, what else can I do? I can't stay here!

LADY: Don't go.

STRANGER: I have to—to straighten out all these things. I'll go to say good bye to the old people; then I'll come back to you! So: I'll be back in a moment! *(Goes)*

LADY *(stands as if turned to stone; then goes to the door and looks out):*
No, he went away! away! *(She collapses and sinks to her knees)*

[CURTAIN]

THE ASYLUM

The refectory in an old cloister; resembles a simple whitewashed round-arched church, but the walls are covered with spots of dampness, which form strange figures.

Dining tables with bowls. At the end of a table a pulpit for the reader. At the back a door leading to the chapel. Lighted candles on the tables. On the left wall a painting of Michael slaying the Devil.[44]

By a long dining table to the left the STRANGER *is sitting in white hospital garb, alone next to his bowl. At the table to the right sit: The brown-clad mourners from Act I; the* BEGGAR; *a* WOMAN *in mourning with two children; a* WOMAN *who resembles the Lady but is not the Lady and who is crocheting instead of eating; a* MAN *who resembles the Doctor but is not he; a* MAN *resembling Caesar;* PEOPLE *resembling his mother and father; the* PARENTS *of the "prodigal son"; and others. All are dressed in white but covering the white garments are veils in different colors. The faces are waxen yellow, corpselike; there is something ghostlike about their beings and their gestures.*

When the curtain goes up, all complete a "Pater Noster" [the Lord's Prayer]—except the STRANGER.

STRANGER *(rises; goes up to the* ABBESS, *who stands by the serving table):* Mother, let me speak a moment.

ABBESS *(in the Augustinian black and white garb):* Yes, my son. *(They go down stage)*

STRANGER: First, let me ask: Where am I?

ABBESS: In the cloister "The Good Help."[45] They found you on the mountains above the Ravine, with a cross that you had broken from a calvary and with which you were threatening someone up in the clouds, someone you imagined you could see. You had a fever, and you fell down a precipice. You were found unharmed but delirious; so you were brought here to the asylum and put to bed. Since then you've been delirious, and in spite of your complaining about pain in one hip, they haven't been able to find any injury.

STRANGER: What did I rave about?

ABBESS: The usual dreams all people sick with fever have: you accused yourself of everything possible and saw your victims as you called them.

STRANGER: And then?

ABBESS: Well, you've been thinking mainly about money. And you wanted to pay for your stay at the asylum. I tried to calm you by pointing out we don't take pay but do everything out of charity . . .

STRANGER: I don't want any charity—I don't need it!

ABBESS: It is surely more blessed to give than to take, but it takes a great spirit to be able to receive and be grateful.

STRANGER: I don't need to receive and I ask for nothing . . . I don't want to be forced to be grateful.

ABBESS: Hm! hm! hm!

STRANGER: But tell me why not one of this whole company wanted to sit at the same table as I? They get up, go away . . .

ABBESS: I suppose they're afraid of you.

STRANGER: Why?

ABBESS: You look so . . .

STRANGER: How . . . I . . . look! But that crowd over there— what do they look like? Are they real?

ABBESS: If you mean actual, they have a terrifying reality. That you see them in a strange way probably depends on your still being feverish or . . . on something else.

STRANGER: But I seem to know them, the whole lot! And I see them as if in a mirror; and they only pretend to eat . . . Is it a play that's being put on? . . . There's a couple resembling my parents, but only slightly.

I've never been afraid of anything before, because life was indifferent for me, but now I'm beginning to be afraid!

ABBESS: If you don't believe they're real people, we'll ask the Con-fessor to come over to present them to us. (*Signals to the* CONFESSOR, *who approaches*)

CONFESSOR *(in Dominican garb, black and white):* Sister!

ABBESS: Tell this patient who are at the table over there!

CONFESSOR: That's soon done.

STRANGER: Let me ask you first: Haven't we seen each other before?

CONFESSOR: Yes, I sat by your sickbed while you were feverish and received your confession—at your request . . .

STRANGER: What! My confession!

CONFESSOR: Yes, but I couldn't give you absolution because I had the impression it was only a matter of feverish dreams . . .

STRANGER: Why?

CONFESSOR: Since there was hardly a crime or a vice you didn't confess, and they were moreover, matters of such a nasty nature that one usually submits to strict penance before one asks for forgiveness. Since you have come to your senses again, I ought to ask if there were any basis to your self accusations.

The ABBESS *goes away.)*

STRANGER: Do you have the right to ask such questions?

CONFESSOR: No, I haven't, it's true!—On the other hand, you wanted to know in whose company you find yourself! Well, it isn't the happiest. There we have, for example, the madman, called Caesar who has lost his reason through reading the works of a certain author, whose notoriety was greater than his deserved fame; and then there's the beggar, who didn't want to admit he was a beggar because he had studied Latin and had been set free! And the doctor who's called the werewolf, who has a well-known past, and then a couple of parents, who worried themselves to death over a degenerate son, who raised his hand against them. That he didn't go to his father's funeral and in a drunken state profaned his mother's grave he'll have to answer for himself. There's his poor sister, whom he drove out into the snow in winter, with good intentions according to what he says. There sits a deserted wife with two unsupported children, and there sits another wife crocheting . . . so they're all old well-known acquaintances. Go over and say hello to them!

(During the latter part of the preceding speech, the STRANGER *has turned his back to the company. Now he goes to the table at the left his back always to the company and sits down. When he lifts his head, he sees the painting of Michael and lowers his eyes.)*

CONFESSOR (*goes up and stands behind the* STRANGER. *In the chapel is heard a Catholic requiem. The* CONFESSOR *speaks softly to the* STRANGER *while soft music is played*):

> *Quantus tremor est futurus*
> *Quando judex est venturus*
> *Cuncta stricte discussurus,*
> *Tuba mirum spargens sonum*
> *Per sepulchra regionum*
> *Coget omnes ante thronum,*
> *Mors stupebit et natura,*
> *Cum resurget creatura*
> *Liber scriptus proferetur*
> *In quo totum continetur*
> *Unde mundus judicetur.*
> *Judex ergo cum sedebit*
> *Quidquid latet apparebit*
> *Nil inultum remanebit.*

(He goes up to the pulpit by the table to the right. Opens the breviary. The music stops.)

CONFESSOR: Now we continue the reading.[46] "If thou wilt not hearken unto the voice of the Lord thy God, to observe to do all his commandments and his statutes which I commend thee this day; that all these curses shall come upon thee and overtake thee:

"Cursed *shalt* thou *be* in the city, and cursed *shalt* thou *be* in the field.

"Cursed *shall* be thy basket and thy store. . . .

"Cursed *shalt* thou *be* when thou comest in, and cursed *shalt* thou *be* when thou goest out."

COMPANY *(softly):* Cursed!

CONFESSOR: "The Lord shall send upon thee cursing, vexation, and rebuke, in all that thou settest thine hand unto for to do, until thou be destroyed, and until thou perish quickly; because of the wickedness of thy doings, whereby thou hast forsaken me."

COMPANY *(loudly):* Cursed!

CONFESSOR: "The Lord shall cause thee to be smitten before thine enemies; thou shalt go out one way against them, and flee seven ways before them: and shalt be removed unto all the kingdoms of the earth.

"And thy carcass shall be meat unto all fowls of the air, and unto the beasts of the earth, and no man shall fray *them* away!

"The Lord will smite thee with the botch of Egypt, and with the emerods, and with the scab, and with the itch, whereof thou canst not be healed.

"The Lord shall smite thee with madness, and blindness, and astonishment of heart: And thou shalt grope at noonday, as the blind gropeth in darkness, and thou shalt not prosper in thy ways: and thou shalt be only oppressed and spoiled evermore, and no man shall save *thee*.

"Thou shalt betroth a wife, and another man shall lie with her: thou shalt build a house, and thou shalt not dwell therein: thou shalt plant a vineyard, and shalt not gather the grapes thereof.

"Thy sons and thy daughters *shall* be given unto another people, and thine eyes shall look, and fail *with longing* for them all the day long: and *there shall be* no might in thine hand.

"And among these nations shalt thou find no ease, neither shall the sole of thy foot have rest: but the Lord shall give thee there a trembling heart, and failing of eyes, and sorrow of mind:

"And thy life shall hang in doubt before thee; and thou shalt fear day and night. . . .

"In the morning thou shalt say, would God it were even! and at even thou shalt say, would God it were morning! . . .

"Because thou servedst not the Lord thy God with joyfulness, and with gladness of heart, for the abundance of all *things;*

"Therefore shalt thou serve thine enemies which the Lord shall send against thee, in hunger, and in thirst, and in nakedness, and in want of all *things:* and he shall put a yoke of iron upon thy neck, until he have destroyed thee."

COMPANY: Amen!

(*The* CONFESSOR *has read the above quickly and loudly, without directing it to the* STRANGER; *the* COMPANY, *aside from the* LADY, *who is crocheting, have listened and cursed, but have not pretended not to notice the* STRANGER. *The latter has been sitting with his back to the* COMPANY, *quietly lost in thought.*)

(*The* STRANGER *rises to leave.*)

(*The* CONFESSOR *approaches him.*)

STRANGER: What was that?

CONFESSOR: Why, that was Deuteronomy.

STRANGER: So that's what it was! But I seem to remember that He blesses, too!

CONFESSOR: Yes, those who keep His commandments!

STRANGER: Well-l!—I can't deny it shook me for a moment, but are they temptations that have to be resisted or warnings that ought to be heeded? . . . Now I am certain I'm still feverish, and I'm leaving to find a real doctor.

CONFESSOR: Yes, but be sure it's *the* right one!

STRANGER: Of course, of course!

CONFESSOR: The one who cures "the blessed pangs of conscience."

ABBESS: If you ever need mercy, you know where to find it.

STRANGER: No, I don't!

ABBESS (*softly*): Well, I'll tell you! In a rose chamber by a large, running river.

STRANGER: That's true! In a rose chamber. Let me see: How long have I been here sick in bed?

ABBESS: Exactly three months today!

STRANGER: A quarter year! Have I been sleeping, or where have I been? (*Looks out through the window*) Why, it's fall. The trees are bare, and the clouds look cold!—Now I'm beginning to re-member!—Do you hear a mill that's grinding? A horn that's sounding? A river rushing, a forest whispering—and a woman weeping! Yes, you're right; that's the one place where I can find mercy! Farewell! (*Goes quickly*)

CONFESSOR (*to the* ABBESS): That fool! that fool!

[CURTAIN]

THE ROSE CHAMBER

The curtains have been taken away; the windows gape like black holes against the darkness outside; the pieces of furniture are covered with brown slip covers and have been pulled out to the center of the room; the flowering plants are gone; a large black iron stove is lighted. The MOTHER *is standing ironing white curtains in the light of a single candle.*

Someone knocks on the door.

MOTHER: Come in!

STRANGER *(enters):* Good evening?—Where's my wife?

MOTHER: So, it's you!—Where did you come from?

STRANGER: From hell—I think!—But where is my wife?

MOTHER: Which one?

STRANGER: Your question is justified. Everything's justified, except me!

MOTHER: There are reasons for that, I suspect, but it's a good thing you've noticed it. But where have you been?

STRANGER: Whether it was a poorhouse, an insane asylum, or an ordinary hospital I don't know, but I'd like to think it was a dream. I've been sick in bed, have lost my memory, and can't believe three months have passed. But where's my wife?

MOTHER: I ought to ask you that! When you deserted her, she left—to look for you, but I don't know if she got tired of looking.

STRANGER: It looks terrible here! Where's your father?

MOTHER: No one has any sorrow where he is.

STRANGER: He's dead, you mean.

MOTHER: Yes! He's dead!

STRANGER: You say it as if you'd like to add him to my "victims."

MOTHER: Maybe I'd be right if I did . . .

STRANGER: He didn't look that sensitive and showed he could sustain a royal hatred.

MOTHER: No, he could hate only evil—in himself and others.

STRANGER: So I'm wrong about that, too!

(Pause)

MOTHER: What do you seek here?

STRANGER: Mercy!

MOTHER: At last! How did you have it at the hospital? Sit down and tell me.

STRANGER *(sits down):* I don't want to recall that! Besides, I don't know if it was a hospital.

MOTHER: Strange! But what happened after you left here? . . .
STRANGER: I fell down a precipice and injured my hip and fainted
  . . . If you speak nicely to me, I'll tell you more.
MOTHER: I'll talk nicely!
STRANGER: Well then! I woke up in a bed with steel bars which
  were painted red, and three men were pulling in a line which
  ran between two blocks; and everytime they pulled, I seemed
  to get two inches taller . . .
MOTHER: You had dislocated something, and they were setting it
  straight . . .
STRANGER: That's true. I hadn't thought of that! But afterwards
  . . . well, I was lying there seeing my whole past roll by in a
  panorama, from childhood, through youth, way up to . . . and
  when it was over it started over again; and the whole time I
  heard a mill grinding . . . I still hear it . . . yes, it's here, too,
MOTHER: Those weren't pleasant pictures you saw.
STRANGER: No! And I finally came to the conclusion—that I was
  a terrible scoundrel.
MOTHER: Why do you use that expression?
STRANGER: I know you wanted me to say "a wicked human being,"
  but, you see, the person who says that about himself seems to
  me to be bragging, and there's an absolute certainty about that
  judgment I haven't won yet.
MOTHER: You still doubt?
STRANGER: Yes, some things and many things. But one thing's
  beginning to clear up . . .
MOTHER: What?
STRANGER: That there are things . . . and powers . . . that . . .
  I haven't believed in before.
MOTHER: Have you noticed, too, that it's neither you nor any
  other human being who controls your unusual destiny?
STRANGER: That's what I seem to notice!
MOTHER: Then you're on the way.
STRANGER: But I'm bankrupt, too: I've lost my ability to write;
  and I can't sleep at night . . .
MOTHER: Why, what's wrong?
STRANGER: They call it the nightmare, I think . . . and last and

worst: I don't dare to die, for I'm not sure any more that would end the whole miserable state.

MOTHER: Well-l!

STRANGER: But the worst of all: I've come to despise myself so I'd like to be free of myself, but I don't see any possibility of that. If I were a Christian, I couldn't keep the first commandment, "Love my neighbor as myself," for then I'd hate my neighbor, and I suppose I do. It's probably true I'm a big scoundrel and have always suspected that, but since I haven't wanted to be fooled by life, I've kept a watchful eye on "the others," and, when I've seen the others weren't any better than I, I've been furious when they've tried to tell me what to do.

MOTHER: Yes, but you've misunderstood the whole thing when you've thought it was something between you and the others. This is a matter between you and Him . . .

STRANGER: Who?

MOTHER: The Invisible One, who has controlled your destiny.

STRANGER: May I get to see Him!

MOTHER: Then you'll die!

STRANGER: Oh no!

MOTHER: Where have you got this damnable rebellious spirit? If you won't bend as the rest of us, you'll have to be broken as a reed!

STRANGER: I don't know where I've got this damnable defiance. It's true I can tremble before an unpaid bill but if I were going to climb Mt. Sinai [47] and meet the Eternal One, I wouldn't cover my face!

MOTHER: Mary, Mother of Jesus!—If you talk like that, I'll think you're the child of the devil!

STRANGER: That seems to be the general opinion of me around here. But I've heard that those who are close to the devil usually are rewarded with honor, possessions and gold, especially gold! Do you think I deserve the suspicion?

MOTHER: You'll bring a curse on my house!

STRANGER: Then I'll leave your house . . .

MOTHER: At night! No!—Where do you intend to go?

STRANGER: I'll go to find the only one I don't hate.

MOTHER: Are you sure she'll receive you?
STRANGER: Absolutely!
MOTHER: But I'm not sure.
STRANGER: But I am!
MOTHER: Then I'll have to awaken your doubts.
STRANGER: You can't!
MOTHER: Yes, I can.
STRANGER: You're lying!
MOTHER: We're not talking nicely now—so we'll stop.—Can you sleep in the attic?
STRANGER: Anywhere at all; I can't sleep anyway!
MOTHER: Then I say good night to you whether you think I mean it or not!
STRANGER: There aren't rats in the attic, I hope! I'm not afraid of ghosts, but rats are unpleasant.
MOTHER: It's good you're not afraid of ghosts, for . . . no one has slept through one night up there, what ever's wrong.
STRANGER *(hesitates for a moment; then):* You're the meanest person I've ever run across, but that's because you're religious!
MOTHER: Good night!

[CURTAIN]

THE KITCHEN

It's dark, but the moon throws moving shadows of the bars at the windows on the floor when storm clouds pass.

In the corner to the right under the crucifix, where the OLD MAN *used to sit are hanging on the wall: hunting horns, gun, hunting bag. A stuffed bird of prey stands on the table. Since the windows are open, the curtains are fluttering, and kitchen rags, scrubbing aprons, and towels hanging on a line in front of the stove move in the wind. The sighing of the wind can be heard along with the roar of a distant waterfall. Now and then there's a pounding on a wooden floor.*

STRANGER *(enters, half-dressed, carrying a lighted candle in his hand):* Is there anyone here?—No one! *(Comes forward with the candle,*

which somewhat weakens the play of shadows) What's that moving
on the floor?—Is there anyone here?—*(He goes toward the table,
but when he catches sight of the bird of prey, he stops as if turned to
stone)* Good God!

MOTHER *(enters; dressed, with a candle in her hand):* Are you still
up?

STRANGER: Yes, I couldn't sleep!

MOTHER *(gently):* Why not, my son?

STRANGER: Someone was walking above this room.

MOTHER: Impossible—there isn't any room above this one.

STRANGER: That's what disturbed me!—But what's that moving
like snakes on the floor? . . .

MOTHER: It's the moonlight!

STRANGER: Yes, it's the moonlight! And there's a stuffed bird!
And scrub rags! Everything's so simple and natural, but that's
just what disturbs me.—Who's pounding in the night? Has anyone
been shut out?

MOTHER: No, it's a horse stamping in the stable.

STRANGER: I've never heard any mention of that!

MOTHER: Well, there are horses that are hagridden.

STRANGER: Who does it?

MOTHER: Who knows!

STRANGER: Let me sit down for a moment!

MOTHER: Sit down and let me talk seriously with you. I was nasty
last night and I apologize, but you see just because I'm so thoroughly mean, I use religion as I use the hairshirt and the stone
floor. To avoid offending you, I'll answer what makes me hagridden—it's my evil conscience. If it's I or someone else that punishes
me I don't know and I don't think I have the right to try to
find out!—Now tell me what happened to you in that room.

STRANGER: Really . . . I don't know . . . I haven't *seen* anything,
but when I went in, I felt that someone was in there. I looked
about—with my candle lighted, but found no one. Then I went
to bed. Someone began to walk with heavy footsteps above my
head . . . Do you believe in ghosts and those who walk again?

MOTHER: No . . . my religion forbids that, but I believe our own
sense of right has the ability to create means of punishment . . .

STRANGER: Well! After a while an icecold stream of air hit my chest, searched until it found my heart—so that became cold—and I had to get up . . .

MOTHER: And then?

STRANGER: Then I had to stand there on the floor watching my whole life pass in review, everything, every blessed thing . . . and that's the worst of all.

MOTHER: Yes! I know all this—I've gone through it, too. That sickness has no name, and there's only one cure . . .

STRANGER: And that is?

MOTHER: You know! You know what children must do when they've been bad!

STRANGER: What?

MOTHER: First, ask for forgiveness!

STRANGER: And then?

MOTHER: Try to set things right . . .

STRANGER: It isn't enough to suffer as one deserves?

MOTHER: No, that's only revenge!

STRANGER: Well, what else?

MOTHER: Can you restore a life you've destroyed? Can you undo a wicked deed? Undo?

STRANGER: No, that's true!—But I was forced to do it, I was forced to take when no one gave me the right; but shame to the one who forced me! (sighs—highly disturbed; his hand on his chest) Now he's here, in this room; and he's tearing the heart out of me!

MOTHER: Bow down!

STRANGER: I can't!

MOTHER: On your knees!

STRANGER: I don't want to!

MOTHER: May Christ have mercy on you! Lord, have mercy on him!—(To the STRANGER) On your knees before the Crucified Lord! Only He can undo it!

STRANGER: No, not before Him! Not before Him! And if I'm forced to do it, I'll take it back . . . afterwards!

MOTHER: Down on your knees! My son!

STRANGER: I can't get down on my knees! I can't . . . Help me, Eternal God! (Pause)

MOTHER: *(hastily murmurs a prayer; then says):* Is it better?

STRANGER *(pulls himself together):* Yes! . . . But do you know what that was? It wasn't death; it was annihilation.

MOTHER: Annihilation of the divine—what we call spiritual death.

STRANGER *(seriously, without irony):* So that's what you mean . . . then I'm beginning to understand.

MOTHER: My son, you've left Jerusalem, and you're on the way to Damascus. Go there! the same way you came, and place a cross at each station but stop at the seventh. You don't have fourteen as He did!

STRANGER: You're speaking in riddles!

MOTHER: Yes! Go—seek out those to whom you have something to say—your wife first.

STRANGER: Where?

MOTHER: Seek her—But don't forget to look after the one—you call the werewolf—

STRANGER: Never!

MOTHER: That's what you probably said when you were to come here . . . and, as I told you, I expected you.

STRANGER: What reasons did you have for that?

MOTHER: I had no tangible reasons . . .

STRANGER: Just as I had seen this kitchen in a—state of ecstasy if you will . . .

MOTHER: That's why I regret I wanted to separate you and Inge-borg, for you were destined to meet each other . . . But go find her. If you do, that's fine; if you don't, that would probably be as it was intended.—But dawn has come, morning is here, and night is over!

STRANGER: And what a night!

MOTHER: You'll remember it!

STRANGER: Not all of it, but some of it!

MOTHER *(looks out through the window; as if to herself says):* Beautiful morning star, why have you fallen from Heaven? [48]
    (Pause)

STRANGER: Have you noticed that before the sun comes up, a human being shivers. Are we children of darkness since we tremble before the light?

MOTHER: Do you never get tired of questioning?
STRANGER: No, never! You see, I long for light!
MOTHER: Go and seek it then! And peace be with you!

[CURTAIN]

ACT IV

IN THE RAVINE

The same landscape as before, but it is autumn; the trees are leafless.
Work is going on in the smithy; the mill is going.
THE SMITH *stands in the door to the left; the* MILLER'S WIFE *in*
the door to the right.
THE LADY *is dressed in a jacket and leather hat; she is in mourning.*
THE STRANGER *is dressed in a south German alpine outfit: a coat*
of mixed shades, knee pants, alpine shoes, staff; a green hunter's hat
with grouse feathers. Over these he is wearing a brown "Imperial mantle"
with cape and hood.
LADY *(enters; dressed for traveling; tired and distressed):* Has any gentle-
man dressed for traveling gone by here?
(*The* SMITH *and* MILLER'S WIFE *shake their heads negatively.*)
LADY: Can I stay here overnight?
(*The* SMITH *and* MILLER'S WIFE *shake their heads negatively.*)
LADY (*to the* SMITH): May I stand in the door to warm myself for
a moment?
(*The* SMITH *pushes her back.*)
LADY: May God reward you as you deserve!
(*Goes; can be seen shortly afterwards on the footbridge; and then*
disappears.)
STRANGER *(enters; dressed for traveling):* Has any lady dressed for
traveling crossed the stream?

(*The* SMITH *and* MILLER'S WIFE *shake their heads negatively.*)

STRANGER [*to the* MILLER'S WIFE]: May I buy some bread? See—
I have the money!

(*The* MILLER'S WIFE *rejects the money.*)

STRANGER: No mercy!

ECHO *(in the distance imitates his voice):* Mercy!

(*The* SMITH *and* MILLER'S WIFE *burst into prolonged, loud laughter, the end of which* ECHO *answers.*)

STRANGER: I like that—an eye for an eye, a tooth for a tooth! [49]
That eased my conscience a bit!

(Goes into the ravine.)

[CURTAIN]

THE HIGHWAY

The same landscape as before but in autumn dress. The BEGGAR
*is sitting by an atonement chapel with a glue-covered switch and a bird
cage with a starling in it.*

STRANGER *(enters; dressed as in the preceding scene):* Have you seen
any lady dressed for traveling go by, Beggar?

BEGGAR: I've seen five hundred traveling ladies go by, but, seriously
speaking, will you quit calling me Beggar? I do have work now.

STRANGER: So it's you?

BEGGAR: *Ille ego qui quondam . . .*

STRANGER: What are you working at?

BEGGAR: I have a starling that whistles and talks . . .

STRANGER: That's to say: he's the one who works!

BEGGAR: Yes, I've become my own man!

STRANGER: Do you catch birds, too?

BEGGAR: The glued switch, eh? No-o, I keep that for the sake of
appearance only!

STRANGER: So appearance is important to you?

BEGGAR: Yes, what else should be? What doesn't show is only
pure—nonsense.

STRANGER: And that's the summary of your whole philosophy of life?

BEGGAR: My whole philosophy! My point of view can certainly seem old-fashioned but . . .

STRANGER: Say one single serious word: Say something about your past.

BEGGAR: Nah! What would be the point of digging up that old stuff! Keep on going, sir; just keep going! Do you think I'm always this cheerful? No, it's only when I meet you, for you're so damned funny.

STRANGER: How can you smile when you've wasted your whole life?

BEGGAR: Now you're getting impertinent!—But if you can't smile at your misery, not even at others', then life's pointless!—Listen; If you follow that wheel track in the dirt, you'll get to the lake, and that's where the road ends! Sit down and rest there, and you'll get another view of the whole thing! There are so many accidents, religious objects, and unpleasant memories here, you can't think straight about the Rose Chamber. But just follow the tracks, only the tracks! If it gets a little dirty occasionally, just lift your wings and flap them!

Concerning flapping: Once I heard a bird sing something about Polykrates' ring and having received all the glory of the world but not knowing what to do with it. So he prophecied in the east and in the west about the great nothingness he had been in on creating out of the empty universe. I wouldn't insist it was you if I didn't believe it so much I could swear to it: and once when I asked you if you knew who I was, you answered that that didn't interest you. I offered my friendship to you, but you refused it with one single little word *shame!* Well, I'm neither touchy nor unforgiving, so I'll give you a bit of advice as food for thought on the way: Follow the tracks!

STRANGER *(turns to the side):* No, you won't deceive me again!

BEGGAR: You believe only evil; that's why you get only evil! Try for once to believe good. Try!

STRANGER: I want to try! But if I'm fooled, I have the right to . . .

BEGGAR: You never have the right to do that!

STRANGER *(as if to himself):* Who is it that reads my secret thoughts? Who turns my soul inside out? Who is persecuting me? Why do you persecute me?

BEGGAR: Why do you persecute me? Saul! [50]

(*The* STRANGER *makes a gesture of horror; goes.*)

(*The chord from the funeral march is heard as before.*)

LADY *(enters):* Have you seen a gentleman dressed for traveling go by?

BEGGAR: Yes, there was a poor soul just now, who limped on.

LADY: The one I'm looking for doesn't limp.

BEGGAR: This one didn't either, but he seems to have got something wrong with his hip, which made his walking a little difficult. No, I won't be mean!—Look there—in the dirt of the road!

LADY: Where?

BEGGAR *(points):* There! Where you see the tracks of a wagon, and alongside them the impression of a rough shoe that has tramped heavily . . .

LADY *(examines the tracks):* It's he! Yes, those steps are heavy . . . but will I be able to catch up with him?

BEGGAR: Follow the tracks!

LADY *(takes his hand and kisses it):* Thank you, my friend! *(Goes)*

[CURTAIN]

BY THE SEA

The same landscape as before but in winter garb. The sea is very dark; on the horizon the clouds take forms of towers resembling heads of giants. In the distance can be seen the three white stripped masts of a wrecked ship; they resemble three white crosses. The table and the bench under the tree are still there, but the chairs are gone.

There is snow on the ground.

Now and then a buoy can be heard.

(*The* STRANGER *enters from the left; stops for a moment and looks out to sea; then he goes out to the right back of the cottage*).

(*The* LADY *enters from the left; is following The* STRANGER'S *footprints in the snow; goes out to the right in front of the cottage.*)

(*The* STRANGER *enters from the right; goes toward the left; discovers the* LADY'S *footprints; stops; looks back toward the right.*)

LADY (*enters, rushes into his arms, but draws back*): You push me away?

STRANGER: No! But there seemed to be someone between us!

LADY: I suspect there is!—But what a meeting!

STRANGER: Yes, it has become winter, as you see!

LADY: And I feel how coldness radiates from you!

STRANGER: I almost turned to ice in the mountains!

LADY: Won't spring ever come again?

STRANGER: Not for us! Driven out of the Garden of Eden we'll have to wander on among the stones and thistles; and when we've cut our feet and had our hands pricked, the need to sprinkle salt in each other's wounds will come. And that mill is grinding, and it'll never stop, for it won't run out of water.

LADY: Most likely you're right . . .

STRANGER: Yes, but I don't want to give way to the unavoidable; I don't want us to tear each other to pieces, but I will rip myself open as a sacrifice for reconciliation with the gods. I'll say: The blame is mine; I was the one who taught you to loosen the bonds; I was the one who enticed you; and then you can blame me— for everything; the act itself and its consequences . . .

LADY: You can't bear that burden!

STRANGER: Yes, there are moments, when I feel I bear within me all the sin and sorrow and filth and shame in the world; there are times when I think the wicked act, the sin itself is a punishment placed upon me! You know I was sick with fever recently and, among other things, well, a lot happened—I dreamt I saw a crucifix without the Crucified One; and when I asked the Dominican—there was a Dominican there among many others—well, I asked him what that could mean, and he answered: "You don't want to have Him suffer for you—so suffer yourself!" And that's why people have become so sensitive about their own suffering!

LADY: And that's why conscience begins to be so heavy when no one helps carry . . .

STRANGER: So you, too, are there?

LADY: Not there—but on the way!

STRANGER: Put your hand in mine, and we'll wander on together.

LADY: Where?

STRANGER: Back—the same way we came! Are you tired?

LADY: Not any more!

STRANGER: I've been on the verge of collapse several times, but I met a strange beggar . . . well, you probably remember him— the one who's supposed to be like me; and he asked me to try to believe his intentions were good. I believed—I really tried . . . and . . .

LADY: And?

STRANGER: Things went well for me! . . . And since then I feel I have the strength to go on . . .

LADY: Let's go on!

STRANGER *(turned toward the sea):* But it's turning dark, and the clouds are piling up . . .

LADY: Don't look at the clouds . . .

STRANGER: And below them? What's that?

LADY: It's only a sunken ship!

STRANGER *(whispers):* Three crosses!—What new Golgotha [51] lies ahead for us?

LADY: But they're white; that bodes well!

STRANGER: Can anything good happen to us any more?

LADY: Yes, but not right away.

STRANGER: Let's go on!

[CURTAIN]

THE HOTEL ROOM

As before. The LADY *is sitting beside the* STRANGER *crocheting.*

LADY: Say something!

STRANGER: No, I have only unpleasant things to say since we came into this room.

LADY: Why couldn't you wait to get into this terrible room?

STRANGER: I don't know! That was what I wanted least of all, and that's why I began to long to get here to be tortured.

LADY: And you have been tortured . . .

STRANGER: Yes! I don't hear any songs any more and see nothing beautiful. During the day I hear the mill grinding and see the large panorama that has grown into a cosmorama, and at night . . .

LADY: Yes, why did you scream in your sleep?

STRANGER: I had a dream . . .

LADY: A real dream . . .

STRANGER: A terrifyingly real dream . . . but here's the curse; I feel a need to tell it, and to whom but you? But you won't let me, because then I touch the door to the closed room . . .

LADY: The past . . .

STRANGER: Yes!

LADY *(simply):* There's always something crazy in a secret room like that!

STRANGER: Yes, I suspect there is! *(Pause)*

LADY: Tell me!

STRANGER: I'm afraid I have to!—Well then, I dreamt I saw— your former husband married to—my former wife. My children who had got him as their father . . .

LADY: Only you could ever imagine that!

STRANGER: If it were only that!—But I saw him mistreat them. *(Gets up)* And when I naturally choked him to death . . . no, I can't go on . . . But I won't get any peace before I've learned the truth; and to get that I have to go to him in his own home!

LADY: So you've come that far!

STRANGER: I've been on my way toward that, and now I can't stop . . . I have to see him!

LADY: But if he won't receive you?

STRANGER: I'll go to him as a patient and tell him about my sickness . . .

LADY *(frightened):* Don't tell him that . . .

STRANGER: I understand: you mean he might feel he'd have to detain me as an insane person . . . well, I'll have to risk that

. . . and I have a need for taking risks about . . . everything, freedom, life, well being! I need emotional experience so strong it will bring my ego to the surface; I long for torture that'll restore the balance in this situation so I don't need to go around feeling guilty. So down into the snakepit—as soon as possible!

LADY: If I could go with you . . .

STRANGER: You don't need to: my agony will do for both of us!

LADY: Then I'll call you my liberator, and the curse I uttered over you once will turn into a blessing!—See, it's spring again?

STRANGER: I've seen it on that Christmas rose that has started withering.

LADY: But don't you feel there's spring in the air?

STRANGER: Yes, I seem to feel the chill in my heart beginning to let up . . .

LADY: Maybe the werewolf can cure you completely!

STRANGER: We'll see! Perhaps he isn't so dangerous.

LADY: He certainly isn't as cruel as you!

STRANGER: But my dream! Imagine . . .

LADY: . . . if it were only a dream!—But now I have no more yarn and my useless work is done! It has become dirty . . .

STRANGER: But it can be washed!

LADY: Or colored!

STRANGER: Rose red!

LADY: Never!

STRANGER: It looks like a manuscript roll . . .

LADY: With our story on it . . .

STRANGER: Written in the dust of the highway, in tears and blood . . .

LADY: Well, the story's soon over! Go and prepare the last chapter!

STRANGER: Then we'll meet again at the seventh station! Where we began!

[CURTAIN]

ACT V

AT THE DOCTOR'S

The setting approximately as before. But the woodpile is smaller by half. On a bench by the porch are surgical instruments, knives, saws, tongs, etc.

The DOCTOR *is busy polishing his instruments.*

SISTER *(comes out from the porch):* A patient wants to see you!

DOCTOR: Do you know him?

SISTER: I haven't seen him, but here's his card.

DOCTOR *(looks at the card):* You know . . . this goes beyond anything I've ever been in on . . .

SISTER: Is it he?

DOCTOR: It's he! Though I don't despise courage, I find this directness cynical—I feel it's like a challenge. Still let him come!

SISTER: Do you really mean that?

DOCTOR: Absolutely! But if you want to, you can talk with him a little in your simple, candid way.

SISTER: I had intended to . . .

DOCTOR: Fine! You do the rough work, and I'll follow up with the finishing plane.

SISTER: Yes, rely on me—I'll tell him everything your good heart forbids you to say.

DOCTOR: Hush—about that heart of mine, and hurry up so I don't lose my calm. But shut the doors!

(The SISTER *goes.)*

DOCTOR: What are you up to by the garbage can again, Caesar?

(CAESAR *comes up.)*

DOCTOR: Listen, Caesar! If your enemy comes and puts his head in your lap, what would you do?

CAESAR: I'd cut off his head!

DOCTOR: That's not what I've taught you!

CAESAR: No, you've said one ought to put live coals on it, but I think that's shameful.

DOCTOR: I think so, too, really, for it's more cruel and more cunning.—Can you tell me if it isn't better to revenge oneself a little so the other fellow gets straightened out and sort of feels vindicated?

CAESAR: Since you understand that better than I do, why do you ask me?

DOCTOR: Silence! I'm not talking to you!—So: we'll cut off his head and then . . . we'll see!

CAESAR: It depends on how he behaves.

DOCTOR: Quite right!—how he behaves!—Sh-h!—Go away!

STRANGER *(comes down from the porch; distressed but with a certain resigned self-control):* Doctor!

DOCTOR: Yes!

STRANGER: You're amazed to see me here . . .

DOCTOR *(seriously):* I quit being amazed long ago, but I'll have to begin again, I see.

STRANGER: May we speak confidentially?

DOCTOR: About everything considered suitable between civilized people! Are you ill?

STRANGER *(slowly):* Yes-s!

DOCTOR: Why do you come to *me?*

STRANGER: You should be able to guess that.

DOCTOR: I don't want to!—What is your illness?

STRANGER *(hesitantly):* I can't sleep.

DOCTOR: That's not an illness; that's merely a symptom. Have you seen any other doctor about it?

STRANGER: I've been bedridden in—an institution, had fever ———But it was an extremely strange fever . . .

DOCTOR: What was strange about it?

STRANGER: May I ask you this: Can one be on one's feet and still be delirious?

DOCTOR: Yes, if one's insane, but only then!—
   (*The* STRANGER *gets up; sits down again.*)

DOCTOR: What was the name of the hospital?

STRANGER: The Good Help.

DOCTOR: There's no hospital with that name!

STRANGER: Is it a cloister then?

DOCTOR: No, it's an insane asylum!

(*The* STRANGER *gets up.*)

DOCTOR *(gets up; calls out):* Sister, shut the street entrance! And the little gate to the highway! (*To the* STRANGER) Please sit down!—I have to keep them shut because of the many tramps around here.

STRANGER *(becomes calmer):* Doctor, an honest question: Do you think I'm insane?

DOCTOR: People don't usually get honest answers to that question, you know; and no one who has that trouble believes what one says. So it's absolutely all the same to you what I think.—But, on the other hand, if you feel your soul is sick, look for a priest.

STRANGER: Won't you take on that job for a moment?

DOCTOR: No, I lack the calling.

STRANGER: If——

DOCTOR *(interrupts him):* Besides I haven't time, for we're getting ready for a wedding.

STRANGER: My dream . . .

DOCTOR: I thought it would comfort you to hear I've consoled myself, as they say, that it would delight you, actually—that's how it usually is . . . but I see it increases your suffering!—There's something behind this! Now I'll have to find out . . . How can it affect you unpleasantly that I'm marrying a widow?

STRANGER: With two children?

DOCTOR: Oh ho! Oh ho!—I get it! That's an infernal thought, worthy of you! Listen, if there were a hell, you'd head it—you have a gift for dreaming up punishments beyond anything I could come up with—and I'm called the werewolf.

STRANGER: Well, it can seem . . .

DOCTOR: For a long time I hated you, as you may know, because you gave me an undeserved bad reputation through your unforgivable act, but when I got older and more sensible, I understood that if the punishment was unjust that time, I deserved it because of other sins that weren't discovered, and besides you were a child who had enough of a conscience to punish yourself, so that matter needn't bother you either! Is that why you came?

STRANGER: Yes!

DOCTOR: Would you be satisfied if I let you go without any condition?

(*The* STRANGER *looks at him questioningly.*)

DOCTOR: Or did you perhaps think I intended to lock you up? Or saw into you with my instruments over there? Kill you, perhaps? One should put such wretches out of their misery, of course!

(*The* STRANGER *looks at his watch.*)

DOCTOR: You'll catch the boat!

STRANGER: Will you shake hands with me?

DOCTOR: No, I can't! I mayn't! Besides, what good would it do for me to forgive you, when you don't have the strength to forgive yourself?—There are things, of course, that can be helped only by being undone; this one can't!

STRANGER: "The Good Help."

DOCTOR: That wasn't so bad!—You challenged fate, and you lost no disgrace in a good fight. I did so, too, but like you I've haggled about my woodpile; I don't want thunder indoors, and I don't play with the lightning any more.

STRANGER: One station more—and I'm there.

DOCTOR: One never gets there!—Farewell!

STRANGER: Farewell.

[CURTAIN]

THE STREET CORNER

As in Act I, the STRANGER *is sitting on the bench under the tree writing in the sand.*

LADY *(enters):* What are you doing?

STRANGER: I'm writing in the sand, still.

LADY: Don't you hear any songs coming?

STRANGER *(points toward the church):* Yes, but from in there!— There's someone I've been unjust to without knowing it!

LADY: I thought our wandering was almost over when we happened to get back here . . .

STRANGER: Where we started . . . on the street, between the tavern, the church—and the post office. The post office! P-, o-, s-, t- . . . Didn't I decide not to pick up a registered letter here . . .

LADY: Yes, because it had only nasty news . . .

STRANGER: Or legal documents about the trial. *(Strikes his forehead)* That's it!

LADY: Go in and believe it's a good letter!

STRANGER *(ironically):* Good?

LADY: Yes! Try to imagine that!

STRANGER *(going into the post office):* I'll try!

(*The* LADY *walks about on the sidewalk, waiting.*)

(*The* STRANGER *comes out with a letter.*)

LADY: Well-l?

STRANGER: I'm ashamed!—It was the money!

LADY: You see!—And all this suffering, and all these tears—in vain . . .

STRANGER: Not in vain!—It looks mean, this game, but it probably isn't! It was the Invisible One I was unjust to when I misjudged . . .

LADY: Sh-h! Don't! Don't blame anyone!

STRANGER: No! It was my own stupidity, or wickedness . . . I didn't want to be fooled by life, so I was!—But the elves . . .

LADY: Have undone what they did!—Let's go.

STRANGER: Yes, let's go and hide ourselves in the mountains with our misery . . .

LADY: Yes, the mountains conceal!—But first I must go in to light a candle for my blessed St. Elizabeth . . .[52]

(*The* STRANGER *shakes his head.*)

LADY: Come!

STRANGER: Well, I can go through, of course, but I won't stay!

LADY: You don't know that!—Come!—You'll hear new songs in there.

STRANGER *(follows her toward the church entrance):* Perhaps!

LADY: Come!

[CURTAIN]

Notes on
'To Damascus, I'

1. According to Acts, Saul, persecutor of the followers of Christ, set out for Damascus, now the capital of Syria, to bring back believers in Christ there as prisoners to Jerusalem for punishment. See Acts, Chapter 9, for an account of the miracle that took place on Saul's journey to Damascus, noting particularly Saul's certainty about knowing the truth and his trying to force truth as he saw it upon others, his being laid low on the road to Damascus, his being struck blind, his being rebuked by the Lord, his deliverance from blindness, and his being given a very special mission or assignment. Verses such as "he is a chosen vessel unto me, to bear my name before the Gentiles, and kings . . . . For I will shew him how great things he must suffer for my name's sake" suggest parallels Strindberg believed he saw between his Inferno experiences and those of Saul or, as he is more commonly known, St. Paul.

2. The "characters" are not individualized as the "characterless characters" or dynamic, complex human beings Strindberg discussed in the Preface to *Lady Julie* are but may, for want of a better term, be called types, even abstractions of aspects of a specific person.

3. The funeral march is the one composed by Felix Mendelssohn-Bartholdy (1809–47) as Strindberg makes clear later.

4. The Swedish *Den okände* is, literally translated, the Unknown One, the person who does not really know himself and whom others do not know either or, if you will, a stranger to himself and others.

5. *De profundis,* "out of the depths," is the beginning of Psalm 130: "Out of the depths have I cried unto thee, O Lord."

6. *En bortbyting* (a changeling) is, according to folklore, a child, deformed physically or otherwise, that troll or elf parents have secretly exchanged for a normal unbaptized human child.

7. *Älvorna* (the elves) are in folklore less unattractive than *troll*. Both are, of course, supernatural creatures, according to popular notions.

8. Eve is the first woman, the wife of Adam, and the first mother; for

90

Strindberg the name represented the epitome of the eternally feminine, the complement of the masculine that was to reconcile him to life.

9. Strindberg's parents had married September 24, 1847, after living together for several years. Strindberg was born on January 22, 1849. The first volume of his autobiography, *The Son of a Servant,* contains detailed information about his family with some emphasis on less happy aspects of family life. Two brothers, Carl Axel and Oscar, were born before their parents were married.

10. The Church of Sweden is the official national church and has had great power over Swedes, including in Strindberg's day a powerful voice in preliminary hearings and divorce trials. See *The Bond* for one use Strindberg made of these facts.

11. See any biography for an account of Strindberg's fear that he might be losing his mind. *A Madman's Defense* has information about the importance of this fear in the breakup of his first marriage.

12. Market fairs.

13. Strindberg was humiliated when Knut Hamsun, the Norwegian novelist, issued a successful public appeal for financial aid to Strindberg during the depths of the Inferno. Nathan Söderblom, then pastor of the Swedish Church in Paris and later archbishop of Uppsala, had also collected money for Strindberg. Such help, Strindberg felt, reduced him to the level of begging.

14. According to legend, Polykrates, the dictator of Samos in the second half of the sixth century B.C., threw a ring, his "most precious" possession, into the sea to appease the gods' jealousy of his good fortune.

15. The mandrake *(Mandragora officinarum)* was used as a narcotic in medicine and as a magic device in love potions and the like. Figures resembling human beings made out of its root were used as good luck pieces. The Christmas rose is apparently the herb *Helleborus niger* with white or purple flowers.

16. *A Madman's Defense,* essentially an account of his first marriage, was certainly inappropriate reading for Siri von Essen's successors.

17. Bluebeard, the epitome of the cruel, jealous husband, forbade, according to the popular legend, each of his wives to open a door to a room in which he kept the bodies of his wives who had disobeyed his order and had therefore been killed.

18. See any encyclopedia for accounts of Medea's inhuman acts including her persuading the daughters of King Pelias to try to rejuvenate their father by cutting him up and cooking him with magic herbs in a kettle. Medea did not supply the daughters with the proper herbs.

19. A species of carpenter ant.

20. "Ave Maris Stella" ("hail, thou star of ocean") is one of the earliest and most popular Marian hymns.

21. By the time these matters came up in Strindberg's life he had been subjected to two actual and major trials: the blasphemy trial which followed the publication of *Giftas I* (1884; *Being Married;* translated as *Married,* 1917, and as *Getting Married,* 1973), and the divorce trial. Both were highly disturbing for Strindberg.

22. Any Strindberg biography contains information about the Powers, the supernatural forces that meant a great deal to Strindberg from the Inferno Period (1894–97) on. Martin Lamm's *Strindberg och makterna (Strindberg and the Powers),* (Stockholm: 1936) is the best Swedish introduction to this matter.

23. According to folklore, a werewolf is a man who willingly or through magic has been transformed into a wolf, i.e., a bloodthirsty animal.

24. *The Inferno* (1897) or its continuation *Legender* (1897–98, *Legends*) would fit this nicely. Some contemporaries believed the two volumes proved that Strindberg had "crossed the line" into insanity.

25. July 27 used to be called the Seven Sleepers' Day. The legend of the seven sleepers is the story of seven brothers who slept for about two hundred years and were then awakened by God to testify about the resurrection. Folklore says the weather on that day determines the weather for the following seven weeks.

26. See Genesis 19 for the account of the destruction of sinful Sodom. Note particularly verse 26: "But his [Lot's] wife looked back from behind him, and she became a pillar of salt."

27. At a Swedish commencement *(promotion)* each new Ph.D. and each new recipient of an honorary or jubilee doctorate was crowned with a laurel wreath in Strindberg's day; today those in the humanities are so crowned; those in the sciences and medicine receive the doctoral hat. Even actors and musicians received laurel wreaths. See *The Dance of Death,* for an example.

28. The scene is a distorted reflection of disturbing details from Strindberg's and Frida Uhl's getting married on Heligoland, 16 May 1893. See any biography.

29. See a biography or *The Inferno* for an account of Strindberg's attempts at making gold.

30. According to the ancient Greeks, the three fates are Clotho, who spins the thread of life; Lachesis, who determines its length; and Atropos, who cuts it off.

31. One's Achilles' heel is his most vulnerable point. According to the legend, Achilles the famous Greek hero had been dipped into the River Styx to make him invulnerable but, unfortunately, Thetis (his mother and goddess of the sea) had held him by the heel which was consequently not touched by the water.

32. The Angelus (so called from its first word *Angelus Domini* or Angel of the Lord) is the prayer to be recited morning, noon, and evening. The ringing of the church bells to summon the faithful to prayer is also known as the Angelus.

33. Her parents' home was at Mondsee on the Danube in Austria.

34. Frida Uhl Strindberg's parents were "divorced" shortly after Frida's birth. Her father then became the editor of *Wiener Zeitung;* her mother returned to her parents' home, the estate on the Danube.

35. See Luke 15: 11–32 for the parable of the prodigal son. The prodigal son was, of course, a wastrel and a sinner: "Father, I have sinned against heaven, and before thee! And am no more worthy to be called thy son."

36. The hill on which Christ was crucified is a skull-like elevation in Jerusalem.

37. The great river is the Danube. See note 34.

38. The river sprite *(näcken* or *strömkarlen)* is, according to folklore, a supernatural figure who entices human beings into drowning in the river through his playing of the violin. A person can protect himself from the river sprite by throwing a stone into the water.

39. See note 34. Strindberg's divorce from his first wife Siri von Essen became final in 1892.

40. "The *blessed* mill" has the symbolic significance implicit in the statement, "the mills of the gods grind slowly."

41. See note 46.

42. Lent, the period of fasting in preparation for Easter, is a penitential time extending from Ash Wednesday to Easter.

43. See Genesis 32 for the account of Jacob's successful wrestling: "I will not let thee go, except thou bless me." Note Jacob's lameness.

44. Revelations 12: 7–9: "And there was war in heaven: Michael and his angels fought against the dragon; and the dragon fought and his angels. And prevailed not; neither was their place found any more in heaven. And the great dragon was cast out, that old serpent, called the Devil and Satan . . ."

45. The Swedish name is *Den Goda Hjälpen* (literally, the Good Help).

46. Deuteronomy 28:15 ff.

47. Mt. Sinai, on which the law was given to the Israelites, is in the southern part of the Sinai peninsula.

48. Apparently an allusion to Satan or the rebel archangel Lucifer rather than Venus, the morning star of astronomy. Lucifer was the light bringer, "the morning star," before his fall.

49. See Exodus 21:22–25.

50. As a young authority on the law, Saul persecuted the Christians. See Footnote 1.

51. Golgotha with its three crosses was the place where Christ was crucified. See the four gospels.

52. Probably the German noblewoman (1207–37) who was canonized in 1235.

Introduction to
'To Damascus, II'

IN A JUNE 5, 1898 letter to the great Swedish poet Gustaf Fröding (1860–1911), Strindberg wrote:

> Don't use the word hallucination (not even the word delirium) as signifying something unreal. Hallucination and delirium have a certain kind of reality or they are evocations in the imagination deliberately designed to frighten, summoned by the Invisible Ones, and all of them have symbolic meaning. For example: You note that projections in alcoholic delirium are constant: flies and rats. Direct offspring of filth. (The king of flies, etc.) So if people want to eliminate the significance of visions by simply saying "It's only delirium," they are mistaken and the matter is not thereby disposed of.

and:

> As far as my religion goes: Well, I'm a Christian by name, I suppose; an amateur Catholic, a confessionless Theist, I don't know! Yet! but through occultism, Swedenborg, Saint-Martin, Eliphas Levi, and Kabbala I have a completely satisfactory explanation, a scientific explanation of miracles, and I believe in all miracles, for they happen every day, and I take notes on them.

Both quotations reveal Strindberg's post-Inferno fascination with inner experience, his continual struggle to come to terms with himself and the forces he labeled Powers, and his deliberate concentration on and use of his experiences and observations, "real" and imagined.

To Damascus, I had by no means exhausted the wealth of confessional material from his Inferno period and the decades of pre-Inferno experience. While the plan for the companion play, *To Damascus, II*, did not discard or disregard his personal way to the cross as part of the pilgrimage to submission and salvation, it was designed to examine the tests to which the Stranger was exposed by the Invisible One and the Powers in driving him through humiliating chastisement to admission of his own inadequacy and the acceptance of Christ as *the* source of help.

Strindberg noted very carefully in his list of characters that the Confessor, the Beggar, and the Dominican are the same person or, if you will, different aspects of the same person. *To Damascus, I* clearly suggests that the Beggar is the Stranger in one of his manifold roles: the gifted human being who must survive almost exclusively on the humiliating charity of others. The first play suggests, too, that the Confessor is the Stranger as the recipient of his own admissions of guilt and as the one who tests the validity of these admissions and metes out penance. In the nightmarish reality of *To Damascus, II,* the Dominican is the Stranger in the role of tester, judge, and disciplinarian. In a play in which the action takes place essentially in the mind, thought, and memory of the Stranger, every "character" takes on aspects of the Stranger or are distorted in his observation and thought. They all apparently serve in various ways as agents of the Eternal One and the Powers in bringing the Stranger to submission and acceptance.

The tests and the humiliations the Stranger is exposed to are by no means exceptional: torture through analysis of one's situation by a willing and even eager agent (his mother-in-law) and his judging, testing self; and torture by a wife who has mastered the art of humiliating her husband (having him unwittingly wear his predecessor's garments, exacting promises, opening and withholding his mail, isolating him to keep him from getting arrogant, making him "analyze" himself and his actions, arousing his guilt feelings, doubting him, and, perhaps worst of all, making him doubt himself and his sanity). All these are matters introduced in the first scene of *To Damascus, II* to set the mood of a play that deals essentially with what Strindberg had called psychic murder and psychic suicide in his essay "Psychic Murder apropos *Rosmersholm.*"

When the Mother-in-law speaks of "a reality you could never have dreamed up," Strindberg is apparently referring to the nightmare that human beings make of reality by consciously or unconsciously distorting human relationships at the expense of others *and* themselves! In his search for self-satisfaction, the Stranger has been forced to substitute the pursuit of gold and honor for the marital happiness denied to him. But that pursuit has not eliminated his concern with his own emotional problems, particularly his guilt feelings about his predecessor:

> We have murdered a soul, and we are murderers.

Pursued by the Dominican, the Stranger not only is self-convicted of psychic murder but sees himself as the arrogant destroyer, subversive, and arsonist. Faced by the Lady who should have been his other half, the Stranger admits:

> There's someone in me who rejoices over your suffering; but it isn't I!

and clarifies the object of his quest—the identification of his *real* self:

> It's as if someone had taken control of my soul, and I'd like to commit suicide to get the life out of the other one.

The contradictions in life, the confrontations with others and with one's selves and one's ambivalent desires are the very meat of what might be called a study of psychic murder and psychic suicide or, if you will, of what people do to each other and to themselves.

The banquet-tavern scenes are superb illustrations of Strindberg's use of dream experience. Both are appreciably the black and white "creations" of Strindberg's imagination, not attempts at reporting faithfully on gray reality: on the one hand, the formal banquet of recognition, the very sort of thing the Swedes do so beautifully, and, on the other, its contrasting travesty or nightmare version. In this materialization of a nightmare one should note with extreme care the details of the fading of what seems to be a state dinner in honor of *the* man of the century into a "drinking" society's subscription dinner: dignity, formality, and good taste with its table settings, speeches, laurel wreath, and garb becoming or exposed as humiliating vulgarity and pretense.

Perhaps an accurate statement of what Strindberg has done would be to suggest that the Strindbergs of this world—the sensitive human beings—live in fear that they may be robbed of what Strindberg considered a human being's greatest possession: faith in himself. Strindberg's imagination was superbly able to conjure up a vision of what might well happen if he were ever to attend a banquet in his honor: the stripping away of every pleasant but distorted appearance to reveal the very opposite—revolting reality.

Just what Strindberg meant by calling the Damascus plays dream plays (See the preface to *A Dream Play)* is beautifully illustrated in the banquet-tavern and the jail scenes. His stage directions are direct and to the point. For example:

> *Dark on stage: a confusion of scenes: landscapes, palaces, rooms are raised and shot forward while people and furniture disappear, last of all the* STRANGER, *who seems to be standing as if frozen still sleeping; finally even he is concealed; and out of the confusion appears a prison cell.*
>
> *A door to the right; above the door a barred opening through which the sun casts a ray, which forms a light spot on the left wall, where a large crucifix is hanging.*
>
> *The* STRANGER, *dressed in brown cape and hat, is sitting by the table watching the spot of sunlight.*

It is precisely in matters such as these that the Expressionists found not only sources of inspiration but also structure and substance to exploit or imitate frequently slavishly, and on occasion to distort beyond belief.

In the jail scene is an excellent illustration of inner dialogue, Strindberg talking with Strindberg, or, by extension, any human being talking with himself. The Stranger and the Beggar are different aspects of one being or different selves touching on sensitive vulnerable personal spots. Two speeches summarize the Stranger's reactions to his real *and* imagined experiences in prison and in the tavern: "In hell, I think—either that or I've dreamt the whole thing" and "What doesn't burn up is, unfortunately,—the memory—of—the—past."

Note that it is one of the multiple personalities speaking to what must be considered the central self that makes the principal point of *To Damascus, II* clear:

BEGGAR: . . . Give up your pretensions now!

STRANGER: Yes! Now I give up! . . . I'm through concerning myself about others since I saw that the powers which control the destinies of human beings can't stand having any assistants. And it was my crime that I wanted to set people free.

BEGGAR: . . . set people free from their duties and sinners free from feelings of guilt so that they haven't any pangs of conscience. You're not the first nor the last who helps out in the devil's work. *Lucifer a non lucendo!* But when that fox gets old, he becomes a monk—that's how wisely it's arranged, and then he has to attack himself and drive Beelzebub out with his own Baal sacrifice.

STRANGER: So that's where I'm to be driven!

BEGGAR: Yes! Where you didn't want to go! You're to get up and preach on housetops and chimneys against yourself; you're to unravel your web thread by thread; you're to flay yourself alive at every street corner and show what you look like inside!

Strindberg has expressed through his own personal experiences, real and imagined, what an arrogant human being must do to receive relief from his burden of guilt, to achieve some degree of inner tranquility, to come to terms with forces within and outside himself, and to approach identification of self. Tested again and again and punished or chastised in almost every conceivable way a human being can be disciplined, the being who is a stranger not only to others but to himself has been brought as low as Job. But he has gained enough insight into his ambivalent self to say "Come priest, before I change my mind."

This is a decidedly rich drama of religious and psychological experience that touches on and explores an amazingly wide range of universal human dilemmas and frustrations, hopes and disappointments, defeats and victories, and the ultimate realization of the finite human being's helplessness and confusion. Strindberg's use of counterpoint, symbols, music, and the blend of the actual and the imagined creates a play as rich in structure and technique as in substance. *To Damascus, II* is a worthy companion to its predecessor.

To Damascus, II

Characters

THE STRANGER
THE LADY
THE MOTHER
THE CONFESSOR
THE BEGGAR
THE DOMINICAN
THE DOCTOR
CAESAR
[and others]

} *the same person*

Settings

ACT I: *Outside the cottage.*
ACT II: *The laboratory. The Rose Chamber.*
ACT III: *The tavern—The banquet. The prison. The Rose Chamber.*
ACT IV: *The tavern. The ravine. The Rose Chamber.*

ACT I

OUTSIDE THE COTTAGE

To the right a terrace, on which the cottage lies. Below it the highway goes toward the backdrop, which shows a heavy evergreen forest with heights, the lines of which intersect each other. To the left suggestions of the river bank, without any view of the river itself.

The cottage is white with small windows set in sandstone frames and supplied with bars. Grape vines and climbing roses on the walls. Outside up on the terrace a well; along the edge of the terrace gourd plants which hang down with large yellow blossoms. Fruit trees along the highway; and a cross commemorating an accident.

A stairway goes through the terrace down to the highway—on the balustrade flowering plants in jars; below the stairway a bench.

The highway comes in from the right in the foreground and winds past the terrace, which juts out like a headland and then extends back toward the backdrop.

Full sunlight from the left.

The MOTHER *from the left.*

The MOTHER *is sitting on the bench. The* DOMINICAN *is standing in front of her.*

DOMINICAN: You've called me about an important family matter. Tell me about it.

MOTHER: Life has tried me severely, Father, and I don't know in what I've failed to be struck so by the disfavor of Providence.

DOMINICAN: It's a sign of grace to become the object of the Eternal One's tests—Triumph awaits the victor!

MOTHER: That's what I've told myself now and then, but there are limits to suffering . . .

DOMINICAN: There aren't any limits! Suffering is boundless, like grace!

MOTHER: First, my husband ran off with another woman.

DOMINICAN: Fine! He'll come back—on his knees!

MOTHER: Then as you know, my only daughter was married to a doctor. She left that husband and dragged home a stranger, whom she presents as her new husband.

DOMINICAN: That I don't understand—divorce isn't permitted in our church.

MOTHER: No, but they went to another country where the laws are different, and he who isn't an orthodox Catholic got a minister to marry them.

DOMINICAN: It's not a legal marriage, and it can't be dissolved since it has never existed, but it can be declared invalid.—Who is your present son-in-law?

MOTHER: Frankly: If I only knew! I know one thing, and that's enough to top the whole wretched situation: he's divorced and his wife and children are living in near misery.

DOMINICAN: This is a difficult case, but we'll straighten it out most likely. What does he usually do?

MOTHER: He's a poet—apparently he's famous in his own country . . .

DOMINICAN: And godless, of course?

MOTHER: Yes—at least he was. But since he got married the second time he hasn't had one happy day: what he calls fate took hold of him with a hard hand, and he has been driven here with an iron whip like a destitute beggar. Misfortune struck him blow upon blow so I was touched with pity just when he fled from here. He wandered about lost in the forest, he had a fall out there, was rescued by merciful people and taken into an asylum, where he lay sick for three months without our knowing where he was!

DOMINICAN: Wait a minute—last year a man was admitted under circumstances you describe to the cloister The Good Help where I'm confessor. In his fever, he opened his heart, and there's hardly a sin he didn't admit to! When he became rational, he said he didn't remember anything. To test him I used the secret apostolic power granted us and tried the minor curse. You see, when a secret sin has been committed, Deuteronomy's curse is said over the suspect. If he's hit then as St. Paul says,[1] his body is delivered to Satan to be punished so that his soul may improve and be saved.

MOTHER: Oh God! It's he!

DOMINICAN: Yes—your son-in-law! The ways of Providence are strange.—Was he thoroughly hit?

MOTHER: Yes, and then . . . He slept here overnight, but was awakened from sleep by an inexplicable power that turned his heart to ice, he said . . .

DOMINICAN: And then he had terrifying visions?

MOTHER: Yes!

DOMINICAN: And was pursued by the thoughts of anxiety of which Job [2] speaks: "When I say, my bed shall comfort me, my couch shall ease my complaint; then Thou scarest me with dreams, and terrifiest me through visions: So that my soul chooseth strangling, and death rather than my life." That's quite as it should be! But did he get his eyes opened?

MOTHER: Yes, but only to get his sight twisted. When his misfortunes piled up and he couldn't explain them naturally any longer and no doctor could cure him, he began to see that he was struggling with higher conscious powers

DOMINICAN: Who wanted to do him evil and therefore were evil. That's the way it usually goes . . . And then?

MOTHER: Then he found some books that taught him these evil powers could be overcome.

DOMINICAN: So! He's now looking into what's concealed, what's to be hidden! Well, has he succeeded in appeasing the spirits of punishment?

MOTHER: He says he has, and he seems to be able to sleep at night again.

DOMINICAN: Well, he thinks he has, but you see since he hasn't accepted the love of truth, God will send him a powerful delusion so he will believe lies.

MOTHER: Let him take his chances, but he has changed my daughter's frame of mind, too. She certainly wasn't either warm or cold before, but now she's on the way to becoming evil!

DOMINICAN: How do they get along?

MOTHER: Half the time like angels; the rest of the time they torture each other like devils.

DOMINICAN: That's the way: they're going to torture each other to the cross.

MOTHER: Just so they don't leave each other.

DOMINICAN: Already!

MOTHER: They have left four times each, but have come back; it's as if they were chained to each other, and that would be a good thing—their child is on the way.

DOMINICAN: Let the child come—little ones usually freshen up stale souls!

MOTHER: If it only would! But the child is a new cause for quarreling. They're already arguing about the child's name; they quarrel about its christening; and she's already jealous of his children by his first wife, and he can't promise to love this child as much as the others, and she wants him to promise to without qualifications. There's no end to their hellish life!

DOMINICAN: Oh yes! Just wait! If he's once let himself in against the Powers,[3] we have him, and our prayers will be stronger than his resistance; they go to work just as effectively as they do secretly!

(*The* STRANGER *appears up on the terrace. He is dressed in a hunting jacket and an English-Indian summer hat and has an alpine staff in his hand.*)

DOMINICAN: Is that he—up there?

MOTHER: That's my present son-in-law.

DOMINICAN: Strangely like his predecessor!—But look—see how he's behaving . . . He hasn't noticed me yet, but he senses my presence. (*The* DOMINICAN *makes the sign of the cross in the air.*) See how uneasy he's getting . . . and he's stiffening like an icicle . . . there! He'll soon scream.

STRANGER (*has stopped abruptly and has become immovable; feels toward his heart; calls*): Who's down there?

MOTHER: It's I!

STRANGER: But you're not alone!

MOTHER: No, I have company!

DOMINICAN (*makes the sign of the cross*): Now he's become silent and struck to the ground like a felled tree!

(*The* STRANGER *collapses and falls to the ground.*)

DOMINICAN: Now I'll go! For if he became aware of me, he'd burst. But I'll soon be back. You see, he's in good hands! Farewell! And peace be with you! *(Goes).*

STRANGER *(gets up and comes down the stairway):* Who was here?

MOTHER: A wanderer! Sit down—you look pale!

STRANGER: I had a fainting spell . . .

MOTHER: Always new names which don't say anything new. Sit down here on the bench!

STRANGER: No, I don't like sitting there—people are always going by.

MOTHER: And I've been sitting here since I was a child watching life go by like the river down there. I've seen people pass by on this highway playing, taking advantage of each other, begging, cursing, dancing. I love this bench and I love the river down there, though it hurts us and gnaws away at our land. Last year it took all our hayfields so we had to sell our cattle. Our property has lost half its value the last few years, and when they finish lowering the lake up in the mountains and the swamp is drained, the river will rise and sweep away our house. We've had lawsuits in court for ten years and have lost on every level and we'll have to go under: That's as unavoidable as fate.

STRANGER: Fate is not unavoidable!

MOTHER: Be careful if you think you can control that!

STRANGER: I already have!

MOTHER *[sighs]:* So you're back to that! You don't learn anything from the chastisement Providence gives you.

STRANGER: Yes, to hate. Can one love evil, what does evil?

MOTHER: I'm not learned as you know, but I read yesterday in a dictionary that the Eumenides [4] mean the Well-intentioned Ones!

STRANGER: That's true, but it's a lie that they're well intentioned. I know only one well-meaning fury, and she's my own!

MOTHER: Are you calling Ingeborg a fury?

STRANGER: Yes, because that's what she is, and she's a really great one! Her imaginative ability to come up with ways to torture me surpasses the most infernal notions I can concoct, and, if I get out of her hands alive, I'll get out of the fire pure as gold.

MOTHER: You got what you deserve. You were going to make her over as you wanted to, you said, and you have!

STRANGER: Absolutely!—But where is my fury?

MOTHER: She went up the road a while ago.

STRANGER: In that direction?—Then I'm on my way to being ruined!

(Goes toward the back)

MOTHER: You can still joke? Just wait!

(*The* MOTHER *is alone for a moment until the* STRANGER *has disappeared. Then the* LADY *comes in from the right. She is dressed in summer clothes and is carrying the mail bag as well as some opened letters in her hand.*)

LADY: Are you alone, Mother?

MOTHER: I have been for a moment!

LADY: Here's the mail! And it's Job's!

MOTHER: Do you open his letters?

LADY: I open all his letters, for I want to know with whom I've united my destiny, and I keep back all news that could puff up his arrogance. In a word: I'm isolating him so he gets to keep his energy with the danger of his being blown to pieces!

MOTHER: How learned you've become!

LADY: Yes, when he's foolish enough to tell me almost everything, I'll soon have his fate in my hands! Imagine, he's working with electricity now and says he can tame lightning so it will give him light, heat, and power. That would do, but I see in one of today's letters he's corresponding with goldmakers.

MOTHER: Is he going to make gold? ⁵ Is he sane?

LADY: That's the big question. The little one is: Is he a charlatan?

MOTHER: Do you suspect he is?

LADY: I think he's capable of everything evil and of everything good—on the same day.

MOTHER: What else is new?

LADY: This—my former husband, whose plans for remarriage haven't worked out, has become despondent, has left his practice, and is wandering about on the highways.

MOTHER *[sighs]:* Too bad—all the same he was my son-in-law, and under a rough exterior hid a warm heart.

LADY: Yes, that's right! And I called him werewolf only in his role as my husband! I felt all right about him as long as I knew he was calm and was about to remarry. Now he'll haunt me like a bad conscience itself.

MOTHER: Do you have a conscience?

LADY: I didn't, but since I've been reading what my husband has written, my eyes have been opened so I can tell the difference between good and evil!

MOTHER: He did forbid you to read his books, but he didn't count on the consequences of your disobedience.

LADY: Who can take into account all the consequences of an act?

MOTHER: What more evil do you have in that bag, Pandora? [6]

LADY: The worst of all!—Can you imagine, Mother, his first wife is about to remarry?

MOTHER: But that ought to please both of you?

LADY: Don't you know his worst fear is that she'll remarry and his children will get a stepfather?

MOTHER: If he can bear that alone, I'll get strange thoughts about him!

LADY: You think he's that sensitive? Doesn't he say himself that a gentleman nowadays isn't amazed by anything?

MOTHER: People say a lot, but when it gets down to . . .

LADY: But at the bottom of Pandora's box lay a gift which wasn't a misfortune! Look at this, Mother! It's a picture of his six-year-old son!

MOTHER *(looks at the picture):* He looks like an angel!

LADY: He's so attractive I feel good just looking at it!—Do you think my child will be just as attractive? Do you?—Say yes, or I'll be unhappy! I already love this little fellow, but I feel I could hate him if my child weren't as attractive! Yes, I'm already jealous!

MOTHER: I had hoped when you came here from your unfortunate wedding trip you'd be over the worst, but I see now that was merely the introduction to what was to come.

LADY: Nowadays even I am prepared for everything; I think this tangle can't be straightened out—it has to be cut.

MOTHER: But you've made it harder for yourself by not giving him his mail . . .

LADY: In the old days when I went about as a sleepwalker, I could straighten out everything just by blowing on it; but since he made me think, I'm beginning to hesitate. *(She stuffs the letters into her pocket)* There he comes! Don't say anything!

MOTHER: One thing! Why do you let him go about like a ghost in your first husband's summer suit?

LADY: It amuses me to torture and humiliate him! I've made him think it's becoming to him and that it belonged to Dad.—When I see him in the werewolf's clothes, I feel I have both of them in my claws!

MOTHER: God save us! How cruel you've become!

LADY: That probably was my role if I do have a role in this man's life!

MOTHER: I sometimes wish the river would rise and take us all away in our sleep; and if it washed and flushed away for a thousand years, maybe the sin on which this house is built could be washed away.

LADY: So it's true Grandfather, the notary, grabbed other people's property unjustly? They do say this estate has been built up from widows' and orphans' inheritances, from judgments over ruined people, from dead people's estates, from bribes paid by those suing each other . . .

MOTHER: Don't say anything more about that; the tears of the survivors have formed a lake, and that's the one, the people say, which is to be drained and make the river wash us away.

LADY: Can't you prevent that legally? Isn't there any justice on earth any more?

MOTHER: Not on earth, but in heaven, and it's that justice which is going to drown us, the children of the doers of evil. *(Goes up the stairs)*

LADY: Then it isn't enough one has to put up with one's own tears; one has to inherit others, too.

STRANGER *(enters):* Did you call me?

LADY: No, I only lured you without actually longing for you.

STRANGER: I felt you were playing with my destiny in a way unpleasant for me. You've learned my tricks quickly.

LADY: And others, too.

STRANGER: But I beg you—don't touch my destiny with your clumsy hands. I'm Cain,[7] you see, and am under the curse of the Powers, but they don't let mortals interfere with their work of vengeance. See—I'm marked! *(Lifts his hat)* That mark means: "*Mine* is the vengeance, saith the Lord." [8]

LADY: Is the hat too tight?

STRANGER: No, but it burns me! just as the coat does! And if I didn't want to please you, I'd have thrown the whole outfit in the river.—You know when I walk about the neighborhood, people call me doctor. It's your husband, the werewolf, who's meant, I suppose. And I have bad luck. If I ask who planted this tree, they answer: "You did, Doctor." If I ask who owns the green fish container, they answer: "It's yours, Doctor." And when it isn't the doctor's, it's the doctor's wife's! That's you! This confusion of me and him makes my stay here unbearable; and I'd like to leave . . .

LADY: Haven't you tried to leave this place six times and failed?

STRANGER: Yes, but I'll succeed the seventh time!

LADY: Try!

STRANGER: You say it as if you were sure it would fail.

LADY: I am sure!

STRANGER: Torture me in another way, dear fury.

LADY: I can do that, too! . . .

STRANGER: In some new way. Try to say something nasty "the other one" hasn't already said.

LADY: "The other one"—you mean your first wife! You certainly show good taste in reminding me of her . . .

STRANGER: Everything that lives and moves, everything that is dead and still, reminds me of the past . . .

LADY: Until the one who will erase the dark past and bring light comes.

STRANGER: You mean your child that we're expecting!

LADY: Our child!

STRANGER: Do you love it?

LADY: I started to love it today!

STRANGER: Today? What has happened then? Five months ago you wanted to go to a lawyer to get a divorce because I didn't want to go with you to a quack to have the unborn child killed.

LADY: That was then! Now it's different!

STRANGER: Now? *(Looks about as if trying to "sniff out" the truth)* Now?—Has the mail come?

LADY: You're more cunning than I still, but the pupil will soon surpass the master.

STRANGER: Was there a letter for me?

LADY: No!

STRANGER: Give me the printed stuff then, since your conscience makes such a fine distinction between letter and printed matter.

LADY *(takes up the mail bag, which she has had hidden behind the bench):* Look!

(*The* STRANGER *picks up the photograph, observes it carefully, and then puts it into his breast pocket.*)

LADY: What was it?

STRANGER: The past!

LADY: Was it beautiful?

STRANGER: Yes, so beautiful as the future can never be!

LADY *(darkens):* You shouldn't have said that!

STRANGER: No, I shouldn't have, I admit, and I'm already suffering because I did . . .

LADY: Can you suffer?

STRANGER: Doubly—nowadays, for I sense when you suffer. When I hurt you in self-defense, it's I who get fever in my wound.

LADY: In other words: you're defenseless against me?

STRANGER: Yes, and still more now when you're protected by the innocent being you're carrying under your heart.

LADY: That will be my avenger.

STRANGER: Or mine!

LADY *(with tears in her voice):* Poor little thing—born in sin and shame, born to avenge, through hate.

STRANGER: I haven't heard that tone in your voice for a long time.

LADY: Oh yes!

STRANGER: It was this voice that captivated me once, because it resembled a mother's when she talks to her child!

LADY: When you say the word *mother,* I feel as if I could believe only good of you, but the next minute I think: That's just a new way of deceiving me.

STRANGER: What harm have I really done you?

(LADY *at a loss.*)

STRANGER: Tell me! What harm have I done you?

LADY: I don't know.

STRANGER: Think of something! Say something like this: I hate you because I can't fool you.

LADY: Can't I? It's too bad about you!

STRANGER: Then you have some poison in your pocket.

LADY: Yes, I have!

STRANGER: What can that be?—Who's that coming on the highway over there?

LADY: That's a forerunner!

STRANGER: Is it a real human being or a ghost?

LADY: From the past!

STRANGER: He's dressed in tails and a laurel wreath, but he's barefooted.

LADY: It's Caesar.

STRANGER *(confused):* Caesar? Why, that was my nickname in school.

LADY: Yes, but it's the nickname of the madman who was staying with my . . . former husband. Forgive the expression.

STRANGER: Is the madman loose?

LADY: It looks like it!

CAESAR *(enters from in back: dressed in tails without a shirt collar; a laurel wreath on his head; barefooted; bizarre in general):* Why don't you greet me?—You should say: Hail, Caesar! for now I'm the master! The werewolf's lost his mind, you see, since the Great Man ran off with his wife, whom he in turn had snatched from her first lover or fiancé, or whatever you should call him.

STRANGER (*to the* LADY): That's enough strychnine for two adults! (*To* CAESAR) Where's your master, or slave, or madman's doctor, or guard then?

CAESAR: He's right behind me, but don't be afraid of him; he has neither poison nor knife with him. On the other hand, he needs only to show up and every living being runs away from him; the trees lose their leaves; and the dust of the highway flees in a whirlwind before him as the pillar of clouds did before the children of Israel . . . 9

STRANGER: Listen . . .

CAESAR: Silence, while I'm speaking . . . And sometimes he thinks he's the werewolf and says he wants to devour a little child who hasn't been born yet and who's really his according to the rights of the first comer . . . *(Goes aside)*

LADY (*to the* STRANGER): Can you lay that demon?

STRANGER: I can't manage devils who can stand sunlight!

LADY: You uttered arrogant words the other day—now you'll have to take them back. You said: "Invisible Ones who steal about at night and fight in the darkness unfairly, come back during the day when the sun is shining!" Now they've come!

STRANGER: And that pleases you?

LADY: Yes, almost!

STRANGER: What a shame I can't rejoice when you get your blows!—Let's sit down on the bench, the bench of the accused— more will probably come!

LADY: Let's leave instead!

STRANGER: No. I want to see how much I can take; besides with every blow of the whip I feel one item on my register of sins has been erased.

LADY: But I can't any more: Look—there he's coming!—Oh God, the man I once thought I loved.

STRANGER: Thought? Yes, because it's only an illusion the whole thing, yet it's not only that. Go away—I'll take it as my duty to stand alone.

(*The* LADY *goes up the stairs, but does not get to the top before the* DOCTOR *can be seen coming from the back*).

(*The* DOCTOR *with long, gray, hanging hair; dressed in an English-Indian hat and a hunting coat exactly like the Stranger's; pretends not to notice the* STRANGER; *sits down on a stone on the other side of the highway directly opposite the* STRANGER *on the bench. Takes off his hat and wipes the perspiration off his forehead.*)

STRANGER *(who has become impatient):* What do you want?

DOCTOR: I want only to see the house, where I was happy once and *my* roses bloomed . . .

STRANGER: A civilized gentleman would select a time when the present occupants are off on a little trip for the attainment of that goal, for example, and you ought to have done that for your own sake so as not to seem ridiculous.

DOCTOR: Ridiculous? I wonder which of us is more ridiculous.

STRANGER: At the moment I suspect it's I.

DOCTOR: Yes, but I think you don't know how contemptible you really are.

STRANGER: What do you mean?

DOCTOR: This—you want to possess what I have possessed.

STRANGER: Go on!

DOCTOR: Have you noticed that we're dressed alike?—Fine! Do you know why? Well, because you're wearing my clothes which I forgot to take along when the catastrophe struck. A civilized gentleman at the turn of the century shouldn't expose himself to that sort of thing!

STRANGER *(throws off his hat and coat):* Damned woman!

DOCTOR: You're welcome! Castoff men's clothes have always been fatal ever since the famous Nessus outfit.[10] Go on in—change your clothes; I'll sit here and listen while you settle that business with the damned woman privately.—Don't forget the cane!

(*The* LADY *has hurried up toward the house, but falls in front of the stairs.*)

STRANGER *(stands, at a loss).*

DOCTOR: The cane! The cane!

STRANGER: I beg for mercy, not for the woman's sake, but for the child's!

DOCTOR *(beside himself):* So! There's a child, too! *Our* house, *our* roses, *our* clothes, the bedclothes included, and *our* child. You'll have me within your doors, I'll sit by your table, lie on your bed; I'll be in your blood, in your lungs, in your brain; I'm everywhere, and you can't get at me. When the clock strikes midnight, I'll blow cold on your heart so that it'll stop like a wornout watch; when you sit working, I'll come with opium you can't see, and it'll put your thought to sleep, confuse your reason so you'll see visions that you can't tell from reality; I'll lie like a stone on your path so you'll stumble; I'll be the thorn that pricks your hand when it wants to pick the rose; my soul will stretch like a spider's web over yours and through the woman you've stolen from me; I'll lead you like a steer; your child will be mine, and I'll talk through its mouth; you'll see me in its eyes so that you'll push it away like an enemy. And now: farewell, little house, and farewell, Rose Chamber; no happiness that I'll need to envy will blossom there! (*Goes. In the meanwhile the* STRANGER *has sat down on the bench where he has listened as an accused who has no answer.*)

[CURTAIN]

ACT II

THE LABORATORY

A rococo garden pavilion; high windows. In the middle of the floor a large writing desk with various chemical and physical apparatus. Two copper wires run down from the ceiling to an electroscope which stands in the middle of the table and is equipped with small bells to note the tension of the electricity in the air.

On a table to the left a large, old-fashioned electric machine with a glass disk, brass conductors, Leyden battery; the posts are lacquered red and black.

To the right a large, old-fashioned open stove with tripods, crucibles, tongs, bellows, etc.

At the back a door leading out to a landscape; it is cloudy and dark but now and then red sunlight shines into the room.

A brown cape with collar and hood is hanging by the stove; next to it are a suitcase and alpine staff.

STRANGER: Where is . . . Ingeborg?

MOTHER: You know that better than I do!

STRANGER: Well . . . she's at the lawyer's to get a divorce . . .

MOTHER: Why?

STRANGER: Because . . . No, it's so crazy you'd think I'm lying.

MOTHER: Tell me!

STRANGER: Well, she wants a divorce because I didn't beat up the mentally unbalanced man. She says that was cowardly . . .

MOTHER: I don't believe you.

STRANGER: No, there you are!—You believe only what you like to; the rest is only lies.—Now, is it in your interest to believe she has stolen letters from me?

MOTHER: I don't know anything about that.

STRANGER: It wasn't a question of knowing but of believing!

MOTHER *(interrupts him):* What are you up to in here?

STRANGER: Experimenting with the electricity in the air.

MOTHER: And you've brought the lightning rod in on the desk!

STRANGER: Yes, but there's no danger because the bells start ringing when there's a disturbance in the air.

MOTHER: This is blasphemy and black magic: Watch out!—And what are you making in the stove?

STRANGER: Gold.

MOTHER: Do you believe you can?

STRANGER: You assume I'm a charlatan? I can't blame you, but don't be too quick to judge; I may have the certification of my analysis at any moment.

MOTHER: That may be, but what do you intend to do if Ingeborg doesn't come back?

STRANGER: She'll come back once more, but when the child comes, she'll probably get away . . .

MOTHER: You're very sure.

STRANGER: As I said: I'm still sure . . . one feels that as long as the bond holds, but, when it has broken, then one feels it so unpleasantly clearly.

MOTHER: But when you're free of each other, perhaps you'll both be bound to the child; you don't know about that sort of thing ahead of time.

STRANGER: I've protected myself against that by having a great interest which'll fill the emptiness in my life.

MOTHER: Gold and honor, you mean!

STRANGER: Exactly! for a man the most lasting of all illusions . . .

MOTHER: You're still building on illusion?

STRANGER: On what else can I build since everything is illusion?

MOTHER: When you do awaken from that dream, you'll see a reality you could never have dreamed up.

STRANGER: I'll wait until then.

MOTHER: Yes, wait!—Now I'll go to shut the windows before the thunder starts. *(Goes toward the back)* That will be interesting.

STRANGER *(A hunting horn can be heard in the distance.):* Who's blowing that again?

MOTHER: No one knows, but it doesn't bode well. *(Goes)*

STRANGER *(works with the electroscope so his back is to the open window; then he takes a book and reads aloud):* "When the giant family of Adam had increased so they considered themselves great enough in number to dare to storm the heavens, they began to build a tower, which would reach up into heaven. Then the powers above were seized by fear, and to protect themselves they destroyed the conspiracy by confusing the conspirators' tongues and minds so that when two people met, they could not understand each other even when they spoke the same language. Since then those above govern through dissension: Divide and govern. And the dissension is kept up through imagining that the truth has been found, but when any prophet is believed, he is a false prophet. If on the other hand, any mortal succeeds in discovering the secrets of those higher up no one believes him, and he is made insane so no one will believe him. Since then mortals are more or less crazy, those considered wise most of all, and the insane are the only sensible people; for they see, hear, feel what is invisible, what cannot be heard, what is not felt, but can never communicate experiences to others."—So says *Sohar,* the wisest of all books of wisdom, which no human being believes in.[11]

I won't build any Tower of Babel, but I'll lure the powers into my rat trap, and afterwards I'll send them down to the powers below to be neutralized. The upper Schedin [12] have placed themselves between mortals and the Lord Jehovah; that's why joy, peace, and happiness have disappeared from earth.

LADY (*enters; beside herself, throws herself to her knees before the* STRANGER, *puts her arms about his legs and her head on the floor*): Help me! Help me! And forgive me!

STRANGER: Get up! In God's name, get up! Don't do that! What has happened?

LADY: I've behaved stupidly in my anger, and I'm caught in my web.

STRANGER *(lifts her up):* Get up, foolish child, and tell me what it's all about!

LADY: I went to the public prosecutor and . . .

STRANGER: . . . applied for a divorce.

LADY: . . . That's probably what I intended, but when I got there, I accused the werewolf of invading the privacy of our home and of attempted murder . . .

STRANGER: Yes, but he didn't do either . . .

LADY: No, but I accused him of both . . . and while I was standing there, he showed up himself, and signed a warrant against me for false accusation. Then I went to see the lawyer, and he said I can expect at least a month in jail . . . Imagine: My child's to be born in jail. How'll I get out of this? Help me! You can help me!

STRANGER: I can help you! But, don't take revenge on me afterwards because I've helped you.

LADY: How little you really know me! But hurry up—tell me!

STRANGER: Well, we'll put the blame on me, and say I sent you!

LADY: You *are* good all the same!—And now I'm absolutely out of it?

STRANGER: Wipe your tears, child, and don't worry. But tell me about something quite different. Did you put this purse here?
      (LADY *embarrassed.*)

STRANGER: Speak up!

LADY: Has that been tried before, too?

STRANGER: Yes, my first wife wanted to find out in that way if I stole. I wept then, for I was still a child.

LADY: Oh no!

STRANGER: Right now you're the worst person I've ever known.
LADY: Is that why you love me?
STRANGER: No, not because of that!—You've stolen letters, too? Answer: yes! So you want me to become a thief through this purse.
LADY: What do you have on the table over there?
STRANGER: Thunder! *(There is a flash of lightning but no thunder)*
LADY: You're afraid!
STRANGER: Yes, sometimes, but not of what you fear.
   (*The* DOCTOR's *face with distorted features appears at the window.*)
LADY: Is there a cat in here? I feel uneasy.
STRANGER: No, I don't think so, but I, too, have a feeling someone's in here.
LADY (*turns, catches sight of the face, screams, and rushes up to the* STRANGER *for protection*): It's he!
STRANGER: Where? Who? (*The* DOCTOR's *face disappears*)
LADY: He! There in the window!
STRANGER: I don't see anyone—you're mistaken!
LADY: No, I saw him! The werewolf! Can't one kill him?
STRANGER: Yes, I'm sure one could, but that won't help, for he has an immortal soul which is bound to yours.
LADY: If I had known that before.
STRANGER: It says so in the catechism, I think.
LADY: Let's die then!
STRANGER: That was my religion once, but now that I no longer believe death is the end, all that's left is to keep going—struggling and suffering!
LADY: How long are we to suffer?
STRANGER: As long as he suffers and conscience tortures us.
LADY: Let's try to defend ourselves before our conscience; let's find excuses for our frivolous behavior; let's find out his faults . . .
STRANGER: Try!
LADY: That's easy for you to say! Since I know he's unhappy, I see only his merits, and you lose by comparison.
STRANGER: See how wisely it's arranged! His suffering sanctifies him, but makes me despicable and ridiculous. This is facing what

can't be changed! We have murdered a soul, and we are mur-
derers.

LADY: Who's to blame?

STRANGER: The one who controls human destinies so insanely!
(A flash of lightning; the electric bells ring)

LADY: Mother of God! What's that?

STRANGER: A direct answer.

LADY: Do you have the lightning rod here in the room?

STRANGER: The priest of Baal [13] wants to lure the lightning from
heaven . . .

LADY: Now I am afraid, afraid for you . . . you are terrible . . .

STRANGER: Fine! There you are!

LADY: Who are you who dare defy heaven, and play with the
destinies of human beings?

STRANGER: Stand up and pull your wits together!—Listen to me,
believe me, and give me the respect I deserve; then I'll lift us
both high over this morass where we've almost gone under!
I'll blow on your conscience so it'll heal like a sore. Who I am?
I'm the one who has done what never was done before; I'm
the one who will topple the golden calf and overthrow the tables
of the money changers; I have the fate of the world in my crucible
and in eight days I'll be the richest of the rich poor; gold, the
false standard of value, will have ceased to rule; all people will
be equally poor, and the children of man will crawl about in
confusion like ants when their hill has been leveled!

LADY: How will that help us?

STRANGER: Do you think I made gold to enrich us and the others?
No, to lay waste the whole world order, to destroy, you see! I
am the destroyer, the subversive, the arsonist of the world, and
when everything lies in ashes, then I'll wander starving among
the rubbish piles and rejoice at the thought: This I have done,
I who have written the last page of world history, which can
thereby be considered finished.

   (*The* DOMINICAN'*s face appears in the open window; they do not
notice him.*)

LADY: This was the basic meaning of your last book,[14] which wasn't
poetry then!

STRANGER: Yes! But to be able to do this, I had to double my person with another's, who could take up everything that binds my spirit . . . so that my soul would get back its purity by means of which it could rise toward Ether, pass the principalities, and reach the throne to place humanity's complaints at the feet of the Eternal One . . .[15]

(*The* DOMINICAN *makes the sign of cross in the air and disappears.*)

STRANGER: Who is here? Who is the terrible being who pursues me and cripples my thought?—Did you see anyone?

LADY: No, I didn't!

STRANGER: But I feel him. *(Puts his hand to his heart)* Listen; listen— far, far away, they're reciting a rosary . . . Can you hear it?

LADY: Yes, I hear it, but it's no Angelus—it's the curse of Deuteronomy! Against us!

STRANGER: Then it's in the cloister The Good Help . . .

(*The* LADY *sighs with distress.*)

STRANGER: Darling! What is it?

LADY: Say that word again! Darling!

STRANGER: Are you sick?

LADY: No, but I'm suffering, and I'm filled with joy at the same time. Go and tell my mother to prepare my bed!—But bless me first!

STRANGER: Am I to . . .

LADY: Say that you forgive me: why, I can die if the little one takes my life! Say that you love me!

STRANGER: Imagine—I can't get that word across my lips!

LADY: So you don't love me?

STRANGER: When you say that it seems to be so! It's terrible, but I think I hate you!

LADY: At least give me your hand as one gives it to a person in dire need!

STRANGER: I want to, but I can't: There's someone in me who rejoices over your suffering; but it isn't I! For I'd like to carry you on my arms and suffer your agony, but I'm not permitted to! I can't!

LADY: Hard as stone!

STRANGER *(with a restrained gesture):* Probably not! Probably not!

LADY: Come to me!

STRANGER: I can't move.—It's as if someone had taken control of my soul, and I'd like to commit suicide to get the life out of the other one.

LADY: Think of your child with pleasure . . .

STRANGER: I can't do that either, for it binds me to earth!

LADY: If we've sinned, we're punished! Heaven, isn't it enough soon?

STRANGER: Not soon, but it will be sometime.

LADY *(sinks down):* Help me! Mercy! I'll perish!

   (*The* STRANGER *gives her his hand as if released from paralysis.*)
   (*The* LADY *kisses his hand.*)
   (*The* STRANGER *lifts her up and leads her toward the door.*)

[CURTAIN]

THE ROSE CHAMBER
(See *To Damascus, I*)

A room with rose-colored walls; small windows with iron bars and flowering potted plants. Rose red curtains; furniture in white and rose.

At the back a door to a white bedroom; when the door is opened, one sees a large bed with a canopy and white curtains. To the right, a door leading outside. To the left a stove with coal fire. In front of the fire a bathtub covered by a white cloth; a cradle in white, rose, and light blue.

Tiny infant clothes spread here and there. A green dress is hanging on the wall to the right.

Four sisters of mercy on their knees—facing the door at the back. Their garb the black and white of the Augustinian nuns. The midwife, dressed in black, by the fire. The nurse in black and white Breton folk costume.

The MOTHER *stands listening at the door at the back.*

The STRANGER *is sitting in a chair to the right reading a book. Beside him hangs a hat and a brown cape with collar and hood; on the floor a small suitcase.* SISTERS OF MERCY (*sing a psalm; except for the* STRANGER *the others join in now and then*):

> *Salve, Regina, mater miseri cordiae,*
> *Vita dulcedo, et spes nostra, salve.*
> *Ad te clamamus, exules filii Evae:*
> *Ad te suspiramus gementes et flentes*
> *In hac lacrymarum valle.*

(*The* STRANGER *gets up; goes toward the* MOTHER.)

MOTHER: Stay where you are!—A human being is born, another dies—it's all the same to you.

STRANGER: Who knows?—When I want to come in, I'm not allowed to, and when I don't want to, I'm supposed to. Now I want to go in.

MOTHER: She doesn't want to see you; besides, your presence is superfluous. The child's the most important person now.

STRANGER: For you, yes, but I'm still the most important person for myself.

MOTHER: The doctor has forbidden everyone from going in, because her life's in danger.

STRANGER: What doctor?

MOTHER: Your thoughts are there again!

STRANGER: Yes, and you're the one who made me think of him! An hour ago you let me understand the child couldn't be mine! So you made your daughter out to be a prostitute, but that means nothing to you just so you could hurt me! You're the next to worst person I know!

MOTHER (*to the* SISTERS): Sisters! Pray for this unhappy man.

STRANGER: Make way so I can get in, for the last time—step aside.

MOTHER: Leave this room and this house.

STRANGER: If I should do as you say, in ten minutes you'd be ready to send for the sheriff for my having deserted my wife and child!

MOTHER: Then it'd only be to put you into the asylum—the one you know.

MAID (*in from back*): The mistress asks you to do her a favor, sir.

STRANGER: Yes?

MAID: There's a letter in her dress that's hanging in this room.

STRANGER *(looks about; sees the green dress; goes up to it and takes a letter out of its pocket):* This letter's addressed to me, was opened two days ago: So it was stolen! That is *nice!*

MOTHER: You'll have to forgive a sick person who's your wife!

STRANGER: She wasn't sick two days ago!

MOTHER: No, but she is now!

STRANGER: But wasn't two days ago!—*(Glances through the letter)*—Now I'll forgive her anyway, with the victor's generosity!

MOTHER: The victor's?

STRANGER: Yes, I've made what no one before me has made.

MOTHER: Gold . . .

STRANGER: Here's the certification [16] from the greatest authority alive; and now I'm leaving to meet him personally.

MOTHER: You're leaving now!

STRANGER: On your orders!

MAID: The mistress would like to have you come in, sir!

MOTHER: You hear?

STRANGER: No, I don't want to now! You have made my wife, your daughter, out to be a prostitute and my unborn child the child of a kept woman. Keep them! You've destroyed my honor here; the only thing left for me is to restore it elsewhere!

MOTHER: You can't forgive!

STRANGER: Yes, I forgive you—and leave! *(Puts on the brown cape and hat; picks up the suitcase and cane.)* If I stayed, I'd soon be worse than I am. The innocent being, who was to ennoble the false situation, you polluted in its mother's womb, and that child will be the seed of discord and a punisher and an avenger. Why then should I stay here to let myself be torn to pieces?

MOTHER: You don't have any duties, do you?

STRANGER: Yes! And the first one is to protect myself from total destruction! Farewell!

[CURTAIN]

ACT III

THE TAVERN—THE BANQUET [17]

A banquet room. Long tables set with flowers, candelabras; dishes with peacocks, pheasants with feathers, a wildhog's head, whole lobsters, oysters, salmon, asparagus bunches, melons, grapes.

Elevated platform with eight musicians in the right corner at the back.

At the speaker's table: the STRANGER *in tails; next to him a civilian official with orders; a professor in tails and wearing his orders; the rest in black evening dress with bands, more or less imposing.*

At the second table some men in tails among men in black frock coats.

At the third table men wearing neat everyday suits.

At the fourth table strange-looking ragged figures. The tables are set so that the first is farthest to the left and the fourth farthest to the right; because of this arrangement the STRANGER *cannot see the men at the fourth table. At the fourth table closest to the footlights are sitting the* DOCTOR *and* CAESAR, *both of them shabbily dressed.*

They are now eating dessert, and golden goblets are in front of the guests. The music (pianissimo) is in the middle of Mendelssohn's funeral march. The guests are conversing with each other.

DOCTOR (*to* CAESAR): The atmosphere's a little depressed, and dessert came too early!

CAESAR: And the whole thing smacks of humbug . . . by the way: he hasn't made gold, has he? I suspect that's a lie like everything else.

DOCTOR: I don't know, but they say he has; and in our enlightened times you can expect anything.

CAESAR: There's a professor at the speaker's table—he's the expert, I suppose, but what's he professor of?

DOCTOR: I don't know, but it really ought to be metallurgy and applied chemistry.

CAESAR: Can you see what order he has?

DOCTOR: No, I don't know that order; I suspect it's some minor foreign order.

CAESAR: Well, at a subscription affair like this the company is always rather mixed.

DOCTOR: Hm?

CAESAR: You mean that we . . . hm . . . well, we aren't dressed very elegantly, but as far as our intelligence goes . . .

DOCTOR: Listen, Caesar! You're an asylum inmate under my care and should avoid talking about intelligence as much as you can!

CAESAR: That's the most shameless thing I've heard in a long time! Don't you know, you fool, I've been assigned to keep an eye on you ever since you lost your mind . . .

PROFESSOR *(taps on his goblet):* Gentlemen!

CAESAR: Hear! Hear!

PROFESSOR: Gentlemen!—As our little society has been honored today by the presence of the great man, whom we celebrate as our guest of honor, and as the board . . .

CAESAR *(to the* DOCTOR): That's the administration!

PROFESSOR: . . . as the board selected me to express the feelings that moved it, I was at a loss at first whether I should accept the flattering assignment. But when I compared my own lack of ability with others' I found that neither lost in the comparison really . . .

VOICES: Bravo!

PROFESSOR: Gentlemen! The century of great inventions comes to an end with the greatest of all discoveries—sensed by the Pythagoreans,[18] prepared for by Albertus and Paracelsus, achieved by our guest of honor. Permit me to give the feeble expression of our admiration for the greatest man of the great century. From the community the laurel wreath! (*He places a laurel wreath on the* STRANGER'*s head.*) From the board—this! (*He hangs the brilliant badge of an order about the* STRANGER'*s neck.*) Gentlemen, a cheer for the Great Maker of Gold!

ALL (*except the* STRANGER): Hurrah! (*The musicians play the chords from the funeral march*)

(During the latter part of the PROFESSOR'*s speech waiters have replaced the gold goblets with dark tin goblets and now begin to carry out peacocks, pheasants, etc.*)

(*The musicians play softly. General conversation.*)

CAESAR: Listen! Shouldn't they let us taste that before they take it away?

DOCTOR: It all seems to be humbug, except for the gold making.

STRANGER *(taps):* Gentlemen! For me it has always been a matter of pride not to be easily fooled . . .

CAESAR: Hear, hear!

STRANGER: . . . and not to be easily swept off my feet, but the sincerity which your splendid tribute reflects has moved me; when *I* say moved me, I mean just that!

CAESAR: Bravo!

STRANGER: There are doubters, of course, and there are moments in every man's life when doubt steals in upon even the strongest of us. I admit that; even I have doubted, but after having been the object of this sincere and heartfelt tribute, when I have witnessed this royal banquet, for it is royal, and finally since the administration itself . . .

VOICE: The board! The board!

STRANGER: —The board, if you wish, has given a glowing recognition of my humble merit, which only the future can judge, so I do not doubt anymore—I *believe! (The man in the civil uniform steals out)* Yes, gentlemen, this is the greatest and most beautiful moment in my life, because it has restored to me the most precious thing a man has: his faith in himself.

CAESAR: Splendid! Bravo!

STRANGER: My thanks! A toast to you!

(*The* PROFESSOR *gets up.*)

(All get up and circulate. All but two of the musicians leave.)

A GUEST (*to the* STRANGER): Very pleasant, very!

STRANGER: Excellent!

(All the formally dressed men steal out.)

FATHER (*an old foppish man with a single lorgnette and military bearing goes up to the* DOCTOR *and greets him*): Well, well! So you're here?

DOCTOR: Yes, Father-in-law, I'm here and everywhere *he* is.

FATHER: You mayn't call me Father-in-law at this late date—besides I'm *his* now.

DOCTOR: Does he know you?

FATHER: No, he hasn't had the honor, and I'd like to keep my incognito. Has he really made gold?

DOCTOR: That's what they say, but one thing is sure—he deserted his wife when she was in childbed.

FATHER: That's to say: I can expect still another son-in-law soon? Yes, yes, boys, this isn't nice, and all this uncertainty gives me a distaste for being a father-in-law. Oh well, I haven't anything to say . . . of course, since . . .

The cloths and candelabras have been removed so that the tables of boards and sawhorses are stripped bare. A large stone bowl is carried in and stone mugs of the most ordinary sort are set out on the speaker's table.

CAESAR (*taps; the shabby, ragged men sit down by the* STRANGER *at the speaker's table; the* FATHER *sits down astride a chair and stares at the* STRANGER): Gentlemen! This banquet has been called royal; it's not as if the food and drinks have been royal; on the contrary, they've been miserable; but the man we've honored is a king, a king in the world of the spirit: I alone can judge that . . .

(*A* SHABBY FELLOW *giggles.*)

CAESAR: Quiet, fellow!—but he is more than a king, for he is a man of the people, of the little people, the friend of the oppressed, the guardian of madmen, the delight of fools. If he has made gold, I don't want to know, I don't care about that, and I hardly believe he has . . . (*Murmuring. Two policemen enter and sit down by the door; the musicians come down and sit at a table.*) . . . but assume that he has, then he has solved all the problems the newspapers have tried to crack the last fifty years. But his is just an assumption . . .

STRANGER: Gentlemen!

SHABBY FELLOW: No, don't interrupt.

CAESAR: It's a loose assumption without any real basis, and the analysis *can* be wrong!

ANOTHER SHABBY FELLOW: Don't talk nonsense!

STRANGER: As guest of honor, I should think the bases on which I have constructed my proof should not be without interest for my fellow guests . . .

CAESAR: We don't want to hear that! We don't want to!

FATHER: Wait a minute! I think that justice demands the defendant has the right to explain himself. Won't you as guest of honor tell the society your secret in a few words?

STRANGER: As an inventor I don't want to give away my secret, and it can't really be considered necessary since I have confided the result to a legal expert!

CAESAR: Then it's bosh the whole thing, and we don't believe authorities, for we're all freethinkers.—Have you ever heard anything so shameless as having to honor in blind faith a dealer in secrets, a swindler of patents, a charlatan?

FATHER: Wait a minute, good people!

(*During this scene a beautifully decorated partition screen with palms and birds of paradise has been taken away so that a miserable tavern shelf and counter, back of which the* TAVERNKEEPER'S WIFE *stands pouring up drinks, can be seen. Underworld figures and unkempt women go up to the counter and drink.*)

STRANGER: Have they invited me here to be insulted?

FATHER: Not at all! Our friend here is a little talkative, but he hasn't said anything insulting yet.

STRANGER: Isn't *charlatan* insulting?

FATHER: That wasn't seriously meant.

STRANGER: Even as a joke I consider *swindler of patents* highly insulting.

FATHER: He didn't use that expression.

STRANGER: What's that? I appeal to all of you. Didn't he say *swindler of patents?*

ALL: He did not say that!

STRANGER: Then I don't know where I am!—And in what company I find myself.

SHABBY FELLOW: Is there something wrong with the company? Is there?

(*Murmuring*)

BEGGAR (*on crutches; comes forward; strikes one crutch against the table so mugs are broken*): Mr. Chairman!—I demand the right to speak! (*He knocks still more dishes to pieces*)

I haven't let life fool me easily, gentlemen, but this time I was fooled! My friend in the highseat over there convinced me that I had so thoroughly fooled myself about his judgment and his good common sense that I am moved and touched.

There are limits to sympathy, and there are limits to cruelty—it hurts me to see genuine merit dragged down into the dirt, and this man deserves a better fate than his foolishness has brought him.

STRANGER: What do you mean?

(*The* FATHER *and the* DOCTOR *have stolen out during the foregoing: There are now only shabby figures at the speaker's table; the tavern customers gather in groups and stare at the* STRANGER.)

BEGGAR: This—you who consider yourself the man of the century accept an invitation from a drinking society [19] to let yourself be honored as a scientist . . .

STRANGER *(gets up):* But the board . . .

BEGGAR: Yes, the board of the drinking society granted you its highest degree through the insignia which you'll have to pay for yourself . . .

STRANGER: And the professor?

BEGGAR: That's what he's called, but he isn't any; oh, he does give lessons, I think; and that fellow in the uniform, who must have fooled you most, is only a servant on the palace staff.

STRANGER: *(tears off the crown and the band):* Well!!!—But who was the old gentleman with a monocle?

BEGGAR: That was your father-in-law!

STRANGER: Who set up this joke?

BEGGAR: It isn't a joke; it's absolutely serious. The professor came on behalf of the society; they call themselves the society, and asked if you wanted to be guest of honor at the banquet; you answered yes; so it became serious!

(*Two disreputable women place a garbage can on a pole on the speaker's table.*)

WOMAN I: If you're the one who makes gold, treat us to a drink.

STRANGER: What's the meaning of this?

BEGGAR: It's the last number of your reception: and it means: gold isn't anything but—garbage!

STRANGER: If that were only true, the garbage could be exchanged for gold.

BEGGAR: Well-l, that's only the drinking society's philosophy, and you'll have to take the philosophy where you come.

WOMAN II: (*sits down beside the* STRANGER): Don't you recognize me?

STRANGER: No!

WOMAN II: Oh well: You don't need to get embarrassed this late at night!

STRANGER: You're supposed to be one of my victims, I suspect! I suppose I'm one of your hundred first seducers.

WOMAN II: No, not in the way you mean. But I did get hold of a printed book just when I was being confirmed; and it said it was the duty of each person to let all his instincts be expressed. Oh well, I grew freely, blooming; and here is the fruit in my highly developed personality.

STRANGER *(gets up):* Perhaps I may go now!

TAVERNKEEPER'S WIFE *(comes up with a bill):* Yes, you may, but this bill is to be paid first.

STRANGER: By me? I haven't ordered anything!

TAVERNKEEPER'S WIFE: I don't know anything about that, but you're the last of the company to go.

STRANGER (*to the* BEGGAR): Is this part of my reception, too?

BEGGAR: Yes, it is, and, as you know, everything has its price— even honor—

STRANGER *(takes up a calling card and hands it to the woman):* Here's my card! I'll pay tomorrow!

TAVERNKEEPER'S WIFE *(puts the card in the garbage can):* Hm! I don't know that name and I've put a lot of calling cards in the garbage can before. I want the money.

BEGGAR: Listen, ma'am, I guarantee this man will pay . . .

TAVERNKEEPER'S WIFE: So you dare to kid me, too.—Officer! Come here a minute!

POLICEMAN: What is this all about? The bill, I suppose. Come along to the station, and we'll settle this. *(He writes in his notebook)*

STRANGER: Rather that than standing here bickering . . . (*To the* BEGGAR) I can put up with a joke, but I hadn't expected it to be so cruelly serious.

BEGGAR: You can expect everything when you've challenged such powerful beings as you have! And I'll whisper this to you: Be prepared for what's worse, for the very worst!

STRANGER: To think I could let myself be fooled so . . . so . . .

BEGGAR: These feasts of Balshazzar [20] always end when *a* hand comes forth and writes—a bill; and another hand taps you on the shoulder and takes you to the police station! But royal it has to be!

POLICEMAN (*puts his hand on the* STRANGER): Clear enough?

WOMEN AND SHABBY FIGURES: The goldmaker! The goldmaker can't pay! Hurrah! They'll put him in jail! They'll put him in jail!

WOMAN II: Yes, but he's to be pitied!

STRANGER: You pity me! Thank you for that, though I don't deserve it fully! *You* have pity!

WOMAN II: Yes, and I've learned even that from you!

CHANGEMANG Á VUE [21]

Dark on stage; a confusion of scenes: landscapes, palace, rooms are raised and shot forward while people and furniture disappear, last of all the STRANGER, *who seems to be standing as if frozen still sleeping; finally even he is concealed; and out of the confusion appears a prison cell.*

THE PRISON

A door to the right; above the door a barred opening through which the sun casts a ray, which forms a light spot on the left wall, where a large crucifix is hanging.

The STRANGER, *dressed in brown cape and hat, is sitting by the table watching the spot of sunlight.*

The door is opened; the BEGGAR *is let in.*

BEGGAR: What are you thinking about?

STRANGER: I'm wondering why I'm sitting here, and I'm wondering where I was last night.

BEGGAR: Where do you think you were?

STRANGER: In hell, I think—either that or I've dreamt the whole thing.

BEGGAR: Wake up then for here comes reality.

STRANGER: Go on—only ghosts frighten me.

BEGGAR *(shows him a newspaper):* First—according to this paper, the great expert has retracted his confirmation of your goldmaking—he says he was deceived by you. The consequence—the paper calls you a charlatan!

STRANGER: Hell!—Whom am I struggling against?

BEGGAR: Against difficulties just like other people!

STRANGER: No, this is something else . . .

BEGGAR: Against your own gullibility then?

STRANGER: No, I'm not gullible, and I know I'm right!

BEGGAR: What good does that do when no one else knows it?

STRANGER: If I can get out of here, I'll straighten it all out.

BEGGAR: The case has been dropped since the bill has been paid . . .

STRANGER: Who paid it?

BEGGAR: Most likely the society or the drinking "administration."

STRANGER: Then I can leave?

BEGGAR: Yes, but there's one more matter . . .

STRANGER: Hit away!

BEGGAR: But an enlightened gentleman may not be taken aback . . .

STRANGER: I have a feeling I know . . .

BEGGAR: The announcement's on page one.

STRANGER: That's to say—she's already remarried, and my children have a stepfather. Who is he?

BEGGAR: Whoever he is, don't murder him—for he's not to blame, certainly the man who marries a deserted woman is innocent.

STRANGER: My children!—God in heaven my children!

BEGGAR: That was unforeseen, I take it. But why didn't you look ahead when you were that old! and such an enlightened gentleman to boot!

STRANGER *(beside himself):* God in heaven, my children.

BEGGAR: Enlightened gentlemen do not cry! But listen, old boy: on occasions like this a gentleman usually . . . either . . . well, you say it!

STRANGER: Shoots himself!

BEGGAR: Or?

STRANGER: No, no, not *that*.

BEGGAR: Yes, old boy, exactly that! He puts out an emergency anchor on trial.

STRANGER: This is hopeless! Hopeless!

BEGGAR: Yes, it is! Absolutely hopeless. And you can live for a generation longer to contemplate your villainy.

STRANGER: Have some shame!

BEGGAR: You have some!

STRANGER: Have you ever seen another human destiny like mine?

BEGGAR: Look at mine!

STRANGER: I don't know yours.

BEGGAR: And it has never occurred to you during our long acquaintanceship to ask about my circumstances. You once rejected the friendship I offered you and you fell right into the arms of the drinking society. Welcome to that and farewell until next time!

STRANGER: Don't go!

BEGGAR: Probably you want company when you leave this place?

STRANGER: Why not?

BEGGAR: You haven't considered the possibility I wouldn't want to leave in your company?

STRANGER: No, I haven't!

BEGGAR: But that's how it is. Do you think I want to be suspected of having been in on the immortal goldmaker-banquet that's written up in the morning paper?

STRANGER: You don't want to be seen in my company!

BEGGAR: Even the beggar has a bit of pride and is afraid of ridicule.

STRANGER: You don't want to be seen in my company! Am I that thoroughly bad?

BEGGAR: You ought to ask yourself that, and answer it yourself, too!

(*A mournful cradle song can be heard as if sung at a distance.*)

STRANGER: What's that?

BEGGAR: A mother singing by her child's cradle.

STRANGER: Why should I be reminded of that just now?

BEGGAR: Presumably to let you really feel rather keenly what you left for the sake of a foolish notion.

STRANGER: If it's possible I've made a mistake, then it's the devil's delusion—then I'd lay down my weapons.

BEGGAR: Please do so as soon as possible then . . .

STRANGER: Not yet! *(A rosary can be heard being recited in the distance.)* What's that? *(A long hunting horn melody can be heard)* That's the unknown hunter! *(The chord of the funeral march is heard)* Where am I?

(He remains standing as if in a hypnotic sleep.)

BEGGAR: Bend or break!

STRANGER: I can't bend!

BEGGAR: Break then!

(The STRANGER *falls down.)*

(The same confusion of decorations as before.)

[CURTAIN]

THE ROSE CHAMBER

The same scenery as in Act II. The SISTERS OF MERCY *are now on their knees reading from prayer books . . .* "Exules filii Evae, ad te suspiramus gementes et flentes in hac lacrymarum valle." *The* MOTHER *by the door at the back. The* FATHER *is standing by the door to the right.*

MOTHER *(going up to him):* So you're back again?

FATHER *(humbly):* Yes!

MOTHER: Your beauty has deserted you?

FATHER: Don't be more cruel than necessary!

MOTHER: That's what you, who gave my wedding gifts to your mistress, say, you who were so lacking in decency as to ask me to select gifts for your paramour and for me to teach you about colors and designing her clothes . . . What do you want here?

FATHER: I heard that my daughter . . .

MOTHER: Your daughter's hovering between life and death, and you know she has become antagonistic toward you. So I beg you to leave before she finds out you're here.

Gertrud Fridh and Lars Hanson as the Lady and the Stranger
(Royal Dramatic Theater, Stockholm)

Above, Jan-Olof Strandberg as the Stranger in the Asylum Scene;
below, Anders Ek as the Beggar
(Royal Dramatic Theater, Stockholm)

Above, Jan-Olof Strandberg as the Stranger in the Banquet Scene; *right,* Helena Brodin and Jan-Olof Strandberg as the Lady and the Stranger
(Royal Dramatic Theater, Stockholm)

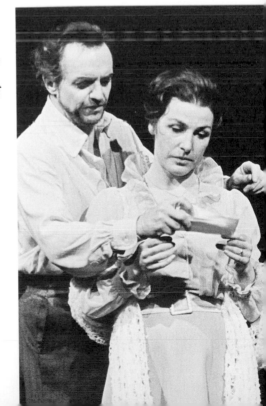

Lars Hanson as the Stranger
(Royal Dramatic Theater, Stockholm)

FATHER: You're right, and I have nothing to say. But let me sit in the kitchen, for I'm very, very tired.

MOTHER: Where were you last night?

FATHER: At the club. But let me ask: Isn't her husband here?

MOTHER: Do I have to stand here revealing the whole mess? Don't you know about your daughter's miserable lot . . .

FATHER: Yes—yes, I do . . . a man like that, a man *like* that . . .

MOTHER: Men like that! Go down and sleep until you're sober . . .

FATHER: The sins of the fathers . . .

MOTHER: You're raving . . .

FATHER: Well, naturally I don't mean my own sins but our ancestors' . . . you know . . . and now they say the lake up there's to be drained and the river will rise . . .

MOTHER *(shoves him out through the door)*: Silence! Misfortune will certainly catch up with us soon enough without your summoning it.

MAID *(enters from in back)*: The mistress is asking for the master.

MOTHER: She means her husband!

MAID: Yes, the man of the house! Her husband!

MOTHER: He went out a while ago!

STRANGER *(enters)*: Has the child been born?

MOTHER: Not yet!

STRANGER *(putting his hand to his forehead)*: What does that mean?— Can it take this long?

MOTHER: Long? What do you mean?

STRANGER *(looks about)*: I don't know what I mean! But . . . how is she?

MOTHER: Just the same as a while ago.

STRANGER: A while ago!

MOTHER: Aren't you going to your goldmaker?

STRANGER: Now I don't understand anything any more! But there's one hope left: that my worst dream was only a dream.

MOTHER: You look as if you were really sleepwalking!

STRANGER: Do I? If I only were! The only thing I feared I'd no longer need to fear.

MOTHER: The one who's looking after your destiny seems to know your vulnerable spots.

STRANGER: At last when I had only one left, he found that, too—fortunately only in my dreams. Blind powers! Impotent powers!

MAID *(comes in again):* The mistress wants you to do her a favor, sir!

STRANGER: She's lying there like an electric eel letting her blows fall at quite a distance! What does she want me to do for her now?

MAID: There's a letter in the pocket of the green jacket.

STRANGER *[sighs]:* No good will come out of that! *(He takes a letter out of the green jacket hanging beside the dress by the stove):* Now I'm dead! I had dreamt this before, but now it's real!—My children have a stepfather.

MOTHER: Whom are you going to blame now?

STRANGER: Myself! Preferably no one!—I have lost my children!

MOTHER: You're getting a new one here!

STRANGER: Think of this—if he's cruel to them . . .

MOTHER: Then you'll get their suffering on your conscience if you have any.

STRANGER: Think of this—if he beats them!

MOTHER: Do you know what I'd do if I were in your place?

STRANGER: Yes, I know what you'd do, but I don't know what I'll do.

MOTHER (*to* NUNS): Pray for this man!

STRANGER: No, don't! Not that! For it won't help, and I don't believe in it!

MOTHER: But you believe in your gold?

STRANGER: Not that either! That's over! Everything's over.

MIDWIFE *(comes in from in back):* The child is born! Praise the Lord!

MOTHER AND THE SISTERS: The Lord be praised!

MIDWIFE (*to the* STRANGER): Your wife has given you a daughter!

MOTHER (*to the* STRANGER): Don't you want to see your child?

STRANGER: No! I don't want to bind myself to anything on earth any more. I'm afraid I'd get to love her, and then you'd tear the heart out of my body. Let me go, out of this air, which is too clean for me. Don't let the innocent child come near me,

for I'm a lost soul, a damned soul, and for me there's no joy,
no peace, no—mercy!

MOTHER: My son, now you're uttering words of wisdom! Without
evil and without deceit! I agree with you, you're not needed
here and you'd be tortured to death among us women. So go
in peace!

STRANGER: The peace is no doubt over, but I'll go. Farewell!

MOTHER: *"Exules filii Evae!"* "A fugitive and a vagabond shalt thou
be in the earth." [22]

STRANGER: Because I murdered my brother!

[CURTAIN]

ACT IV

TIIE TAVERN

*The tavern as in Act III. But disreputable with unpainted wooden
tables and benches. Beggars, criminals, and streetwalkers. Cripples are
sitting here and there drinking by candlelight.*

The STRANGER *and* WOMAN II *are drinking brandy together. The
liquor is in a carafe.*

(*The* STRANGER *is drinking excessively.*)

WOMAN: Don't drink so much!

STRANGER: Huh? Are you moralistic, too?

WOMAN: No, but I can't stand seeing a man I respect degrade
himself.

STRANGER: The reason I came here was to degrade myself, to
take a bath in the dirt to make my skin hard against the pricks
in life, to find an immoral base in my environment. And I chose
your company because you were the most despised woman but
still the one who had kept a spark of humanity. You pitied me
when no one else did, not even I myself. Why did you?

WOMAN: Surely one doesn't know that sort of thing?

STRANGER: But do you know there are moments when you are almost beautiful?

WOMAN: Well, well, listen to the man!

STRANGER: Yes, and then you're like someone who has been dear to me.

WOMAN: Thank you very much!

TAVERNKEEPER'S WIFE: Don't talk so loudly—there's a sick person in bed in there!

STRANGER: Tell me, have you loved anyone?

WOMAN: We don't use that word, but I understand what you mean all the same: yes, I had a lover and we had a child.

STRANGER: That wasn't sensible!

WOMAN: Well, that's what I thought, but he said the time of emancipation had come, when all chains were to be loosened, all barriers fall and . . .

STRANGER *(tortured)*: And then . . .

WOMAN: He deserted me.

STRANGER: He was a scoundrel! *(Drinks)*

WOMAN *(fixes his glance)*: You think so?

STRANGER: Yes, of course he was!

WOMAN: Now you're too strict!

STRANGER *(drinking)*: Am I?

WOMAN: Don't drink so much! I want to see you way up, high above me; otherwise, you can't raise me.

STRANGER: Child, what illusions! I lift! I! who am far, far down there. No, it isn't I, and it isn't I who am sitting here, for I am dead; I know my soul is somewhere else far away, far, far away . . . *(He stares straight ahead lost in thought)* . . . where a large river flows like gold in the sunlight and where the roses bloom with the grape vines on a wall; and where a white baby carriage stands under the acacia, but the child is asleep, for its mother is sitting there crocheting, crocheting a long, long runner, and it says on the runner . . . let's see . . . "Blessed are the sorrowful, for they shall be comforted." But that probably isn't how it is! I'll never get it! . . . Tell me, isn't there thunder in the air? It feels so heavy, so depressing . . .

WOMAN *(looks out the window):* No, I don't see any clouds out there . . .

STRANGER: That's strange! Now the lightning's flashing!

WOMAN: No, you're mistaken!

STRANGER: One, two, three, four, five . . . now it ought to thunder! But it doesn't. I've never been afraid of thunder before today— that's to say, tonight . . . Well, is it day or night?

WOMAN: Why, it's night, dear!

STRANGER: Yes, it is night! Night!

(*During the preceding scene the* DOCTOR *has come in and sat down back of the* STRANGER *without being seen by him.*)

TAVERNKEEPER'S WIFE: Don't talk so loudly—there's a sick person in there!

STRANGER *(to the* WOMAN*):* Give me your hand!

WOMAN *(wipes it on her apron):* Why?

STRANGER: You have a white, a beautiful hand. But . . . look at mine; why it's absolutely black! Can't you see it's black?

WOMAN: Yes, it really is!

STRANGER: Already turned black; probably rotted away, too? I'll feel if my heart has stopped! *(Places his hand above his heart)* It has stopped! So I am dead! And I know when I died!—To think one can walk about dead. But where am I then? Are all these others dead, too? They look as if they had come up from the city sewers or as if the penitentiary, the poor house, or the venereal section of the hospital had let them out. The workers of the night, suffering, moaning, cursing, fighting, torture each other, insult each other, envy each other as if any of them had anything to envy. The flame of sleep runs in their veins, their tongues stick to their gums, which have dried up from their curses, and they put out the fire with water, with fire water, which awakens a new thirst, the firewater which itself burns with a blue flame and burns out the soul like a swamp fire so only the red sand is left. *(Drinks)* Fire up! Put it out! Fire up! Put it out! But what doesn't burn up, is, unfortunately,—the memory— of—the—past! What shall one use to burn up one's memories?

TAVERNKEEPER'S WIFE: Please don't talk so loudly; there's a sick

person in bed in there. Yes, he's so sick he has already asked
for the sacrament.[23]

STRANGER: May he go to hell soon then!

(ALL *murmur disapprovingly.*)

TAVERNKEEPER'S WIFE: Watch out! Watch out!

WOMAN (*to the* STRANGER): Do you know the man who's sitting
in back of you staring at you all the time?

STRANGER (*turns around—the* DOCTOR *and he stare at each other
for a moment without saying anything*): Yes, I used to know him!

WOMAN: He looks as if he wanted to eat you alive.

(The DOCTOR *sits down directly across from the* STRANGER *and
stares at him.*)

STRANGER: What are you looking at?

DOCTOR: At your gray hairs!

STRANGER (*to the* WOMAN): Am I grayhaired, too?

WOMAN: Yes, of course you are.

DOCTOR: And I'm looking at your beautiful companion: sometimes
you do have good taste, sometimes not.

STRANGER: And sometimes you have the bad luck that we have
the same taste.

DOCTOR: That wasn't a kind thing to say! But you have murdered
me twice—keep on murdering.

STRANGER (*to the* WOMAN): Let's leave this place!

DOCTOR: You sense me! You feel me at great distances! But I
get to you as the lightning finds you, even if you laid yourself in the depths of the earth or of the sea . . . try sensing
me!

STRANGER (*to the* WOMAN): Come with me! Guide me—I can't
see . . .

WOMAN: No, I don't want to leave yet, and I don't want to be
bored!

DOCTOR: You're right about that, woman of joy! Life is heavy
enough anyway without having to bear other people's self-in-
flicted suffering, too. But that man doesn't bear his own but
puts it on his wife's back.

STRANGER: What's that? Wait. Her false accusation of violation
of privacy and attempted murder.

DOCTOR: And now he's blaming her!

(*The* STRANGER *puts his head in his hands and lets it sink to the table.*)

(*The following melody is played on a violin and a guitar in the background*):

DOCTOR (*to the* WOMAN): Is he sick?

WOMAN: He's crazy, I think, for he insists he's dead.

(*In the distance reveille is sounded on a drum and then on a horn, but extremely softly.*)

STRANGER: Is it morning? The night has passed, the sun is rising, and the ghosts are returning to their graves—so I'll go. Come!

WOMAN (*moves toward the* DOCTOR): No, I said!

STRANGER: Even you, my last friend! Am I so damnably bad that not even a prostitute wants to keep me company for pay?

DOCTOR: You must be!

STRANGER: I don't believe it even if everyone says it! As far as that goes, I don't believe anything, because everytime I've believed anything I've been fooled.—But tell me one thing: Hasn't the sun come up yet? I heard the rooster crow and the dog bark a while ago and now the Angelus is ringing . . . Have they put out the lights since it's so dark?

DOCTOR (*to the* WOMAN): He's blind . . .

WOMAN: Yes, heavens, I think he is!

STRANGER: No, I see you, but I don't see the lights.

DOCTOR: It's beginning to turn dark for you . . . you've played with the lightning and looked too much into the sun, and no one may do that . . .

STRANGER: One's born with the desire to do that, but one may not. That's merely envy . . .

DOCTOR: What do you have that's worth envying?

STRANGER: I have what you never will understand and what only I can appreciate.

DOCTOR: You mean the child . . .

STRANGER: You know I didn't mean that, for if I had, I'd have put it like this: I have what you couldn't get . . .

DOCTOR: So you're at that again! Then I'll speak as bluntly: you took what I had rejected.

WOMAN: For shame! No, I don't want to be with such pigs! *(Gets up and takes another seat)*

STRANGER: We've gone pretty low! But I think the farther I sink, the closer I get to a goal: the end!

TAVERNKEEPER'S WIFE: Don't talk so loudly—there's a dying person in there.

STRANGER: Yes, I, too, think it smells of dead bodies in here.

DOCTOR: Probably we're the dead.

STRANGER: Can one be dead without knowing it?

DOCTOR: The dead say one doesn't know the difference.

STRANGER: You frighten me! If that were possible! And all these shadow figures, whose faces I seem to recognize as youthful memories from the schoolroom, from the swimming school, from physical education classes . . . *(Puts his hand to his heart. Sighs)* No, he's coming, the terrible one who sucks my heart out of my breast . . . He's coming, the invisible one, who has pursued me for years . . . Now he's here! *(Beside himself)*

   (The doors are opened; a choir boy carries a lantern with blue glass, which throws a blue light on the customers; he rings the silver bell: All give a howl as if they were wild animals; then the DOMINICAN *enters with the sacramental [vessels]; the* TAVERNKEEPER'S WIFE *and the* WOMAN *fall to their knees; the rest howl. The* DOMINICAN *lifts the monstrance; all fall to their knees; the choir boy and the* DOMINICAN *go into the room to the left.)*

BEGGAR (*enters; goes toward the* STRANGER): Come away from here! You're sick, and officers with warrants are looking for you.

STRANGER: Warrants? From whom?

BEGGAR: Your wife!

DOCTOR: The electric eel! delivers her blows at quite a distance. She sued me once for libel because she couldn't stay away at night.

STRANGER: Away at night?

DOCTOR: Yes—s! Do you know whom you've been married to?

STRANGER: They said she was engaged before she married— you!

DOCTOR: Yes, that's how they put it, but actually she was the mistress of a married man, whom she sued for rape later on after she had forced her way into his studio and been his model in the nude.

STRANGER: And you married *her?*

DOCTOR: Yes, she sued me for breach of promise after she seduced me, and then I had to marry her, but she had two plain-clothesmen there to see to it I didn't run away.—And *you* married her!

STRANGER: That's because I learned early there's no need to be selective when all of them are alike.

BEGGAR: Come away from here! Or you'll regret it!

STRANGER (*to the* DOCTOR): Was she always religious?

DOCTOR: Always!

STRANGER: And tender, good-hearted, self-sacrificing . . .

DOCTOR: Absolutely!

STRANGER: Can anyone ever get to understand her?

DOCTOR: No, you can go crazy if you think about her, so I took her as a fact: charming and intoxicating as a fact!

STRANGER: Of course, but that's why one's defenseless against one's pity, so I don't want any trials in court for I can't defend myself without accusations against her, and I don't want to do that.

DOCTOR: You've been married before . . . how was it?

STRANGER: Exactly the same!

DOCTOR: Why, it's like Hyoscyamus,[24] that love; a person sees suns where there aren't any and stars where there aren't any. But it is fun while it lasts!

STRANGER: But the day after? Oh, the day after!

BEGGAR: Come, you unfortunate soul—he's sitting poisoning you, and you don't see what he's up to! Come!

STRANGER *(gets up):* Is he poisoning me? Do you think he's lying?

BEGGAR: He has lied every word!

STRANGER: I don't believe it.

BEGGAR: No. You believe only lies! But you have that coming!

STRANGER: Has he been lying? Has he?

BEGGAR: You can't believe your enemy, of course.

STRANGER: Why, he's my friend since he has told me the bitter truth.

BEGGAR: Eternal powers: save his mind when he believes everything evil to be true! Come, or you're lost!

DOCTOR: He's already lost, but now's he to be beaten into foam, dissolved into atoms, and become part of the ingredients of the great nothingness. There: now go to hell! *(To all the people in the tavern):* Howls from hell for his victims!

(CUSTOMERS *howl.*)

DOCTOR: And no womanly pity any more! Howl, woman!

(*The* WOMAN *makes a gesture of rejection with her hand.*)

STRANGER *(to the* BEGGAR*):* That man doesn't lie!

[CURTAIN]

THE RAVINE

A ravine with a brook in its middle; a footbridge over the brook; in the foreground a collapsed smithy and a mill. Fallen trees over the brook.
The background a starry sky over an evergreen forest; Orion [25] *can be seen plainly.*

The STRANGER *and the* BEGGAR *enter.*

The foreground covered with snow; the background summer green.

STRANGER: I'm afraid! The stars are hanging so low tonight, I feel they want to fall down on me like drops of molten silver. Where are we?

BEGGAR: By the brook in the ravine. You really ought to know them.

STRANGER: Do I? Do I ever recognize them! Why, I remember my wedding trip!—But where is the smithy? and the mill?

BEGGAR: In ruins! Ruins! The Lake of Tears was drained eight days ago; the brook rose, the river rose, and everything was laid waste in meadows, fields, and orchard!

STRANGER: And the guest house?

BEGGAR: It was washed clean of old sins, but the walls are still standing.

STRANGER: And the people in it?

BEGGAR: They've gone to the colonies,[26] so that story's over!

STRANGER: Then my story's over, too, and so thoroughly there isn't one pleasant memory left. The last one was covered by dirt by that poisoner . . .

BEGGAR: For whom you had prepared the poison! Give up your pretensions now!

STRANGER: Yes! Now I give up!

BEGGAR: Then you're close to the final settlement.

STRANGER: I think it can be considered settled now; for if I have done wrong, I have been punished.

BEGGAR: But the others don't seem to think so!

STRANGER: I'm through concerning myself about others since I saw that the powers which control the destinies of human beings can't stand having any assistants. And it was my crime that I wanted to set people free . . .

BEGGAR: . . . set people free from their duties and sinners free from feelings of guilt so that they haven't any pangs of conscience. You're not the first nor the last who helps out in the devil's work. *Lucifer a non lucendo!* But when that fox gets old, he becomes a monk—that's how wisely it's arranged, and then he has to attack himself and drive Beelzebub out with his own Baal sacrifice.

STRANGER: So that's where I'm to be driven!

BEGGAR: Yes! Where you didn't want to go! You're to get up and preach on housetops and chimneys against yourself; you're to unravel your web thread by thread; you're to flay yourself alive at every street corner and show what you look like inside! But that takes courage; the one who has played with lightning isn't afraid! Oh, sometimes, when night comes and the invisible powers that can be seen only in the dark dance on one's chest, then he becomes afraid, afraid even of the stars, but most of all of the mill of sin, which grinds and grinds the past, the past, the past. But one of the seven and seventeen wise men says that the greatest victory is over oneself, but the foolish don't believe that, so they get fooled, too, for they believe only what the nine and ninety fools have said a thousand times!

STRANGER: That's enough!—Tell me one thing: Isn't there snow on the ground here?

BEGGAR: Yes! It's winter here!

STRANGER: And it's green over there?

BEGGAR: It's summer there!

STRANGER: And it's turning light over there?

(Clear light can be seen over the footbridge.)

BEGGAR: Yes, it's light over there, and over here it's dark.

STRANGER: And who are coming over there? *(Three summer-clad children, two girls and a blond boy come out on the footbridge from the right.)* Hello! My children!

(The CHILDREN *come to attention and look at the* STRANGER *without recognizing him.)*

STRANGER *(calls out):* Gerda! Erik! Thyra!—It's I!

(The CHILDREN *now seem to recognize him; turn away to the right.)*

STRANGER: They don't know me any more! They don't want to have anything to do with me!

(MAN and WIFE *enter from the right; the children dance off toward the left and disappear.)*

(The STRANGER *falls, face down, to the ground.)*

BEGGAR: You have to expect things like that! That's how it can happen! Get up again!

STRANGER *(gets up):* Where am I? Where have I been? Is it spring, winter, or summer? In which century am I living and in which universe? Am I a child or an old man, a man or a woman, a god or a devil?—Who are you? Are you you or are you I? Are these my intestines I see about me? Are those stars or nerve endings in my eye? Is that water or my tears? Sh-h! Now I was jerked a thousand years forward in time, and I'm beginning to shrink, to be concentrated, to be crystalized! Wait a little! I'll soon be created over again, and out of the dark water of chaos the lotus flower will raise its head into the sunlight and say: It is I!—I must have slept a couple thousand years, and I dreamt I exploded and became ether, felt nothing any more, didn't suffer any more, had no joy, but had entered into rest and the state of equilibrium! But now! I suffer as if I were all mankind. I suffer and do not have the right to complain . . .

BEGGAR: Go ahead, suffer—then it will be over sooner . . .

STRANGER: No, these are the eternal pangs . . .

BEGGAR: And only a minute has passed . . .

STRANGER: I can't stand it!

BEGGAR: Then you'll have to accept help!

STRANGER: What's coming now? It isn't over yet!

(*It turns light over the footbridge,* CAESAR *comes rushing in over the footbridge; then the* DOCTOR, *bareheaded, enters from the right, looking wild. Gestures as if he wanted to plunge into the brook.*)

STRANGER: He has avenged himself so thoroughly I haven't any pangs of conscience because of him!

(*The* DOCTOR *exits to the left; his sister, searching for him, enters from the right.*)

STRANGER: Who's that?

BEGGAR: Well, that's his unmarried sister who's now without a home and means of support and is in despair and sorrow since her brother lost his mind.

STRANGER: That hits me harder! Poor soul, what shall I do about that? Even if I suffer her pangs, is she helped by that?

BEGGAR: No, she isn't!

STRANGER: Pangs of conscience, why do you come afterwards and not before?—Can you help me out of this?

BEGGAR: No, no human being can! Let's go on!

STRANGER: Where?

BEGGAR: Just come!

[CURTAIN]

THE ROSE CHAMBER

The LADY *is sitting by the cradle crocheting. The green dress is hanging by the door to the right.*

(*The* STRANGER *enters; looks about with amazement.*)

LADY (*simply, gently, without a hint of amazement*): Walk softly and come here and you'll see something beautiful.

STRANGER: Where am I?

LADY: Sh-h! Look at the little stranger who came while you were gone.

STRANGER: They told me the river had swept everything away.

LADY: Why do you believe everything they tell you? The river did flood, but this little human being has someone who protects her and hers . . . Don't you want to see your daughter?

(*The* STRANGER *approaches the cradle.*)

LADY (*lifts the top*): Do you see how beautiful she is? Isn't she?

(*The* STRANGER *darkens.*)

LADY: Take a look!

STRANGER: Everything is poisoned, everything!

LADY: Yes, perhaps!

STRANGER: Do you know *he* has lost his mind and is wandering about in the neighborhood followed by his sister . . . who's looking for him. To top that: he's in want and is drinking . . .

LADY: Oh God, my God!

STRANGER: Scold me!

LADY: No, you do that sufficiently yourself. I'd rather give you a bit of good advice: Go to the cloister The Good Help—a man's there who can set you free from the evil you fear.

STRANGER: There in the cloister, where they pronounce curses and bind . . .

LADY: They set people free, too!

STRANGER: Frankly speaking, I think you want to fool me—I don't believe you any more.

LADY: And I don't believe you! So: consider this your visit to say goodbye . . .

STRANGER: That's what I had intended, I think, but I wanted to find out first if we agreed . . .

LADY: You certainly see we can't build any happiness on other people's sufferings; so we have to part; that's the only means for relieving *his* suffering. I have my child to fill my life, and you have the great goal of your ambition . . .

STRANGER: So you're still mocking me?

LADY: No! How do you mean? You have solved the big problem, haven't you . . .

STRANGER: Sh-h! Say no more about *that,* even if you believe it!

LADY: But when everybody else believes . . .

STRANGER: Nobody believes that any more . . .

LADY: Why, it says in today's paper they've made gold in England and that that's confirmed!

STRANGER: You've been deceived!

LADY: No!—Oh God, he doesn't believe in his own good fortune.

STRANGER: I don't believe in anything any more!

LADY: Take the paper in the pocket of my dress over there!

STRANGER: The green witchdress that bewitched me once between the tavern and the church one Sunday afternoon. That doesn't bring any good!

LADY *(goes over to the dress and takes up the newspaper and a large envelope):* See for yourself!

STRANGER *(tears the newspaper to pieces):* I don't need to!

LADY: He doesn't believe! He doesn't believe! But the chemists have arranged a banquet for next Saturday for you . . .

STRANGER: So! It's written up there, too! . . . About the banquet!

LADY *(hands him the envelope):* And here's the diploma of honor! Read it, man!

STRANGER *(tears the envelope to pieces):* Maybe the administration order is there, too!

LADY: Well! The one the gods wish to destroy they strike blind! You had no good intention in making your discovery, so you weren't allowed to make it alone!

STRANGER: Now I'll leave for I don't want to stand here exposing my shame! I've become a laughing stock, so I want to hide, bury myself alive, for I don't dare to die.

LADY: Go, my friend! We're leaving for our summer retreat in a few days!

STRANGER: So at least that was true!—Then the answer's coming.

LADY: The answer to the problem: why we had to meet?

STRANGER: Why did we have to meet?

LADY: To torture each other!

STRANGER: Is that all?

LADY: You were to free me from a werewolf who wasn't a werewolf, so you became one yourself; and I was to free you from evil by taking your evil on myself, and I did, I think, but with the result you became still more evil. Poor liberator, now you're standing there bound hand and foot, and no magician can release you.

STRANGER: Good bye, and thanks for everything!

LADY: Good bye, and thank you for this! *(She points to the cradle)*

STRANGER *(goes toward the back):* Perhaps I should say good bye to them in there!

LADY: Do that, my friend!

(*The* STRANGER *goes out through the door at the back.*)

(*The* LADY *goes to the door at the right and admits the* DOMINICAN [*the* BEGGAR].)

CONFESSOR: Is he prepared now?

LADY: That unfortunate human being hasn't anything left but leaving the world and burying himself in the cloister.

CONFESSOR: So he doesn't believe he's the great inventor he is?

LADY: No, he can't believe good about anyone, not even about himself . . .

CONFESSOR: Well, that's the divine punishment; that he'd believe the lie because he didn't want to believe the truth.

LADY: But lighten his burden of guilt a little if you can.

CONFESSOR: No—then he'd become arrogant right away and accuse God of evil and injustice. And the man is a demon who must be kept captive; one of the terrible breed of revolutionaries he'd misuse his gifts to do evil, and a human being's capacity for doing evil is unlimited.

LADY: Because of the . . . affection you've had for me, lighten his burden of guilt a little where he's most pressed and most without guilt.

CONFESSOR: I can't, but you shall do it so that he leaves you with the belief there is something good in you and that you're not what your former husband said you were. If he believes in you, I'll set him free later, as I bound him once, when he once confessed to me in the cloister The Good Help while he was ill.

LADY *(goes toward the back; opens the door):* Well then!

STRANGER *(enters):* There's that terrible person! How did he get here?—But you're the beggar, aren't you?

CONFESSOR: Yes, I'm your terrible friend, who has come to fetch you.

STRANGER: Have I . . .

CONFESSOR: Yes. You sold your soul to me once . . . when you were sick and felt insanity coming on. Then you promised to serve the good powers, but, when you got well, you broke your promise; so you were struck with anxiety and have wandered about without peace, crushed by your conscience.

STRANGER: Who are you really, who dares touch my destiny?

CONFESSOR: Ask her!

LADY: This man was my first bridegroom, who has since devoted his life to the service of Christ since I deserted him . . .

STRANGER: And if that were true . . . ?

LADY: Then you don't need to think so badly about your deeds when you became the punisher of my faithlessness and my other husband's lack of conscience.

STRANGER: His crime can't offset mine! Besides it's probably a lie like everything else, and you're saying this just to comfort me!

CONFESSOR: He's a lost soul . . .

STRANGER: And damned!

CONFESSOR: No! (*To the* LADY) Say something good about him!

LADY: He doesn't believe if I say anything good; he believes only evil!

CONFESSOR: Then I'll say a good word! Once upon a time a beggar came to him and asked for a drink of water, and he gave him wine instead of water and let him sit at his table. Do you remember that?

STRANGER: No, I don't remember little things like that!

CONFESSOR: Arrogance, arrogance!

STRANGER: Say arrogance! It's the very last trace of our divine origin! Come along before it gets dark!

CONFESSOR: "The whole world had clear light and was unhindered in its deeds; only over these rested a deep night, which was like the darkness, which was to come over them! But they themselves were more difficult than the darkness."

LADY: Don't hurt him!

STRANGER *(passionately):* Imagine—how beautifully she can talk and how evil she *is!* Look at those eyes—they can't weep, but they can caress, pierce, lie! Yet: "Don't hurt him!"—Look, now she's afraid I'll awaken the child, the little monster who took her from me! Come, priest, before I change my mind!

[CURTAIN]

Notes on

'To Damascus, II'

1. See I Corinthians, 5:4–5, particularly 5: "To deliver such an one unto Satan for the destruction of the flesh, that the spirit may be saved in the day of the Lord Jesus." For Deuteronomy's curse, see note 46, p. 93, or Deuteronomy 28:15 ff.

2. Job 7:13–15.

3. Strindberg's point of departure for his concept of the Powers was the many Biblical references to "the powers of the world" and "the powers of heaven." See note 22, p. 92.

4. The Eumenides or the Erinyes or the Furies are, as *Webster's Collegiate Dictionary* says, "three avenging spirits, snaky-haired women who pursued evildoers and inflicted madness." The idea implicit in "the Well-Intentioned Ones" is that they were disciplinarians forcing the individual to avoid transgression and to follow the path meted out to him by fate.

5. See any biography or *The Inferno* for an account of Strindberg's attempts at making gold.

6. Furious because Prometheus had stolen fire from heaven for the use of mankind, Zeus or Jupiter avenged himself on man by having Vulcan fashion a godlike being, Pandora (all gifts), from earth and water and by having the gods endow her with good and evil qualities. Among these gifts were beauty, artistic qualities, artfulness, and cunning. When Prometheus saw her, he rejected her, but his gentler brother, Epimetheus, married her. Their union was happy until Mercury put into her care a box which he forbade her to open. Overcome with curiosity, she opened it, releasing the sufferings, vices, sins, and other afflictions of mankind. In her terror, Pandora closed the box and thereby saved Hope for mankind.

7. See Genesis 4 for the account of Cain, son of Adam and Eve and slayer of his brother Abel. Note particularly Genesis 4:11–12: "and now *art* thou cursed from the earth, which hath opened her mouth to receive thy brother's blood from thy hand; when thou fillest the ground, it shall

not henceforth yield unto thee her strength; a fugitive and a vagabond shalt thou be in the earth."

8. See Genesis 4:15. Romans 12: "Vengeance is mine . . . saith the Lord."

9. Exodus 13:20–22, part of the account of the Israelites' fleeing from Egypt: "And the Lord went before them by day in a pillar of a cloud, to lead them the way; and by night in a pillar of fire, to give them light; to go by day and night: He took not away the pillar of the cloud by day, not the pillar of fire by night, *from* before the people."

10. According to Greek mythology, Nessus was shot by Hercules for trying to seduce Deianira, his wife. The dying Nessus persuaded her to steep her husband's shirt in Nessus' blood as a love charm. When Hercules put it on, it caused him so much pain and agony that he killed himself.

11. See Genesis 10:10 and 11:4, 9 for the biblical story of the Tower of Babel. The thirteenth-century book called *Sohar* is extremely important to cabbalistic interpretations of the secret significance and nature of God, the universe, creation, the scriptures, etc.

12. Powers.

13. Baal, chief god of the Phoenicians, was worshipped by the Israelites, who were to worship no other god but Jehovah.

14. This apparently has to do with Strindberg's conviction that when he had discovered how to make gold he could upset the whole economic system. See his *Inferno* and *Legender.*

15. Ether is the region beyond the atmosphere of the earth as Strindberg uses the term here. The principalities are the various orders of angels.

16. Strindberg believed experts would attest to his discovery of the secret of making gold. See *The Inferno.*

17. The opening of the scene is remarkably reminiscent of Swedish banquets designed to honor people for their achievements. Strindberg had been a guest on occasion of various organizations that along with serious and even idealistic goals supplemented their pursuits by indulging in good food and drink. Perhaps the most prominent Stockholm club of that kind was *Sällskapet* (founded 1800).

18. The Pythagoreans are the followers of the Greek philosopher Pythagoras (582–507 B.C.), who may have developed the doctrine of metempsychosis or the transmigration of souls. Albertus (ca. 1206–80) was the German philosopher, theologian, and scientist who believed that the metals could be transformed. Paracelsus (1490–1541) was the Swiss physician and scientist who emphasized the role of chemical change.

19. See note 17.

20. See Daniel 5:1, 9, 22, 29, 30; 7:1; 8:1 for the account of the fall of Babylon, for whom Daniel interpreted the handwriting on the wall: God hath numbered thy kingdom and finished it. Thou art weighed in the balances, and art found wanting. Thy kingdom is divided, and given to the Medes and Persians *(Mene, Mene, Tekel, Uphärsin)*.

21. This phrase, which Strindberg used to indicate a change of scene, is reproduced exactly as it appeared in the original Swedish edition.

22. Genesis 1:4.

23. The last rites, or extreme unction, or the sacraments of penance, communion, and consecration collectively.

24. *Hyoscyamus niger* or belladonna or henbane, a poisonous herb used not only as a poison but as a means for dilating the pupil of the eye, relieving spasms, etc.

25. Orion, the constellation represented on the charts by the figure of a hunter with belt and sword.

26. Colonies here refer to outlying farming or gardening areas away from the main or home farm. Swedish parallels would be the *fäbod* or summer upland pasture and the areas set aside particularly on the outskirts of cities for summer gardening and even living.

27. Beelzebub was the pagan deity believed to be the prince of demons. See note 13.

Introduction to
'To Damascus, III'

THE PRODUCTION OF *To Damascus, I* at the Royal Dramatic Theater in November, 1900 may have been the primary stimulus for Strindberg's renewed interest in dramatizing further his Damascus (and Inferno) experiences. Certainly the predominantly friendly and even enthusiastic reception of the production by critics and theatergoers alike did not lessen his interest in the set of personal problems which the Inferno crisis had intensified or raised and which had never really been resolved. (Nor had he claimed that they had been: *To Damascus, I* ends with his willingness to walk through the church and his firm assertion that he will not stay, and *To Damascus, II* with the decidedly inconclusive words, "Come, priest, before I change my mind!")

His letters reveal his continuing concern with personal difficulties and his failure to achieve inner peace and tranquility or what he calls reconciliation *(försoning)*. On January 24, 1899, he wrote to Carl Larsson, the brilliant artist:

> That you have such forbearance with my faults can demonstrate that you consider me irresponsible *(oansvarig)* or [that I] deserve to [have them] overlooked. That probably has some secret basis just as my never being able to forgive myself an unworthy act and my never being able to accept praise. The latter seems to me to be for someone else, and I don't believe it. But my life is a cripple lacking a half ell in the backbone, of course. My years between twenty and thirty are missing—the best bits and I don't understand my destiny. At nineteen I discovered [I had] the gift of writing plays, a gift not common in Sweden. I was then a half-pious soul who on his knees thanked God for the special favor and began dutifully to cultivate my precious talents. But imagine if you painted colossal canvases which were never

accepted for exhibition but which you had to roll up and carry up
to the attic where they would remain to become old-fashioned. That's
what I've had to do several times over. And it isn't true that I've
misused my gifts, for the most beautiful plays—*The Secret of the Guild,
Lord Bengt's Wife, To Damascus,* and *Advent* are not played while the
uglier ones are put on only to disappear leaving a wet spot behind!
   At this point in time I know wherein I have sinned and admit it,
but where I am without guilt!—about that I used to become angry,
very angry! Nowadays not so much—I just keep asking what it means!

Strindberg called what he wrote to Larsson his jeremiad, a lamenta-
tion which indicated extremely well that indulgence in public confession in the first two Damascus plays had not proved a lasting or
even appreciable remedy.

   His letters reveal constant self-scrutiny, indulged in certainly for
sources of material for his creative writing, but obsessive because
of his genuine concern with his "spiritual" or psychic condition.
Take, for example, part of a letter written to his friend in Lund,
Axel Herrlin, the philosopher, on December 11, 1900:

> Here [in Stockholm] I live more alone than in Lund. Have pleasure
> only in my work. The results, even the good ones, do not have the
> ability to delight me. And I still seem to be in some disciplinary state
> of penance. For I'm isolated in such a way that when I seek out human
> beings, they hurt me without wanting to, so that I withdraw. If I
> seek out a pleasure, it fails. If I have a friend, he's taken from me.
>   It goes slowly on my way to sanctification. When I think I've pro-
> gressed a bit, I fall down again. I seem to have won a little seriousness
> though. I do not believe that sin (crime) itself is punishment. But
> that I despise it and myself is good for the moment of death which
> always represents the moment of release. The seventh chapter of the
> epistle to the Romans seems to have solved the puzzle for me. "Who
> shall deliver me from the body of this death?" [The Swedish version
> says literally: Who shall release me from this body of sin?]
>   The longing for purity and beauty appears most powerfully just
> after sinning! That is strange! Is that the function of sin, *that?*

Strindberg, a seeker for perfection, was keenly aware not only of
his very special gifts but also of his imperfections. He was fascinated
and disturbed by his very human ambivalence and backsliding, his

fluctuating faith and doubt, his inability to maintain a constant control in his own pursuit of his spiritual goal of reconciliation with humanity and the Powers.

The successful production of *To Damascus, I* in 1900 provided him with a delightful temptation to which he succumbed with great pleasure: to try again to be reconciled with humanity through woman. Harriet Bosse played the part of the Lady and was soon to receive what is perhaps a unique proposal: "Miss Bosse, do you want to have a child with me?", and who was to curtsey and say, "Yes, thank you!" That third attempt at marriage was a most important reason for writing a third Damascus play, for it very quickly became clear to him that his relationship with Harriet was anything but perfect. But that tie provided him with much material for speculation and creative writing and played an important role in the completion of the Damascus trilogy.

Although the manuscript indicates he had originally intended to divide *To Damascus, III* into acts, he settled for a division into nine scenes:

1. The shore of the river: below the monastery
2. The crossroad
3. The terrace
4. The mountainside
5. The dining room
6. The dining room the morning after
7. The chapter room
8. The art gallery
9. The chapel

As a close reading of the whole play will suggest, it is a thoroughly Strindbergian combination of (1) the actual reality experienced during the time preceding and in the time of composition and (2) his projection through his imagination of what might happen if he solved his problems by forsaking the world and entered a monastery.

To Damascus, III is a dream play in that Strindberg speculates about what might be and puts the results into perceptible form. That speculation was firmly based, of course, on such actualities as his third marriage. A rather good indication of what Strindberg did with his materials can be suggested by a few chronological facts: he probably began writing the play very late in 1900, he let Harriet Bosse read what he had written at the end of February, they were married on May 6, 1901, and he completed the play toward the end of June!

Strindberg was not only actively creating material for exploitation in his writing but was also trying to come to terms with himself, his fellow human beings, and with what he calls the Eternal One and the Powers. While he had dealt with his efforts to achieve that goal in the two earlier Damascus plays, he had not claimed to have achieved it. While he was still trying to achieve "reconciliation" *(försoning)* through woman, he apparently doubted whether he would and considered the possibility of "being buried alive and reborn" in a monastery as the means that might work. To a degree he may have attained a partial settlement through his "Both . . . and . . . ," that is, his sensing that he would have to accept humanity for what it is and resign himself to the facts of the human condition.

A great many personal problems continued to torture him, problems that he would have liked to overcome or at least to put up with: his difficulties in accepting guidance and directives; his sense of his own worth in contrast to what he had been led to believe by "religious" people; his feeling that the Powers had always treated him as a stepchild; his longing for his children that had been taken away from him; his continuing concern with women; his feeling of guilt about his past (unpaid debts of various kinds, the corrupting effects of his writings); his speculation about the origin of evil; his difficulty on occasion of distinguishing between opposites; his ambivalent attitude toward his sexuality; and his fear that he was committing psychic suicide.

It is not particularly amazing that much of what troubled *and* interested him stemmed directly from his sexuality and that of others. Note the range of his treatment of marriage in this play: the beautiful lyric apostrophes to women and the exquisite wedding-day scene and the contrasting analytic tearing apart in the morning-after scene. Note his concern with the possibility that he may have corrupted the younger generation, including the young fellow he believes is his own son. In no other work has Strindberg been so brutally blunt about sex:

> TEMPTER: I've understood a lot, but not this . . . What mighty love, which is the wedding of souls, has to do with reproduction! . . . I've never understood how a kiss, which is an unborn word, speech without sound, the silent speech of souls, can through a sacred act be exchanged for———a surgical operation! Which always ends with weeping and gnashing of teeth. I've never grasped how the sacred night, the first one, when two souls should kiss each other in love, why that night should end with shedding of blood, quarreling, hatred, mutual contempt—and bandages.

It is a presentation re-enforced by many other matters: Sylvia's "development," the venereal-disease patients, the court trial, to mention the most striking ones.

To Damascus, III presents Strindberg's considered defense against the continuing charge that he was forever changing his mind and his point of view on God, man, and the universe—a point about the play that has never been emphasized. He had long known, of course, that no matter how he behaved or what he said, people were ready to criticize, but the charge that he did not accept a set of beliefs and remain faithful to them disturbed him. His apologia consists of demonstrating, quite effectively I think , that the people he had considered among the greatest of human beings—Uriel Acosta, Hegel, Boccaccio, Luther, Gustav Adolf, Schiller, Goethe, Voltaire, Napoleon, Victor Hugo, Kierkegaard, Stolberg, La Fayette, and Bismarck—had changed their beliefs as they developed. It is a remarkably telling defense of a dynamic evolution in his thinking:

> The developing Powers promulgate the spirit of the time in *seeming* circles! . . . Hegel, the philosopher of his time, a dimorph, because they swear in the name of a Leftist Hegel and a Rightist Hegel, has solved the contradictions of life, history, and spirit best with his magic formula: thesis, affirmation; antithesis, denial; synthesis, summation! . . . Young man, relatively young man! You began life by affirming everything; then you denied everything by principle. Finish by summing up! So: Don't be exclusive any longer! Don't say: Either—or —but: Both—and! In a word or two: Humanity! and Resignation!

For the Strindberg student his promise has a special significance:

> PRIOR: . . . But will you now promise to forget your own story of torture and never tell it again?
> STRANGER: I promise!

Strindberg's major works have been labeled autobiographical and confessional. In a very real sense Strindberg exploited his own life, "real" and imagined, to a degree at least equal to that of any other creative artist—many would say far more. Titles such as *The Son of a Servant, A Madman's Defense,* and *Inferno* indicate that he thought his life story had indeed been primarily a story of torture. It can be added that the Stranger did not promise to refrain from telling stories about other people's torture. Many of his works after the Damascus plays present testimony about others as perceived and understood by Strindberg!

To Damascus, III

Characters

THE STRANGER
THE LADY
THE CONFESSOR
THE PRIOR
THE TEMPTER
THE FIRST WIFE
HER PRESENT HUSBAND
ERIK
THYRA
GERDA
Minor characters

Settings

1. *The shore of the river*
2. *The crossroad*
3. *The terrace on the monastery mountain*
4. *Higher up on the mountain*
5. *The newlyweds' dining room*
6. *The newlyweds' dining room*
7. *The chapter room*
8. *The portrait gallery*
9. *The chapel*

[SCENE 1]

*The foreground is one shore of the great river; to the right a point
with old willow trees juts out; in the middle the river flows quietly on;
the background is the other shore, a high forest-covered mountain; above
the crowns of the deciduous trees rises the cloister, a colossal oblong perfectly
white building with two rows of small windows; its facade is broken
by the cloister church with two towers in Jesuit style; the church door
is open so that the monstrance on the altar can be seen at a given
moment lighted by the sun.*
    *On the low sandy shore in the foreground are growing purple and
other varieties of loosestrife; there is a rowboat on the shore.*
    To the left is the ferryman's cottage.
    *It is an early summer evening when the sun is low; the foreground,
the river, and the lower part of the background are in shadow; on the
other shore the deciduous trees move before a light breeze; the cloister
alone is in sunlight.*
    The STRANGER *and the* CONFESSOR *enter from the right; the*
STRANGER *is dressed in alpine style with a brown cape with collar
and hood; he has a staff and an overnight bag; he is limping somewhat.
The* CONFESSOR *in the black and white Dominican garb. They stop
so that a willow conceals the view of the cloister.*
STRANGER: Why are you leading me about on these winding hilly
    roads that never end?
CONFESSOR: That's how the road up here *is*, my friend! But we'll
    soon be there.
    (*Brings the* STRANGER *forward*)
    (*The* STRANGER *catches sight of the cloister; is fascinated by the
    view; lifts his hat; puts down his overnight bag and his staff.*)
CONFESSOR: Well-l?
STRANGER: I've never seen anything *that* white in this dirty world

167

except in my dreams; yes, this is my youthful dream of a house
in which peace and purity dwell!—Hail, white house . . . now
I am home!

CONFESSOR: Fine, but we have to wait for the pilgrims here in
the place called the shore of parting since a person generally
says farewell here before the ferryman takes him over.

STRANGER: Haven't I had enough partings? Hasn't my whole life
been a thorny path of partings? Inns, steamboat landings, railroad
stations with waving of tear-drenched handkerchiefs?

CONFESSOR: Yes, yet your voice trembles with the pain of the
thought of loss!

STRANGER: I don't miss anything; I don't want anything back!

CONFESSOR: Not even your youth?

STRANGER: That least of all! What would I do with its ability to
suffer?

CONFESSOR: And to enjoy?

STRANGER: I've never enjoyed anything, for I was born with a
thorn in my flesh so that every time I stretched out my finger
for pleasure my finger hurt and the devil slapped me down!

CONFESSOR: Pitiful pleasures!

STRANGER: Not so bad: my own home, wife, children, duties, con-
sideration for others!—No, I was born in disfavor, brought up
as the stepchild of life, hounded, hunted, in a word damned.

CONFESSOR: Because you didn't obey the commandments of God
. . .

STRANGER: That no one *can* obey, according to what St. Paul [1]
says. But what no one can, I was to do. Why I alone? Because
I was to be the dupe! Because they demanded more of me than
of the rest—*(Screams)*—Because they were unjust to me!

CONFESSOR: Are you back to that again, rebel?

STRANGER: Yes, back to *that,* always back to *that!*—Let's cross the
river!

CONFESSOR: Do you think you can go up to that white building
unprepared?

STRANGER: I am prepared; test me!

CONFESSOR: Fine! The first vow is humility!

STRANGER: And the second is obedience! Neither has been my

virtue exactly, but that's why I want to try the test of strength.

CONFESSOR: And show your pride in your humility!

STRANGER: Anything at all: I'm indifferent to everything!

CONFESSOR: Everything? The world and its finest gifts: innocent childlike joy, the delightful warmth of home, recognition by your fellow human beings, the satisfaction of duties fulfilled—everything's indifferent.

STRANGER: For me . . . because I was born without the sense for joy. There have been times when I've been envied, but I've never understood why people envied me: my agony in misfortune, my fear that success wouldn't last long?

CONFESSOR: That's true: Life gave you everything you wanted, even a little gold toward the end. And you even got a bust if I remember rightly?

STRANGER: I got a bust! Yes!

CONFESSOR: Do you believe in busts, in statues? You?

STRANGER: Not at all, but all the same a monument does express a well-deserved recognition which neither envy nor misunderstanding can take away.

CONFESSOR: Really? I seem to have noticed that human greatness exists in other people's opinions, and a shift in opinion can quickly reduce greatness to less than zero.

STRANGER: Other people's opinions have never meant anything next to mine.

CONFESSOR: Really? Really?

STRANGER: And no one has been as strict with himself as I! And no one as humble! Everybody has demanded respect from me while they've all tramped on me and covered me with spit. When I finally discovered I had duties to the immortal soul I had been given, I began to demand respect for my immortal soul and was then labeled the proudest of the proud—and by whom? by the proudest of all among the humble and the little people.

CONFESSOR: You're entangled in contradictions . . .

STRANGER: Even I! Yes, because life has been nothing but contradictions: the rich are the spiritually poor; the many little people have the power and the great ones serve the many little ones; and I've never met more arrogant people than the humble; I've never met an uneducated person who hasn't believed he could judge learning and do without it; I've always run into the most unpleasant mortal sin among the most religious—I mean self-righteousness, and I was religious myself when I was young, but I've never been as bad since! The better I thought I was, the worse I became!

CONFESSOR: Then what are you looking for here?

STRANGER: What I said a bit ago, but I'll add: I'm seeking death without dying!

CONFESSOR: Dying from your flesh, dying from your old ego! Fine!—Keep calm; the pilgrims are now coming on their timber floats to celebrate Corpus Christi . . .[2]

STRANGER *(looks toward the right . . . becomes amazed):* What is this?

CONFESSOR: People who believe in something . . .

STRANGER: Help my disbelief then! *(The sun strikes the monstrance up in the church so that it glows like a window pane in the sunset.)* Has the sun entered the church or . . .

CONFESSOR: The sun has entered the church! . . .

(The first float comes from the right. White-clad children with wreaths on their heads and lighted candles in their hands stand about a flower-decked altar, on which has been placed a white banner with a golden lily. They sing while the float slowly glides by.)

> Happy is he who fears the Lord,
> *Beati Omnes, qui timent Dominum,*
> Who wanders on His paths.
> *Qui ambulant in viis ejus.*
> You shall eat from the labor of your hands.
> *Labores manuum tuarum quia manducabis.*
> Blessed are you, and blessed be you!
> *Beatus es et bene tibi erit. (exit)*

(The second float with YOUNG BOYS *on the one side and* GIRLS *on the other. A banner with a rose.)*

> Your wife shall be as a fruitful vine
> *Uxor tua sicut vitis abundans,*
> Within the walls of your house.
> *In lateribus domus tuae. (exit)*

(*The third float with* HUSBANDS *and* WIVES; *a banner with fruits:
figs, grapes, pomegranates, melons, ears of grain, etc.*)
> *Filii tui sicut novellae olivarum,*
> Your children as olive branches around your table,
> *In circuitu mensae tuae. (exit)*

(*The fourth float with* OLD WOMEN *and* MEN; *a banner with a
pine with snow on top.*)
> Behold, so is blessed the man,
> *Ecce sic benedicetur homo,*
> Who fears the Lord.
> *Qui timet Dominum! (exit)*

STRANGER: What were they singing?

CONFESSOR: A song of pilgrimage!

STRANGER: Who wrote it?

CONFESSOR: A royal person . . .

STRANGER: Here? What's his name? Has he written anything else?

CONFESSOR: He has written at least fifty songs and his name is David,[3] son of Jesse. But he didn't always write psalms . . . when he was young he was up to other things, yes, yes . . . that's how it can be!

STRANGER: May we go now?

CONFESSOR: Soon, but I have a couple of things to say first!

STRANGER: Go ahead!

CONFESSOR: All right, but don't get sad or angry.

STRANGER: I won't!

CONFESSOR: Well, you see on this side you're a well-known, let's say famous man, but on the other you'll be absolutely unknown among the brothers, consequently nothing but an ordinary simple human being.

STRANGER: Really? Don't they read in the cloister?

CONFESSOR: Not frivolous things, but serious books.

STRANGER: But they surely see newspapers?

CONFESSOR: Not the kind in which there's anything about you!

STRANGER: So nothing of my life's work exists over there?

CONFESSOR: Which work?

STRANGER: I see! Fine! May we go now?

CONFESSOR: Soon! Isn't there anyone you'd like to say good bye to?

STRANGER *(after a pause):* Yes, but that's impossible.

CONFESSOR: Have you ever seen anything impossible?

STRANGER: Really not since I saw my own fate!

CONFESSOR: Well then, whom do you want to meet?

STRANGER: I once had a daughter; I called her Sylvia since she sang all day like a bird . . . I haven't seen her for several years— she ought to be a young woman of sixteen. But I'm afraid if I could see her, life would again have value for me.

CONFESSOR: You're not afraid of anything else?

STRANGER: What would that be?

CONFESSOR: That she has changed!

STRANGER: That could only be a good thing!

CONFESSOR: Are you sure?

STRANGER: Yes!

CONFESSOR: She'll come! *(Goes downstream and waves toward the right)*

STRANGER: Wait! . . . I wonder if this is wise?

CONFESSOR: It can't hurt! *(Waves again).*

(*A boat rowed by a young girl can be seen on the river. She is dressed in summer clothes, is bareheaded with blond loose hair. She gets out of the boat back of the willow. The* CONFESSOR *withdraws to the ferryman's cottage so that he can still be seen by the audience.*)

(*The* STRANGER *has waved to the girl who has waved back.*)

GIRL (*comes on stage, runs into the* STRANGER'S *arms and kisses him*): Dad, dear dad!

STRANGER: Sylvia, my dear child!

GIRL: Where in the world did you come from up here in the mountains?

STRANGER: And you—how did you get here? I thought I had really hidden myself!

GIRL: Why should you hide?

STRANGER: Ask as few questions as possible . . . You've become a big girl . . . and I've turned gray.

GIRL: No, you aren't gray . . . you're just as young as when we parted . . .

STRANGER: When we parted . . .

GIRL: When you left us . . .

(*The* STRANGER *is unable to speak.*)

GIRL: Aren't you glad to see me?

STRANGER *(weakly):* Yes!

GIRL: Well, show it then!

STRANGER: How can I—this is our farewell for life!

GIRL: Why, where are you going?

STRANGER *(points at the cloister):* Up there!

GIRL *(childishly knowingly):* Enter the cloister? . . . Yes, when I think of it, that's probably best.

STRANGER: What do you mean?

GIRL *(pityingly, but well meaning):* I mean when you've made a mess of life . . . *(Caressingly)*—No, now you're hurt! Tell me one thing . . .

STRANGER: You tell me one thing, dear child, about something that has disturbed me more than everything else . . . You have a stepfather . . .

GIRL: Yes!

STRANGER: Well-l?

GIRL: He's a really fine man . . .

STRANGER: Who has all the virtues I lack . . .

GIRL: Aren't you glad we're in better hands?

STRANGER: Good, better, best . . . Why are you bareheaded?

GIRL: Because George has my hat!

STRANGER: Who's George? Where is he?

GIRL: George is my boyfriend, and he's waiting down there by the river.

STRANGER: Are you engaged?

GIRL: No, of course not!

STRANGER: Do you intend to get married?

GIRL: Never!

STRANGER: I see *that* on your painted cheeks which look like a child's when she's got up too early, I hear *that* in your voice which doesn't resemble the garden warbler's any more but the jay's, I feel *that* in your kisses which burned like the sun in May, your set cold glances say that you have a secret you're

ashamed of but would like to brag about . . . And your brothers
and sisters?

GIRL: They're fine, thanks!

STRANGER: Do we have anything else to say to each other?

GIRL *(coldly):* Probably not! . . .

STRANGER: Now you're very much like your mother!

GIRL: How do you know who never could see her as she was?

STRANGER: But you have—you who are so young!

GIRL: I've learned to understand from you! If you only understood
yourself!

STRANGER: Do you have still more to teach me?

GIRL: Perhaps; but that was considered improper in your time.

STRANGER: My time which has been and isn't any more—just as
Sylvia isn't any more, merely a name, a memory. *(Takes a travel
book from his pocket)* Look at this travel book! Do you see the
small spots from your fingers there, and there some from small
damp lips? You made those marks when you were five and sat
in my lap on the train when we saw the Alps for the first time.
You thought it was heaven, but when I told you it was Die
Jungfrau, you asked if you could kiss the name in the book!

GIRL: I don't remember that!

STRANGER: The beautiful memories are lost, the ugly ones last!
Do you remember anything about me?

GIRL: Yes!

STRANGER: Hush! I know what you mean; one night, yes . . .
that terrible night! Yes, that terrible night! Sylvia, child, when
I close my eyes, I see a pale little angel, who slept on my arm
when she was sick, who thanked me when she got a gift . . .
Where is *she,* where is she whom I long for and who doesn't
exist any more though she's not dead?———You, who are standing here, are a stranger, whom I think I've never known and
whom I certainly don't long to see again. If Sylvia were dead
in her grave at least, I'd have a graveyard to go to with my
flowers———Strange! She isn't among the dead, nor among the
living either! Maybe she never existed; perhaps she was a dream
like everything else!

GIRL *(caressingly):* Poor Dad!

STRANGER: There she is!————No, that was only her voice!————
——So you think my life is a failure?

GIRL: Yes, but why talk about that now?

STRANGER: Because I now remember I saved *your* life once.—For
a month you'd been in bed tortured by typhoid fever; your
mother who was a thinking woman urged the doctor to free
you from a painful existence through a strong drug. But I interfered and saved you from death and your mother from the house
of correction!

GIRL: I don't believe it!

STRANGER: But a fact can be true even if you don't believe it!

GIRL: You've dreamt it!

STRANGER: Who knows if I haven't dreamt everything, and if I'm
not standing here dreaming! If I only were!

GIRL: I have to go now, Dad!

STRANGER: Good bye then!

GIRL: May I never write to you?

STRANGER: A dead write to a dead? Letters will never reach me
any more! And I may not receive visitors! But I'm glad we met—
now there isn't anything on earth that binds me any more. *(While
he goes to the left)* Good bye, girl or woman—what shall I call
you?————There's no need for tears!

GIRL: I hadn't thought of weeping though decency would call for
something of the kind. Good bye then! *(Goes out to the right)*

STRANGER *(to the* CONFESSOR): I got out of that nicely, Confessor.
Being able to part with mutual satisfaction is a gift from heaven.
But humanity is advancing with great steps; self-control grows
in proportion to the decrease in the flood of tears. I, who have
seen so many tears in my day, feel almost dismayed by this
drought. That was a strong youngster, just as I wished I could
have been!————And this was the most beautiful thing life had
to give————the child, the angel under the white veils of the
cradle, and there was a blue top over it, when she was sleeping,
blue and arched like the sky . . . that was the best! What would
the worst look like?

CONFESSOR: Don't be upset—you should be glad, but throw away
that stupid travel book since this is the last journey!

STRANGER: You mean this! . . . Fine! *(He opens the book, presses a kiss into it, and throws the book into the river)* Anything else?

CONFESSOR: Yes, if you have anything made of gold or silver, you're to give it to the poor.

STRANGER: I have a silver watch—I never got up to a gold.

CONFESSOR: Give it to the ferryman and you'll get a glass of wine.

STRANGER: The last glass! Why, this is like an execution! Maybe my hair should be cut, too?

CONFESSOR: Yes, later! *(Takes the watch, hands it into the ferryman's cottage where he whispers a few words in the doorway; gets a bottle of wine and a glass in return. He places them on the table.)*

STRANGER *(fills the glass but lets it stand):* Will I never get any wine up there?

CONFESSOR: You'll never see wine and never see women; you'll hear songs but not the kind that have to do with wine and women.

STRANGER: I've had enough of women—they won't tempt me any more!

CONFESSOR: Are you sure?

STRANGER: Absolutely sure————But tell me one thing: What do you think of woman since she can't ever come within your consecrated walls?

CONFESSOR: Are you still asking questions?

STRANGER: And why can't an abbess receive confession, conduct mass, and preach?————

CONFESSOR: I won't give you an answer.

STRANGER: Because the answer has to agree with my thoughts on—the subject.

CONFESSOR: It really wouldn't be a misfortune if we did agree on one point!

STRANGER: Very good!

CONFESSOR: Drink up your wine now.

STRANGER: No, I only want to look at it a last time.—It is beautiful . . .

CONFESSOR: Don't think too deeply.—There are memories at the bottom!

STRANGER: And forgetfulness, and songs, and power—imagined, but just because of that more intense . . .

CONFESSOR: Wait here a little—I'll go order the ferry!

STRANGER: Sh-h! I hear a song and I see it! I see it . . . I saw it for a moment as when a flag unfurls in a puff of wind, only to fall back like a rag against the pole, and one doesn't see anything more than a rag. I saw the whole of my life in a second with its joys and sorrows, beauty and ugliness, but now I don't see anything!

CONFESSOR *(going out to the left):* Wait here a little—I'll go order the ferry!

(*The* STRANGER *comes forward so that the rays of the setting sun coming between the trees to the right throw his shadow over the ground and the river.*)

(*The* LADY *dressed in deep mourning enters from the right so that her shadow slowly is thrown in front of that of the* STRANGER).

STRANGER *(who at first observes only his own shadow):* Ha! The sun which makes me a bloodless image, a giant, who walks on the water, clambers up the mountain, climbs over the cloister church's roof, and . . . now goes out into space . . . to the stars . . . ha, now I'm up in the stars . . . (*Notices the* LADY'S *shadow in front of his own*) But who pursues me, who disturbs my journey to heaven, and tries to climb up on my shoulders? *(Turns)*——
—You!

LADY: I!

STRANGER: That black! Black and cruel!

LADY: Not cruel any more! Sorrow . . .

STRANGER: Whom are you mourning?

LADY: Our Mizi!

STRANGER: My daughter!

(*The* LADY *opens her arms to throw herself into his, but he steps aside.*)

STRANGER: The little one's to be congratulated, I pity you, I'm an outsider!

LADY: Comfort me, too!

STRANGER: Lovely! I'm to comfort my fury, weep with my executioner, play up to my tormenting spirit!

LADY: Are you absolutely without feelings?

STRANGER: Absolutely! The feelings I had I wasted on you and others.

LADY: You're right! Reproach me!

STRANGER: No, I have neither time nor desire for that! Where are you going?

LADY: I'm leaving with the ferry.

STRANGER: That's too bad for me—I'm going the same way!

(*The* LADY *weeps, her handkerchief to her eyes.*)

STRANGER *(takes the handkerchief and dries her tears):* Dry your tears, child, and be yourself, be feelingless as you are!

(*The* LADY *wants to put her arm about him.*)

STRANGER *(strikes her gently on her fingers):* Don't touch! When your words and glances no longer could do it, you always had to touch! Forgive a simple question: Are you hungry?

LADY: No, thank you!

STRANGER: You're tired—sit down!

(*The* LADY *sits down by the table.*)

STRANGER *(throws the bottle and the glass into the river):* Well, what are you going to live for now?

LADY *(sadly):* I don't know!

STRANGER: Where do you intend to go?

LADY *(sobs):* I don't know!

STRANGER: So you've hit pure despair? Don't see any point to living and no end to the misery? The same as I! It's a shame there isn't a cloister for both men and women—we'd make a pair.———Is the werewolf still alive?

LADY: You mean . . .

STRANGER: Your first husband?

LADY: He'll never die!

STRANGER: Like a certain serpent! [4]———Now that we're far away from the world and its narrow points of view, tell me one thing: Why did you leave him and go with me, that time?

LADY: Because I loved you!

STRANGER: How long did that last?

LADY: Until I read your book, and until our child was born.

STRANGER: And after that?

LADY: I hated you! That's to say, all the evil I took from you, I wanted to get rid of but couldn't!

STRANGER: That's probably how it was, but a person doesn't find out how it really was!

LADY: Have you noticed that one never finds out how anything really is, that one can live with a person for twenty years, or with his brothers and sisters, his parents, without really knowing anything about them?

STRANGER: So you've noticed that, too!—Since you notice so well, tell me: how did you happen to fall in love with me?

LADY: I don't know, but I'll try to recall!———*(Pause)* Well, you had the manly courage to be impolite to a lady! You looked for a human being's company in me, not a woman's! I thought that honored me, and you!

STRANGER: Then you can tell me, too, if you found I was a misogynist?

LADY: A woman hater? Every normal man is in his innermost being, and woman worshippers are all abnormal.

STRANGER: I hope you're not trying to be polite to me?

LADY: The woman who's polite to a man isn't normal.

STRANGER: You've thought a lot, I hear!

LADY: That's what I've done least, and when I haven't thought I've understood most.———Besides, what I've said is probably only improvisations as you say and needn't be true at all.

STRANGER: Yes, but since it corresponds to my extensive observations, it becomes *very* believable for me.

(*The* LADY *weeps, her handkerchief to her eyes.*)

STRANGER: Now you're crying again!

LADY: I'm thinking about Mizi!—The most beautiful part of life is gone!

STRANGER: No, the most beautiful was you, when you sat up all night watching your child, who took over your bed because the cradle was too cold! *(Three hard blows on the ferryman's door)* Sh-h!

LADY: What's that?

STRANGER: My company that's waiting for me!

LADY *(returning to the earlier topic):* I didn't think life could give one anything as lovely as a child!

STRANGER: And anything as bitter at the same time!

LADY: What do you mean—bitter?

STRANGER: Well, you've been a child yourself, and you surely remember when we as newlyweds came ragged, dirty, and penniless to your mother's home. I seem to remember she didn't find us very lovely!

LADY: That's true!

STRANGER: And I———well, I've just run across my Sylvia! I had expected to see all the beauty and goodness of the child in full bloom in the young woman———

LADY: Well-l?

STRANGER: I found a withered rose, who seemed to have bloomed too early . . . Her bosom had sunk, her hair was snarled like a neglected child's, and her teeth were in a sad state . . .

LADY: Ugh!

STRANGER: So don't mourn! Don't mourn the little one! You could have had to mourn for the grown ones as I have!

LADY: So that is life, then!

STRANGER: Yes, that is life! And so I'm going to have myself buried alive!

LADY: Where?

STRANGER *(points to the cloister):* Up there!

LADY: In the cloister?———No, don't leave me! Keep me company—I'm so alone in the world and so poor, so very poor! When my child died, my mother made me leave, and I've been living since then in an attic room with a seamstress. She was decent and kind at first, but then the lonely evenings became too long———and she went out to look for companionship———so we parted. Now I'm on the highway and don't have anything more than these clothes I have on, nothing more than my sorrow; I eat that, and drink it, it nourishes me and puts me to sleep, I wouldn't want to lose it for anything in the world!

(*The* STRANGER *weeps.*)

LADY: Now you're weeping!———Let me kiss your eyes!

STRANGER: You've suffered this for my sake!

LADY: Not at all for your sake! And you've never done me any harm, but I've tortured you from house and home and child!

STRANGER: I don't remember that, but imagine your saying so! So you still love me?

LADY: Probably! I don't know!

STRANGER: And would want to start over?

LADY: Start over? Our quarrels? We're not going to do that!

STRANGER: You're right—the troubles would only start again!—
Yet it's hard to part!

LADY: Part? The *word* alone is terrible enough!

STRANGER: What are we going to do?

LADY: I don't know!

STRANGER: No, a person doesn't know anything and hardly that—
that's why I'm going to *believe* from now on!

LADY: How do you know you can get to believe when faith is a
gift?

STRANGER: One can surely get a gift if one prays.

LADY: If I only could pray, but I've never been able to beg . . .

STRANGER: I've had to learn to—why can't you?

LADY: One has to stoop first . . .

STRANGER: Life takes care of that nicely . . .

LADY: Mizi, Mizi, Mizi————*(She has rolled up a shawl she had been
carrying on her arm and puts it like an infant in her lap. Utters
sounds as if lulling the child to sleep. Then:)*————Just imagine, I
can see her . . . look . . . here; she's smiling at me, but she's
dressed in black; she has her sorrow, too, I suppose! How stupid
I am! since her mother's mourning . . . and she has two lower
teeth . . . how white they are . . . her baby teeth . . . she'll
never get any others. . . . Well, but can't you see her when I
can? It's no vision; it *is* she!

CONFESSOR (*enters through the ferryman's door; sternly to the
STRANGER*): Come! Everything is ready!

STRANGER: No, not yet! I have to put my house in order first,
and I have to make arrangements for this woman who once was
my wife.

CONFESSOR: So you want to stay!

STRANGER: No, I don't want to, but I don't want to leave unfulfilled
duties behind me! This woman's deserted on the highway without
a home, without money!

CONFESSOR: How does that concern us? Let the dead bury their
dead!

STRANGER: Is that what you teach?

CONFESSOR: No, what you do!———I, on the contrary, offer to
send a Sister of Mercy down to take care of this unfortunate
woman, who . . . who . . . And that sister will come right away!
STRANGER: I'll rely on that!
CONFESSOR (*takes the* STRANGER *by the hand and draws him along*):
Come then!
STRANGER *(in despair):* Lord Jesus Christ, help us all!
CONFESSOR: Amen!

   (*The* LADY *has not looked at the* CONFESSOR *and the* STRANGER,
but now she looks up and follows the STRANGER *with her eyes as if
she wanted to jump up and keep him there but she is hindered by the
imaginary child, whom she has placed against her bosom.*)

[CURTAIN]

SCENE 2

   *A crossroad up in the mountains. To the right huts. To the left a
pool,* [5] *around which are sitting sick people with blue clothes and vermillion
red hands. Blue vapors and small blue flames rise from the pool now
and then. When that happens, the sick people extend their hands and
cough. The background consists of the mountain covered by an evergreen
forest up to a point where the view is cut off by a stationary gray fog.*
   The STRANGER *is sitting by a table outside a hut.*
   The CONFESSOR *enters from the right rear.*
STRANGER: Finally!
CONFESSOR: Why "finally"?
STRANGER: You left me here eight days ago saying, "Wait until
I come back."
CONFESSOR: So? Hadn't I prepared you for the fact the way up
to the white cloister is long and difficult?
STRANGER: I can't deny that! How far have we come?
CONFESSOR: Five hundred meters!—We have fifteen hundred left!
STRANGER: But where's the sun?
CONFESSOR: Up there, above the clouds . . .
STRANGER: So we have to get through the clouds?

CONFESSOR: Of course!

STRANGER: But what about these sick people? What sort of crowd are they? Why are their hands red?

CONFESSOR: I don't want to sully myself or you with sullied words, so I'll speak in beautiful riddles, which you as a poet ought to understand!

STRANGER: Yes, speak beautifully—there's so much ugliness here!

CONFESSOR: You've noticed, I suppose, that the signs of the zodiac correspond to those of certain metals? Well then! You've seen that Venus is pictured with a mirror; in the beginning this mirror was of copper and that metal was called Venus and bore her sign. But now the reverse of the Venus mirror is coated with quicksilver or mercury! [6]

STRANGER: The reverse of Venus is Mercury! . . . Ugh!

CONFESSOR: Quicksilver then is the other side of Venus. In itself quicksilver is as smooth and untarnished as a calm sea, as an inland lake at high summer, but when Mercury strikes heat and gets burned it turns red, gets red as fresh-flowing blood, as the cloth on the scaffold, as the lips of the prostitute, the prostitute's painted lips, the lips of the prostitute painted with cinnabar. Do you understand?

STRANGER: Wait a minute! Cinnabar is quicksilver and sulphur . . .

CONFESSOR: Well then! Mercury has to be put in the fire when it has come too close to Venus! Have we said enough about this?

STRANGER: So these are sulphur springs?

CONFESSOR: Yes! And the sulphur flames purify or cure everything that's rotten! So when the source of life has been contaminated, one's sent to the sulphur spring . . .

STRANGER: How does the source of life get contaminated?

CONFESSOR: When Aphrodite,[7] born out of the pure womb of the sea wallows in filth! . . . When Aphrodite Urania, the heavenly being, lowers herself to promiscuity and becomes the Venus of the highways.

STRANGER: Why did we get desires?

CONFESSOR: Pure desires are to be satisfied, impure to be suppressed.

STRANGER: What is pure and what is impure?

CONFESSOR: Are you back at that again?

STRANGER: Ask these people . . .

CONFESSOR (*stares directly at the* STRANGER, *who "shrinks"*): Watch it!

STRANGER: You're choking me . . .

CONFESSOR: Yes, I'll take away your breath, which you use to express rebellious words, foul-smelling questions . . . Sit down there—I'll soon be back . . . When you have learned patience and withstood the tests! But don't forget I'll hear you, see you, sense you no matter where I am!

STRANGER: So there'll be tests! That's good to know!

CONFESSOR: But you may not talk to the Venus worshippers!

(OLD MAJA *can be seen at the back.*)

STRANGER (*amazed, gets up*): Whom am I meeting here, at last! Who . . .

CONFESSOR: Whom are you talking about?

STRANGER: About that woman, that old woman!

CONFESSOR: Who is she?

STRANGER (*calls*): Maja!—Listen to me!

(OLD MAJA *has disappeared.*)

STRANGER (*hurrying after her*): Maja, my friend, listen to me. ———She's gone!

CONFESSOR: Who is she?

STRANGER (*sits down*): Oh God! . . . When I finally found her again, she left, or . . . I've been looking for her for seven long years, have advertised, have written . . .

CONFESSOR: Why?

STRANGER: This is how her fate is intertwined with mine! . . . Maja was the nurse of my first children . . . those were hard years . . . I struggled with the Invisible One, who did not bless my work! I wrote at a rate so my brains and nerves dissolved as fat in alcohol . . . but I could never make ends meet; I'm one of those who never can . . . Well, a day came when I couldn't pay the servants . . . it was terrible . . . I became the servant of the servants and they became my masters! Finally . . . yes, to save my soul at least, I fled from superior powers . . . out into the wilderness, pulled my soul together in solitude, and came up again!—My first thought was of—my debts! I looked for Maja for seven years in vain! For seven years I saw her shadow, from train windows, from steamers' decks, in foreign cities, in distant countries, but without being able to catch up with her. For seven years I dreamt about her, for seven years I was ashamed, and, when I drank a glass of wine, I blushed with shame at the thought of old Maja, who was probably drinking water in a poorhouse! I've tried to give to the poor the sum I owed her, but that didn't help! And now—she's found and lost at the same time. *(Gets up and goes searching toward the back)* Explain this to me! I want to pay my debt, am able to pay it at last, but am not permitted to.

CONFESSOR: Fool!—Bend before what can't be explained, and you'll see the explanation will come afterwards.—Farewell! *(Going)*

STRANGER: Afterwards?—Everything comes afterwards!

CONFESSOR: Which doesn't come now! *(Goes)*

(*The* LADY *enters, thoughtful; sits down at the table directly across from the* STRANGER).

STRANGER: You again! . . . The same woman, but quite different . . . How beautiful you've become; beautiful as the first time I saw you and asked to be your friend, your dog . . .

LADY: Your seeing me beautiful—I'm not—shows the mirror of beauty is back in your eye . . . The werewolf never saw anything beautiful in me—he didn't have anything to see beauty with.

STRANGER: But why did you kiss me that time—why did you?

LADY: I've often asked myself why, but I've never been able to get an answer; I just don't know. Now when I've been away from you—and have come up on the road to the heights where the air is purer—and the sun is closer—sh-h!—Now I see that Sunday afternoon when you sat like a helpless, outcast child with bewildered eyes staring at your fate—then I felt like a mother as I never had had a chance to—and pity for a fellow human being overcame me—so I forgot . . .

STRANGER: I'm ashamed! Now I feel that's how it was . . .

LADY: But you thought it was something else! As . . .

STRANGER: Don't say it!—I'm ashamed!

LADY: How badly you misjudged me! Didn't you notice I dropped a veil between you and me, the knight's sword in the bridal bed . . .

STRANGER: I'm ashamed . . . I read my evil thoughts into you!— Ingeborg, you're of better stuff than I. . . . I'm ashamed!

LADY: Now you are handsome. Very, very handsome! . . .

STRANGER: No, no! Not I! You are!

LADY *(ecstatically):* No, you!———Now I saw you back of your mask and false beard . . . Now I see . . . now I see . . . the person you have concealed . . . The one I thought you were . . . the one I looked and looked for . . . Sometimes, I thought you were a hypocrite, but we aren't hypocrites, no, no, we can't pretend . . .

STRANGER: Ingeborg . . . now that we're on the other side of the river, with life under us, behind us . . . how different everything looks . . . Now, now I see your soul, the real you, the angel who because of sin was plunged into the prison of the flesh . . . So there is something up there, and beyond . . . It wasn't the beginning when we began and it isn't the end when we die. It's a fragment, life is, without beginning and end! And that's why it's so hard to grasp!

LADY *(blithely):* So very hard! . . . Tell me, for example—now that we're on the other side of blame and blamelessness—how did you get to hate women?

STRANGER: Let me think! . . . Hate—women?—Hate? . . . I never have! Unfortunately . . . from the time I was eight years old, I've always been infatuated with a woman, and I've been in love three times like an erupting volcano . . . But wait: I have always felt women hated me . . . and they have always tortured me!

LADY: Strange!

STRANGER: Let me think a little more . . . Maybe I have been jealous of my person—been afraid of coming under someone's influence.—My first love made herself my governess and nurse . . . Besides, there are men who can't stand children and men who can't stand women—over them.

LADY *(in a friendly fashion):* But you have called women the enemies of humanity. Do you mean that?

STRANGER: Of course I mean it since I wrote it! And I have written from experience and not from theory . . . I sought in woman an angel who would lend me her wings, and I fell into the arms of the earth spirit, who choked me under covers she had stuffed with my wing feathers—I sought an Ariel [8] and found a Caliban; when I wanted to rise, she pulled me down . . . and she always made us sin . . .

LADY *(cheerfully):* Do you know what Solomon who really knew women says?—"And I find what is more bitter than death—the woman, whose heart *is* snares and nets and her hands as bands: whoso pleaseth God shall escape from her; but the sinner shall be taken by her."[9]

STRANGER: And I was never pleasing in the eyes of God! So it's a punishment? That sounds about right! . . . But I was never pleasing in anyone's eyes, and never got a good word! Didn't I ever do anything good? Is it possible a human being never does anything good?—It's terrible never to get a good word!

LADY: You have, but when people said anything good about you, you pushed it away as if it made you suffer!

STRANGER: That's true—I remember now! But can you explain that?

LADY: Explain? You always demand explanations of what can't be explained! "When I applied mine heart to know wisdom . . . Then I beheld all the work of God, that a man cannot find out the work that is done under the sun: because though a man labour to seek *it* out, yet he shall not find *it;* yea farther; though a wise *man* think to know *it,* yet shall he not be able to find it!" [10]

STRANGER: Who said that?

LADY *(takes a doll out of her pocket):* The Preacher! This is Mizi's doll . . . See how she longs for her little mother; how pale she has become . . . And she seems to know where Mizi is because she always looks up toward heaven no matter how I hold her . . . See . . . her eyes follow the stars as the needle of a compass

. . . this is my compass, which always shows me where heaven is . . . She should be dressed in black, of course, since she's mourning, but we were so poor . . . Do you know why we never had any money? Well, because God was angry with us because of our sins. "The Lord will not suffer the soul of the righteous to famish." [11]

STRANGER: Where did you learn that?

LADY: In the book in which everything is written.—Everything!— *(She wraps the doll in her coat)* See she's beginning to get cold— but it's that cloud up there . . .

STRANGER: How do you dare to wander in these mountains alone?

LADY: The Lord is with me. What can human beings do to me then?

STRANGER: Aren't you tortured by the sick people by the pool?

LADY *(turns toward the pool):* I don't see them—I don't see anything ugly any more!

STRANGER: Ingeborg! I made you evil, and you're on the way to making me good!—You know, it was my dream to gain reconciliation through—a woman! You don't believe that! But it's so! Nothing used to have any value for me unless I could put it at the feet of a woman! As an offering to beauty and goodness, not as a tribute to the power-hungry domineering mistress . . . it was my joy to give, but she wanted to take, not receive, so I hated her; when I was most helpless and believed I was close to death, my longing to fall into the final sleep in a mother's lap by a large bosom where I could bury my weary head and drink the tenderness I've never had . . .

LADY: You didn't have a mother?

STRANGER: Hardly!—And I never felt akin to my father or my brothers and sisters . . . Ingeborg, I was the son of the servant, about whom it is written: "Cast out this bondwoman and her son: for the son of this bondwoman shall not be heir with my son, *even* with Isaac". . .[12]

LADY: Do you know why Ishmael was cast out? It says why just a little earlier . . . because he was a scoffer! And then it says this: "And he will be a wild man; his hand *will be* against every

man, and every man's hand against him; and he shall dwell in
the presence of all his brethren!" [13]
STRANGER: It says that, too?
LADY: Yes, my child, since it says everything!
STRANGER: Everything?
LADY: Everything! There you get answers to all your questions,
even the most inquisitive!
STRANGER: Call me your child and I'll like you—and when I like
anyone I want to serve, obey, be mistreated, suffer, put up
with . . .
LADY: You should love your Creator, not me . . .
STRANGER: He is unkind . . . like my father!
LADY: He is love itself—and you are hate!
STRANGER: You are His daughter, but I'm His rejected son . . .
LADY *(caressingly)*: Sh-h! Don't say anything! You . . .
STRANGER: Do you know what I have suffered the last eight days
. . . I don't know what I have got into!
LADY: What do you mean?
STRANGER: I have a landlady there in the hut who looks at me
as if I had come to consume her last crumb . . . She doesn't
say anything, and that's the worst . . . but I think she starts
saying prayers whenever she catches sight of me . . .
LADY: What sort of prayers?
STRANGER: The kind you read backwards over those who have
evil eyes, and bring misfortune with them . . .
LADY: That's strange!—Have you ever heard people talking about
distorting someone's vision?
STRANGER: Oh yes, but who can do that?
LANDLADY *(up to the table)*: Well, well!—You're the gentleman's
sister, aren't you?
STRANGER: Nowadays, yes—we can say that!
LANDLADY (*to the* LADY): To think I'd meet someone I could tell
this to all the same! You see, that gentleman is so modest one
has a sort of respect for him especially since he seems to have
a secret sorrow . . . But I want to tell his sister the truth, and
he's going to listen to it—from the minute he came into my

house I was lucky. Misfortunes had pursued me; I didn't have a boarder, my only cow had died; my husband was in a home for alcoholics, and my children didn't have anything to eat. I prayed to God that He would send me help from on high—I didn't expect anything down here on earth . . . Then this man came.—Besides paying me twice what I asked, he brought luck with him—and my house became blessed! . . . May God bless you, good sir!

STRANGER *(gets up, disturbed):* Silence, woman! You're blaspheming!

LADY: He doesn't believe! Oh God, he doesn't believe!—Look at me!

STRANGER: Now, when I look at you, I believe!—She blesses me! . . . And I the condemned, have brought blessings with me. How can I believe that? . . . With me, me! *(Falls down at the table, buries his face in his hands and weeps)*

LADY: He's weeping! Tears, rain from heaven which softens up the bedrock, fall on his stone heart!————He's weeping!

LANDLADY: He with his heart of gold, his open hand, who's so good to my children!

LADY: Did you hear? Did you hear that?

LANDLADY: There's only one thing about this gentleman I don't understand; I don't want to say anything bad because of that.

LADY: And that is?

LANDLADY: Well, it's only a little thing, but all the same . . .

LADY: Tell me.

LANDLADY: He can't stand my dogs! 14

LADY: That was nice of him not liking that filthy beast. I despise everything animalistic, in myself and in other people. But I don't hate animals, for I don't hate anything created.————

STRANGER: Thank you, Ingeborg!

LADY: You see—I do have an eye for your good qualities even though you don't believe it!————There's the Confessor!

    (The CONFESSOR *enters.)*

LANDLADY: Then I'll go! The Confessor doesn't like me.

LADY: The Confessor loves all humanity.

CONFESSOR *(comes forward; addresses the Lady):* And you, my child, most of all, for you are goodness itself. If you're beautiful to

look at I can't tell, but you must be since you are good————.
Yes, you were the bride of my youth—and my spiritual wife,
will always be, for you gave me what the others couldn't; I've
lived your life spiritually; I have suffered your suffering, not
enjoyed your joys, for you've had no others but your child . . .
Only I saw the beauty of your soul—our friend here sensed it;
that's why he was drawn to you—but his evil was too strong,
and you had to take it on yourself to set him free.—You had
to suffer all the agonies of hell to be evil, suffer for his sake,
and achieve salvation!—Your work is finished! Go in peace!

LADY: Where?

CONFESSOR: Up there! Where the sun is always shining!

LADY *(gets up):* There's even a place for me up there?

CONFESSOR: There's a place for everyone!————I'll show you the
way! *(He accompanies her toward the back)*

(*The* STRANGER *makes a gesture.*)

CONFESSOR: Are you impatient? . . . Don't be! *(Goes)*

(*The* STRANGER *sits alone.*)

(The VENUS WORSHIPPERS *get up, approach the* STRANGER,
and form a circle around him.)

STRANGER: What do you want of me?

VENUS WORSHIPPERS: Hail! Father!

STRANGER *(extremely pained):* Why?

VENUS WORSHIPPERS: Because we're your children! The children
of your loins!

STRANGER *(tries to flee, but is encircled):* Leave me! Let me go!

VOICE II *(a pale youth).* Don't you recognize me, Dad?

(*The* TEMPTER *can be seen at the back by the left crossroad; laughs.*)

STRANGER *(to* VOICE II): Who are you? I seem to recognize you.

VOICE II: I am Erik, your son!

STRANGER: Erik?—You, here?

VOICE II: Here I am!

STRANGER: May God have mercy on me! . . . And you, my child—
forgive me!

VOICE II: Never! . . . You showed me the way to the sulphur
spring! Is it far to the sea?

(*The* STRANGER *falls down.*)

TEMPTER *(laughs): Jubilate temptatores!*

VENUS WORSHIPPERS: Sulphur! Sulphur! Sulphur! And Mercury!

TEMPTER (*comes forward; touches the* STRANGER *with his foot*): The fool! You can convince that fellow about anything! But that's due to his extreme pride! Doesn't he imagine he's the motor in the universe, that he's the cause of all evil? That fool thinks he has taught young people to worship Venus [15]—as if young people couldn't do that before he was born! . . . His arrogance is unbearable, and he has been presumptuous enough to want to dabble in my profession . . . Give him another round, false Erik!

(*The youngster,* VOICE II, *bends down toward the* STRANGER *and whispers in his ear.*)

TEMPTER: There were seven deadly sins; they have become eight. I thought up the eighth—despair. For doubting goodness and not hoping for forgiveness is calling . . . (*He hesitates saying the word God, which he utters as if it burned his lips*) . . . God evil. That is slander, denial, blasphemy . . . See how he twists!

STRANGER (*gets up hastily, looks the* TEMPTER *in the eye*): Who are you?

TEMPTER: Your brother!———Aren't we alike?———Certain features of yours remind me of my portrait.

STRANGER: Where have I seen your portrait?

TEMPTER: A little everywhere! . . . It's often in the churches, although not among the saints . . .

STRANGER: Can't remember . . .

TEMPTER: Was it that long since you went to church? . . . Well, I used to be portrayed along with St. George . . .[16]

(The STRANGER'S *whole body trembles, and he wants to flee but can't.*)

TEMPTER: I appear with Michael,[17] too, in paintings where I don't have the most favorable position, but that can change; everything can change so that the last becomes the first . . . The same thing with you. You're a bit down at the moment, but that can change, too . . . if you had the common sense to choose better company . . . You've been about skirts too much, my boy! Skirts stir up dust, and dust gets in your eyes and chest.—Come here and sit

down, young man, so we can talk a little . . . (*He leads the*
STRANGER *jokingly by the ear to the table*) Sit down and tremble,
sit and tremble, young man! *(They sit down)* Well-l! What shall
we have? A little wine—and a little woman? No? That's too
old-fashioned; too old-fashioned as Dr. Faust is! [18] Good! We mod-
erns look for intellectual dissipations . . . So, you're on the way
up there to the holy men, who believe the one who is sleeping
doesn't sin; on your way to the timid who have given up the
struggle in life because they've had a few defeats; to the binders
who bind people instead of setting them free. Apropos setting
free! Has a holy man ever set you free from your burden of
sin? No! . . . Do you know why your sins have bothered you
lately? Well, you see through asceticism and abstinence you've
become so weak anybody can throw himself at your spirit and
take it over. And they can do that even at a distance! . . . You
happen to have effaced your own personality so you see with
other people's eyes, think with other people's thoughts. In a
word: you have committed psychic suicide. Weren't you sitting
here just now speaking favorably about the enemies of humanity,
about woman, who made hell out of paradise? You don't need
to answer; I can read your answer in your eyes and hear it on
your lips . . . You talk about pure love for a woman! That is
lust, my boy, lust after every woman, and which we have to
pay for dearly: You say you don't desire her! Why do you want
to be near her then? You want a friend?—Take a man, many
men! . . . You let yourself think you weren't a woman hater!
That little woman gave you the right answer to that: Every normal
man is a woman hater, but can't live without union with the
enemy and gets conflict! All perverse and unmanly men are
woman worshippers! What's wrong with you now?

Well, you got to see the sick people here and thought you
had led them into their misery. Believe me, they're lusty fellows,
who'll be released in a few days to go back to their activities
. . . Yes, yes, that false Erik is a rascal! But you have come so
far you can't tell your own children from others' . . . It was
nice to get out of that mess, eh? You see, I can release, see!
. . . But I'm not a saint either . . .

Now we'll call in Old Maja!———*(He whistles in his hands)*
(OLD MAJA *enters.*)

TEMPTER: See there!—Well, what are you up to here? Do you
have anything unsettled with this fellow?

OLD MAJA: No! He's so kind, so kind, and he always was, but he
had a wicked wife.

TEMPTER *(to the* STRANGER): What do you know! . . . You never
got to hear that before! . . . But the very opposite, I suspect!
She, the good angel that you ruined . . . We've heard that, all
of us! . . . Well, Old Maja, what's this he's talking about here?
He's had pangs of conscience for seven years because he owes
you money.

OLD MAJA: He did owe me a little once, but I got that back, with
high interest, yes, much better interest than at the savings bank.
So that was honest and nice.

STRANGER *(jumps up):* What are you saying? Is it possible I've
forgotten that?

TEMPTER: If you have the receipt on you, Old Maja, hand it over.

OLD MAJA: He has the receipt, I suppose, but I have the savings-
bank book where he put in the money in my name. (*She takes
up an account book and hands it to the* STRANGER, *who examines
it*)

STRANGER: Yes, that's right, and now I remember! . . . But why
these seven years of pangs of shame, of disgrace, these long
sleepless nights of self-reproach, why? Why? Why?

TEMPTER: You may go now, Old Maja! . . . But say something
good about this self-torturer first! Don't you remember some
human trait in this wild beast that people have been tormenting
for years . . .

STRANGER (*to* OLD MAJA): Sh-h! Don't say anything! *(covers his
ears with his hands)*

TEMPTER: Well, Maja!

OLD MAJA: Well-l, I certainly know what they say about him, but
that's because of the sort of thing he writes—and I haven't read
that, because I can't read . . . And no one needs to read what
he doesn't want to . . . But in any case the gentleman was very
kind . . . See, he's covering his ears . . . well, I can't stand

flattery either . . . but I'll tell you, sir . . . (*She whispers to the*
TEMPTER)

TEMPTER: Yes-s! All sensitive people are tormented like wild animals! That's the rule! Good bye, Old Maja!

OLD MAJA: Good bye, gentlemen!————(*Goes*)

STRANGER: Why have I suffered innocently for seven years?

TEMPTER (*gestures with a finger upwards*): Ask up there!

STRANGER: Where I never got an answer!

TEMPTER: Ta! That's how it can be! . . . Do you think I look kind?

STRANGER: I can't say you do!

TEMPTER: You look damnably mean, too! Do you know why we look like that?

STRANGER: No!

TEMPTER: Our fellowmen's hatred and meannesses have attached themselves to us. Do you know there are genuine saints up there who have never done any evil themselves, but who are suffering for others, for relatives who have committed unforgiven sins and the like? These angels who have taken upon themselves the wickedness of others finally look like bandits. What will you give me for that?

STRANGER: I don't know who you are, but you're the first person who answers the questions that could reconcile me with life . . . You are . . .

TEMPTER: Go ahead, say it!

STRANGER: You are the liberator!

TEMPTER: And therefore . . .

STRANGER: Therefore the vulture went at you! . . . But listen, haven't you ever thought there's an adequate basis for this as for everything else? Assume earth is a prison where dangerous criminals are locked up: Is it sensible to set them free? Is it right?

TEMPTER: What are you saying? . . . I've never really thought about that. Hm! hm!

STRANGER: And have you thought about this: that we may have been born with guilt . . .

TEMPTER: That doesn't concern me . . . I stick to the present . . .

STRANGER: Fine! Don't you think we're punished in the wrong place sometimes, and we miss the logical connection though there is one?

TEMPTER: There's no lack of logic, but all of life is such a web of faults, omissions, mistakes, which relatively innocent in terms of human weakness are all the same struck by the most logical punishment. Everything is punished, even our foolish acts. Who forgives? The big-minded human being, occasionally, but divine justice, never!

(*A* PILGRIM *appears at the back.*)

TEMPTER: Look! A penitent! I wonder what he's done! We'll ask him! . . . Welcome to our peaceful neighborhood, gentle wanderer! Sit down at the ascetics' simple table where all temptations are lacking!

PILGRIM: Thank you, fellow wanderer in this vale of tears . . .

TEMPTER: What tears?

PILGRIM: None in particular, quite the opposite! . . . The hour of release has come and I'm going up there to get absolution!

STRANGER: Listen, haven't we seen each other before?

PILGRIM: I'm sure we have!

STRANGER: Caesar! It is Caesar!

PILGRIM: I was, but am not any more!

TEMPTER (*laughs*): Royal acquaintances . . . yes, I'm sure! But tell us, tell us!

PILGRIM: I'll tell you now that I have the right to speak——— and my penance is over.

When we met at a certain doctor's, I was locked up like a lunatic they said was suffering from the notion that he was Caesar. Now the Stranger's going to know the truth: I never believed that, but scruples of conscience made me put up with it . . . A friend, a bad friend, had written proof that I was the victim of a misunderstanding, but he kept still when he should have talked, and I took his silence as a suggestion to keep still—and suffer.

Why I kept still and suffered? Well! . . . When I was young, I was in great need once. I was taken in as a guest in a house far away on an island, the guest of an exceptionally gifted man who had been passed by in his profession because of his unreasonable pride. In his isolation he had speculated out some rather strange notions about himself. I noticed that and kept still.

But one day his wife told me confidentially her husband was crazy at times, and thought he was Julius Caesar. I kept his secret for many years strictly, for I'm not ungrateful by nature.

But life is a joker, and after a certain number of years this Caesar interfered crudely in the most intimate part of my destiny. Furious, I revealed the secret of his Caesar mania and made my former benefactor the butt of ridicule so that his existence became unbearable.

No, hear how Nemesis strikes! A year later I wrote a book— you see, I'm a writer, anonymously.—In that book I happened to depict a few details from my family life, how I played with my daughter Julia—her name was Julia just as Caesar's daughter's was—and with my wife, whom we called Caesar's wife, because no one gossiped about her.———Well, this game in which my mother-in-law participated became costly for me . . . When I was reading proof of my book I saw the danger . . . I said to myself: This will ruin you. I intended to cross it out, but, imagine, my pen refused to do it, and an inner voice told me: Let it stay!

And I let it! And I was ruined!

STRANGER: Why didn't you let your friend make the extenuating letter public?

PILGRIM: No, when misfortune had struck, I felt at once: This is the finger of God, you must suffer this, because of your ingratitude.

STRANGER: And you suffered?

PILGRIM: Not in the least! I smiled to myself and kept up appearances! And because I took my punishment calmly and humbly the Lord lightened my burden. I didn't feel the ridicule.

TEMPTER: That's an unusual story, but it can be like that! . . . Shall we be on our way? We'll be a team now that we've tested real troubles! . . . Tear yourselves up by the roots and we'll ascend the heights!

STRANGER: The Confessor said I should wait for him!

TEMPTER: He'll always find you! And there's a session of the court

in the village up there; a particularly interesting case is coming
up; and I suspect I'll have to be a witness. Come on!

STRANGER: Well, it doesn't make any difference if I sit here or
up there!

PILGRIM (*to the* STRANGER): Who is that fellow?

STRANGER: I don't know! He looks like an anarchist!

PILGRIM: An interesting appearance at any rate!

STRANGER: A skeptical gentleman who has seen life.

TEMPTER: Come, children, and I'll tell you stories on the way!
Come on: *(They go toward the back)*

[CURTAIN]

SCENE 3

*A terrace on the cloister mountain: to the right a ledge and to the
left another like it. In the distant back a birds-eye view of a river landscape
with cities, villages, cultivated areas, woods, and farthest away a glimpse
of the sea. At the front of the stage an apple tree with fruit. Under its
branches a long table with a chair at the short end and benches along
both longer sides.*

To the forward right a corner of the village hall.

The cloud is now hovering directly above the village.

At the table sits the JUDGE [19] *at the short end: the council members
on the benches on the long sides. The* DEFENDANT *is standing next
to the* JUDGE *to the right, the* WITNESSES *to the left, among them
the* TEMPTER.

People, among them the PILGRIM *and the* STRANGER, *are standing
here and there about the table.*

JUDGE: Is the defendant present?

DEFENDANT: Present!

JUDGE: This is an extremely sad case, which has spread sorrow
and shame throughout our little community. Florian Reicher,
twenty-three years old, is accused of shooting Fritz Schlipitska's
fiancée with the deliberate intention of killing her. We have here
a premeditated murder and the provisions of the law are definite

and clear.————Do you have anything to say in your defense, Florian, any extenuating circumstance to present?

DEFENDANT: None!

TEMPTER: Hold it!

JUDGE: Who spoke?

TEMPTER: The defendant's lawyer.

JUDGE: The defendant certainly has the right to have a lawyer, but in this obviously clear case, I think the people's judgment has already been reached through facts, and the murderer will have a hard time regaining their sympathy. Isn't that right?

PEOPLE: He's already condemned!

TEMPTER: By whom?

PEOPLE: By the law and his deed!

TEMPTER: Wait a minute!————As the defendant's lawyer, I represent him and take on the charge myself.————So I ask permission to speak!

JUDGE: That can't be denied!

PEOPLE: Florian has already been condemned!

TEMPTER: He has to be heard first!————Well then: I had reached my eighteenth year—I'm speaking for Florian—my mind, trained under a pious mother's watchful eye, was pure, and my heart harbored no guile, none, for I had seen no evil or experienced any. Then I met—it's Florian speaking—on my way a young girl, who in my eyes, seemed the most beautiful thing I had seen on this sinful earth—for she was goodness itself. I offered her my hand, my heart, and my future . . . She accepted and gave me her vow of faithfulness. I was to serve five years for my Rachel [20]—and I worked, gathered straw by straw the little nest we were going to build.————My whole life was based on this woman's love; and as I kept my faith and promises, I didn't harbor any suspicion . . . During the fifth year————I had built our cottage by then, and gathered furniture————when I discovered she had been unfaithful and had slept with at least three men . . .

JUDGE: Are there witnesses to that?

BAILIFF: Three valid ones,—I, the bailiff am one!

JUDGE: You are all that's needed!

TEMPTER: Then I shot her, not out of revenge, but, because of the unhealthy thoughts her faithlessness had given me, because no matter how I tried to tear her image from my mind, images of her lovers crept forth and stole into me so that I finally thought I was living in a forbidden relationship with three men—through a woman as the link!

JUDGE: So it was jealousy!

DEFENDANT: Yes, it was jealousy.

TEMPTER: Yes, jealousy, that feeling of purity, which didn't want to sully my mind because of her promiscuity . . . If I had put up with that or hadn't been jealous I'd have been party to a vice I wanted nothing to do with. So she had to be put away and my thoughts purified from that mortal sin which alone deserves damnation. I have spoken!

PEOPLE: The dead woman *is* to blame! Let her be unavenged.

JUDGE: The dead woman is to blame for causing the crime!

DEAD WOMAN'S FATHER: Your honor, my dead child's judge, and you, my neighbors, let me speak!

JUDGE: You may!

DEAD WOMAN'S FATHER: You accuse her—let me answer! ————Maria, my child, undoubtedly sinned gravely and caused this man's crime! Undoubtedly!

PEOPLE: Undoubtedly! She's the criminal!

FATHER: Let me as a father say a word in explanation if not in her defense.————At fifteen Maria met a man whose object seems to have been to entice young girls to himself as a birdcatcher lures small birds; he wasn't a seducer in the ordinary sense, because he was satisfied by enslaving their minds, trapping their feelings, in order to push them away afterwards—to see how they with their broken hearts and scorched wings were tortured—tortured by pangs of the heart, which are greater than all other pangs!

For three years Maria was cared for in an institution for the emotionally disturbed. And when she came out, she had gone to pieces, so broken up one could say she was split into several persons. She was a good angel, and she feared God with *one* spirit, and with another she was a demon who blasphemed every-

thing sacred. I saw her go from dancing and carousing to meet
her beloved Florian; I heard her change tongues in his presence
and transform her face so that I could have sworn she wasn't
the same person. But she struck me as sincere—in every case.
———If she's to blame, or is her seducer the guilty one?

PEOPLE: She's without blame! Who is the seducer?

FATHER: He's standing here!

TEMPTER: Yes, it was I!

PEOPLE: Stone him!

JUDGE: Observe the law! Let him be heard!

TEMPTER: Good! Listen, Argives! [21]———Well then!———The
undersigned, born of poor but fairly respectable parents, from
the start belonged to those rare birds who seek their Creator
in their youth—but without finding Him—naturally.—Otherwise
old fellows first seek Him in their old age—and for good reason!
But this youthful seeking was accompanied by a purity of mind,
and a modesty, which aroused ridicule even among the women
who were bringing him up—yes, we can laugh now when we
hear he would change his underwear only in a dark closet! But
even if we're now completely corrupted by the coarseness of
life, we still have to see something attractive in that, and when
we get older, even something touching in it, but as we now
are we stand here laughing at his childish innocence!—Laugh
mockingly, people!

JUDGE *(seriously):* You don't know people!

TEMPTER: Then I'll have to be ashamed!———Oh well, he became
a young man, and ran into a system of traps set for his innocence!
I'm an old sinner, but I blush at this moment—*(Takes off his
hat)*—Yes, look at me—when I think of the insight that young
man got into the world of Potiphar's wife [22] which surrounded
him! There wasn't a married woman . . . No, I'm ashamed on
behalf of humanity and womankind . . . Excuse me!———There
were moments when I didn't believe my eyes but thought the
devil had twisted my sight.———The most sacred bonds
———*(Bites his tongue)*—No, hush! Humanity feels slandered!
———It's enough to say until I was twenty-five I withstood the
struggle, and didn't succumb to the ridicule, not to———yes, I

was called Joseph and I was Joseph!—I was jealous of my virtue,
I felt injured by an unchaste woman's glances————but finally
I fell, seduced in a cunning way! And then I became the slave
of my passions, I sat at Omphale's [23] spinning several times
around, was reduced to the depths of the deepest degradation
and suffered, suffered, suffered! But it was really my body that
was degraded; my soul lived its life—its life of purity I might
say, by itself. And I worshipped young pure virgins innocently,
who most likely sensed the mutual sympathy which attracted us.
For, without bragging, or with, they were attracted.—But I didn't
want to cross the line, but they wanted to; and when I fled from
danger, their hearts broke they said. In a word: I have never
seduced an innocent girl! I swear I haven't!————Am I then
to blame for this young girl's emotional distress which led to
mental illness? Don't I on the contrary have the merit of refusing
to take the step which would have caused her to fall?—Who
wants to cast the first stone at me? No one! Then I haven't known
my fellowmen! And I who thought I stood here as a ridiculous
figure pleading for my manly innocence————I feel young again
and I'd like to beg humanity a little for forgiveness! If I hadn't
happened to see that cynical smile on that woman's lips who
was *my* seducer when I was young. Step forward, woman, and
see your work of destruction, see how it has borne seed. . . .
WOMAN *(steps forward, modestly, with dignity):* It was I!————May
I now be heard and tell my simple story about the man who
was *my* seducer when I was young; fortunately, he is present————
JUDGE: Friends, I'll have to interrupt these proceedings, otherwise
we'd get back to Eve in Paradise. . . .
TEMPTER: Who seduced Adam in his youth! That's exactly where
we wanted to come! Eve! Let's have Eve! Eve! (*He swings his
cape through the air. The trunk of a tree becomes transparent and* EVE
wrapped in her hair, and with a girdle about her hips can be seen)
Well, Eve, mother of mankind,[24] you seduced our father. Accused: What do you say in your defense?
EVE *(simply, with dignity):* The serpent deceived me!
TEMPTER: A good answer! Eve has set herself free! Let's have the
Serpent! the Serpent! (EVE *disappears*)

TEMPTER: Come, Serpent! (*The* SERPENT *can be seen in the trunk of the tree*). Here all of you see our seducer! Well, Serpent, who seduced you?

PEOPLE *(horrified):* Hush, blasphemer!

TEMPTER: Serpent! Answer!

(*A crash of thunder with lightning; all flee except the* TEMPTER, *who falls down; the* PILGRIM; *the* STRANGER; *and the* LADY.)

TEMPTER *(still down but coming to; then sits up in the manner of the statue the Sharpener or the Slave* 25): Causa finalia or the ultimate cause————you see, *that* we're never allowed to know!———— However, when the serpent is to blame, we're relatively innocent—but one may not tell people that!————The defendant seems to have got out of this business at any rate! And the court was dissolved as a cloud of smoke! Yes, yes, don't judge! Don't judge, Judges!

LADY (*to the* STRANGER): Come with me!

STRANGER: But I want to listen to this man————

LADY: Why? Why, he's like a little child: asks about everything which can't be answered.—Haven't you heard how children ask questions?—"Dad, why does the sun rise in the east?"—Can you answer that?

STRANGER: Hm!

LADY: Or this one: "Mom, who created God?" You think that's profound!—Come with me!

STRANGER (*struggling with his admiration for the* TEMPTER): Yes, but that about Eve was new . . .

LADY: Really! I read that in my *Bible History* when I was eight years old; and that we inherit the sins of our parents, why, it says so in our national laws.————Come, my child!

TEMPTER *(rises slowly, shakes his limbs, and limps up on the mountain ledge to the right):* Come and I'll show you the world which you think you know but don't know!

LADY *(goes up on the mountain ledge to the left):* Come here, my child, and I'll show you God's beautiful created world as I've learned to see it since tears of sorrow have washed the dust from my eyes.—Come to me!

(*The* STRANGER *stands at a loss between the two of them.*)

TEMPTER: How did the world look through tears? As the willows

on the shore mirrored in troubled waters! A chaos of winding
lines, in which the trees seem to stand on their tops!————No,
my child, with my binoculars dried by the fire of hate, with
my terrestrial tube I look at everything turned right, exact, and
sharp as the thing is!

LADY: What do you really know about things, child? It's not the
thing which enters your eye but the image of the thing; and
image is appearance, not the matter itself. So you're struggling
about pictures, and about appearances!

TEMPTER: Well, listen to her! A little philosopher in skirts————
by Zeus Chronos [26] what a disputation in the mountains' giant
hall; that does require a fitting auditorium! There!

LADY: I have what's mine here, my friend, my husband, my child!
If you want to listen to me, fine; that would be fine for me,
and for you!————Come here, my friend, for this is the way!
Here is the mountain Garizim [27] where people bless you!—And
there is Ebal where they curse you!

TEMPTER: Yes, this is Ebal, where people curse: "Cursed is the
ground for thy sake, woman, . . . in sorrow thou shalt bring
forth children; and thy desire *shall be* to thy husband, and he
shall rule over thee!"—And then [*to the* STRANGER]: "Cursed
is the ground for thy sake . . . Thorns and thistles shall it bring
forth to thee; and thou shalt eat the herb of the field. In the
sweat of thy face shalt thou eat bread." [28] So spoke the Lord,
not I!

LADY: And God blessed the first couple; and God blessed the seventh day when He had completed His labor—which was good.
But you, but we, made it evil, and so, so————. But the one
who keeps the Lord's commandments dwells on Garizim, where
the blessings are awarded: So saith the Lord: "Blessed *shalt* thou
be in the city, and blessed *shalt* thou be in the field! . . . Blessed
shall be thy basket and thy store. Blessed *shalt* thou *be* when thou
comest in, and blessed *shalt* thou *be* when thou goest out; . . .
The Lord shall open unto thee his good treasure, the heaven
to give the rain unto thy land in his season, and to bless all the
work of thine hand: and thou shalt lend unto thee many nations
and thou shalt not borrow . . . and thou shalt be above only

and not beneath; if thou hearken unto the commandments of the Lord." [29]

So come, my friend, and put your hand in mine! *(She kneels with folded hands)* I beg you by the love, which once united us, by the memory of the child that was our bond, by the power of a mother's love————a mother's, a mother's, for that's how I loved you, child gone astray, whom I've looked for in the dark hiding places in the forest, and whom I've found at last starved, withered for lack of love. Come back, child of sorrow, and bury your weary head next to my heart where you rested before you saw the light of the sun! *(She is now transformed during this scene so that her outer garment falls revealing her as a woman clad in white and with hair free of bonds and with a full motherly bosom.)*

STRANGER: My mother!

LADY: Yes, child, your mother! In life I could never caress you—. The will of Higher Powers denied me that—. Why? I don't dare to ask————

STRANGER: My mother? But she's dead!

LADY: She was, but the dead are not dead; and mother love conquers Death! Did you know that? Come, my child, and I shall make up for what I have broken; I'll rock you to rest on my lap; I'll wash you clean from hate and sins————*(She omits the word that can't cross her lips).* I'll do your hair where the sweat of anguish has made it clammy; and I'll warm white linen by the fire in the home you never got, you peaceless, homeless son of Hagar,[30] of the servant, born of a bondswoman, against whom everyone's hand was lifted!—The furrows they plowed on your back were plowed deep————Come and I shall heal your wounds and suffer your suffering————. Come!

STRANGER (*has wept so that his whole body has shaken. Now he goes over to the left ledge on which the* MOTHER *stands with her arms extended*): I'm coming!

TEMPTER: I can't do anything about that!————But we'll meet again.

(Disappears back of a bush)

[CURTAIN]

[SCENE 4]

Higher up on the mountain; in the cloud a jagged landscape with a swamp about it. The MOTHER *goes ahead up a cliff so that she disappears into the cloud. The* STRANGER *stops at a loss.*

STRANGER: Mother! Mother! Why do you leave me so? At the very moment my most beautiful dream was about to come true!

TEMPTER *(appears):* What did you dream? Tell me!

STRANGER: My precious hope, my vague longing, and my last prayer!———Reconciliation with humanity, through woman

———

TEMPTER: Through Woman, who taught you to hate———

STRANGER: Exactly, because she bound me to earth, like the ball the slave drags about . . . about his foot so he can't flee . . .

TEMPTER: Ha, Woman, always Woman!

STRANGER: Yes, Woman! The beginning and the end—at least for us men. In themselves, they're absolutely nothing.

TEMPTER: So: nothing in themselves, everything for us, through us! Our glory and our shame; our greatest joy, our deepest agony; our salvation and our fall; our reward and our punsihment; our strength and our weakness.

STRANGER: Our shame! You said it! Explain, wise man, that puzzle! Whenever I took a woman, my own, my beauty, the woman I loved, out among people on my arm, I was ashamed as if it were a weakness! Explain that puzzle!

TEMPTER: You were ashamed? . . . I don't know why!

STRANGER: You, without an answer?

TEMPTER: Yes, I have no answer!—But I always suffered in my woman's company among people, because I felt she was sullied by other people's glances and I through her.

STRANGER: And when she commited a shameful act, you got the shame! Why?

TEMPTER: The Greeks called Eve Pandora, created by Zeus out of cruelty to torture men and to control them!———As a wedding gift she got a box which contained all the misfortunes of the world. Perhaps this riddle of the Sphinx [31] is better solved seen from Olympus rather than the Garden of Eden! It will never be fully solved! And I'm just as wise as you! And while I'm thinking about it, I'm still enjoying the loveliest thing creation has given us!—Go thou, and do likewise.

STRANGER: By the finest illusions of Satan, you mean! Because *she,* who is the most beautiful for me, can be terrifying for others! But for me, too, when *she* is evil, she can become uglier than any other woman!—What is beauty then?

TEMPTER: An appearance, a reflection of *your* goodness. *(Covers his mouth with his hand).* What the hell! Now I said it . . . and now . . . now . . . the demon's let loose!

STRANGER: The demon! Well then! But if she's a demon, how can she make me long for virtue and goodness? Because that's how case number one was for me. I saw her beauty, and I was seized by the desire to be like her and thereby be worthy of her. I tried first with exercise and bathing, with care of my body and attractive clothes, but became only ridiculous. Then I began from within: I made it a habit to think beautiful thoughts, to speak beautiful words, and to act nobly! And then, one day, when my exterior had come into keeping with my inner being, I became a copy of her—according to what she said!—And she was the one who first uttered the precious words: I love you! How can a devil ennoble us? How can a spirit from the abyss blow goodness into one? How? . . . No, she was an angel! A fallen angel to be sure; and her love was a broken ray from the great light, the eternal light, which warms and loves!—loves!—loves!

TEMPTER: No, listen, old boy, are we going to stand here like youngsters spelling out the problem of love. . . .

CONFESSOR *[enters]:* What, chatterbox? Your whole life has gone into talk so you've never had time to do anything!

TEMPTER: I should have become a priest, but I didn't get the call!

CONFESSOR: While you're waiting for it, help me look for a drunkard who has drowned himself in the swamp here. He must be here, for I've followed his tracks to this point.

TEMPTER: Then he's the one who's lying under the brush right there!

CONFESSOR *(lifts some branches. They see a fully clothed corpse with a young white face):* Yes, it's he!————*(Sinks into reverie as he observes the dead man)*

TEMPTER: Who was he?

CONFESSOR: Strange!————Strange!————

TEMPTER: He was a fine looking man! Almost a youngster!

CONFESSOR: No, my friends: He was fifty-four! And when I saw him a week ago, he looked sixty-four. His eyes were as grayish yellow as a garden snail's slime and were bleeding at the edges from drunkenness; but also because he wept blood over his vice and his misery. His face was brown and swollen like the liver on a butcher's block, and he hid from people's glances out of shame—even at the last he seems to have been ashamed of the broken mirror of his soul; that's why he concealed his face under these branches. I saw him struggle against his vice; I saw him after he was fired from his position as a teacher down on his knees begging God to be set free . . . But! . . . Well, he's free now! And see, now when the evil has been taken away, his goodness and beauty came back; that's how he looked when he was nineteen!————It's sin placed upon him as punishment . . . Why? We don't get to know that. "They that hate the righteous shall be desolate," [32] hints at it.————Or—I knew him when he was young! And now I recall . . . he was always extremely cruel to those who didn't drink. Judged and condemned and always put his cult of the grape on the altar of the joy of life! . . . Now he's free! free from sin! from shame! from ugliness! . . . Yes, he's handsome in death! the liberator Death!—Listen, Liberator, who can't even set a drunkard free of his evil desires! . . .

TEMPTER: Crime as punishment? Well, that's not bad! That's pretty profound!

CONFESSOR: Yes, I should think so! There you got a new topic for discussion!

TEMPTER: Now I'll leave you gentlemen for a while . . . See you again soon! *(Goes)*

CONFESSOR: Well! I saw you with a woman a while ago! So there are temptations still?

STRANGER: Not in the way you mean!

CONFESSOR: What way?

STRANGER: Of course I could still imagine reconciliation with humanity and woman—through woman!—and through that woman who was my wife once, and is now purified and raised through sorrow and want and has become what I once thought she was. But . . .

CONFESSOR: But? . . .

STRANGER: Experience has taught me the closer, the farther apart, and the farther apart from each other, the closer.

CONFESSOR: I knew that from the beginning—Dante [33] knew it; he possessed Beatrice's soul throughout his whole life, and Beethoven [34] knew it—he was married from a distance to Therese von Brunswick—another man's wife! . . .

STRANGER: And just the same . . . I can find bliss only near her!

CONFESSOR: Be near her then!

STRANGER: You forget one thing: We're divorced!

CONFESSOR: Fine! Start a completely new marriage then! The more promising since you're both new people.

STRANGER: Do you think—anyone would be willing to marry us?

CONFESSOR: Would I? That's asking too much!

STRANGER: I forgot! But it'll go somehow! . . . Another thing to find a home! . . .

CONFESSOR: You're lucky sometimes though you don't want to see it. Down there by the river is a little house, absolutely new, and that the owner has never seen . . . He's an Englishman, who was going to get married, but *she* jilted him at the last minute . . . His notary built it so neither one of them has ever touched it even with a glance. Perfectly intact, you see!

STRANGER: For rent then!

CONFESSOR: For rent!

STRANGER: Fine, then I'll risk it! And try to begin living over again!

CONFESSOR: And you'll descend?

STRANGER: Out of the clouds! . . .Down there the sun is still shining, and up here the air is rather thin.

CONFESSOR: Fine! Then we'll part again—for a while!

STRANGER: Where are you going?

CONFESSOR: Upward!

STRANGER: And I down—to earth, the mother with the soft bosom and the warm lap . . .

CONFESSOR: Until you long for what's stonehard, cold, white.— Farewell! Greet them down there! *(They go out each in his own direction)*

[CURTAIN]

[SCENE 5]

A beautiful paneled dining room with a majolica tile stove. A dining table in the center of the room covered with flowers in vases; two candelabras with many lighted candles. An elaborately carved buffet to the left. To the right two windows. At the back two doors; the left door is open revealing the wife's room in light green and mahogany; a brass upright lamp with a large lemon yellow shade is lighted. The door to the right is shut. To the left back of the buffet is an entrance from the hall.

From the left enter the STRANGER *dressed as a bridegroom and the* LADY *dressed as bride, radiant with youth and beauty.*

STRANGER: Welcome to my house, darling, to your home and mine, my bride, into *your* home, my wife.

LADY: Thank you, darling! Why, it's like a fairy tale!

STRANGER: Yes, a fairy tale! A collection of fairy tales, child, which I have created. *(They sit down on opposite sides of the table)*

LADY: Is this real? It seems too beautiful to me.

STRANGER: I've never seen you so young, so beautiful!

LADY: That's in your eye. . . .

STRANGER: Which has learned! Yes, and it was your goodness which was the teacher . . .

LADY: . . . who learned from sorrow . . .

STRANGER: Ingeborg!

LADY: That's the first time you've said my name!

STRANGER: The first? I've never met you before, Ingeborg; I've never known you before, you who are sitting here in our home.

Home! Beautiful word! The beautiful thing I've never owned
before. Home and wife! You're my first, my only one, because
what was before doesn't exist any more, just as little as the hour
that just passed!

LADY: Orpheus! [35] You've sung life and beauty into these dead
stones! Sing life into me, too . . .

STRANGER: Eurydice, whom I've brought back from the land of
the dead! I'll love life into you, I'll create you, and happiness
will be ours now, for we know the dangers that must be avoided!

LADY: Yes, the dangers! . . . How wonderful it is in here! It's as
if the rooms were filled with invisible guests welcoming us! Good
spirits blessing us and our home!

STRANGER: The candlelight is still with reverence, the flowers deep
in thought . . . but just the same! . . .

LADY: Sh-h! . . . Outside the summer night is at rest, warm and
dark; the stars are suspended—huge, filled with tears in the ever-
greens like Christmas lights . . . this is bliss! Hold on to it firmly!

STRANGER *(absorbed in thought):* Just the same . . .

LADY: Sh-h!

STRANGER *(gets up):* I hear a poem coming! . . . It's yours . . .

LADY: Don't say it, for I see it . . . in your eyes!

STRANGER: Because I read it in yours! . . . Besides, I can't say
it, for it isn't in words! . . . It's in fragrance, in color . . . and
if I put it into words it would die! It's most beautiful unborn!
What hasn't been won is most precious!

LADY: Sh-h! . . . Or our guests will go! *(Silence)*

STRANGER: This is happiness . . . but I can't take hold of it!

LADY: See it, breathe it, for it won't let itself be taken hold of!
(Silence)

STRANGER: You're looking at your little room!

LADY: It's as light green as a meadow at midsummer! And someone
is in there! Several!

STRANGER: My thoughts!

LADY: Your good, beautiful thoughts . . .

STRANGER: Which you have given me!

LADY: I had something to give you then?

STRANGER: You?—Everything! But I didn't have my hands free

to accept your gifts before! Not pure hands to touch your dear
heart . . .

LADY: Darling, reconciliation's near . . .

STRANGER: With humanity and with woman—through woman?
Yes, it is fullfilled and blessed be you among women!

*(The candles and the lamp are extinguished; the room becomes dark,
but one can see a weak glow from the yellow brass lamp in the wife's
room.)*

LADY: Why this darkness?

STRANGER: Where are you, darling? Give me your hand! I'm afraid!

LADY: Here it is, dear!

STRANGER: Your little hand which you gave me in the dark, which
led me over stones and thorns! The soft, kind little hand! Lead
me to the light, to your warm light room, light green as hope!

LADY *(leads him toward the light green room):* You're afraid?

STRANGER: My white dove, the frightened eagle seeks shelter with
you, when the thunder of heaven makes it black below, because
you are safe; you have not challenged the thunder of heaven
. . . *(They have reached the opening of the door. The curtain falls.)*

[SCENE 6]

The same room. The table has been cleared. The LADY *is sitting at
the table doing nothing; she seems to be bored. To the right in the foreground farthest down a window is open. Silence.*

STRANGER *(enters with a piece of paper in his hand):* Now you're
going to listen!

LADY *(absently, obediently):* Are you already done?

STRANGER: Already? Are you serious? Why, I've needed seven
days for this one little poem. *(Silence)* It probably bores you?

LADY *(dryly):* No, of course not!

(The STRANGER *sits down at the table and observes the* LADY.)

LADY: Why are you looking at me?

STRANGER: I want to see what you're thinking!

LADY: But I've told you!

STRANGER: That's nothing; I want to *see!* . . . *(Pause)* For what

one says is usually worthless . . . *(Pause)* May I read them—
No, I mayn't for you don't want anything else from me.
(*The* LADY *looks as if she wanted to speak.*)
STRANGER: Your face tells me: That's enough, you've drained me,
   eaten me hollow, killed what's mine, my self, my personality
   . . . I answer, how, darling? I've killed what's yours, I who
   wanted to give you everything that was mine, who let you skim
   the essence of my bowls filled with my long life's own experiences
   and wanderings through the deserts and groves of art and
   poetry . . .
LADY: I don't deny that, but it wasn't mine!
STRANGER: Yours? What is yours? Other people's!
LADY: And yours! Other people's!
STRANGER: No! What I've lived is mine and nobody else's! What
   I've read has become mine, for I smashed it like glass, remelted
   it, and out of the mass, I blew new glass in new forms.
LADY: Fine! But I can't become yours!
STRANGER: I've become yours!
LADY: What did you get from me?
STRANGER: You ask that?
LADY: And just the same—I don't see you think that! But I feel
   you feel it's like that! You wish I were far away!
STRANGER: I must be far enough away from you to be able to
   see you! Now you're close and your image is indistinct!
LADY: The closer, the farther apart!
STRANGER: That's right! . . . But when we leave each other, we
   long for each other, and when we've got together again, we
   long to be apart.
LADY: Do you think we love each other?
STRANGER: Yes, but not like ordinary people, but like extraordi-
   nary. We're two drops of water that are afraid to get too close
   to each other for fear of ceasing to be two and becoming one.
LADY: This time we knew the dangers and wanted to avoid them
   . . . It looks as if they can't be avoided!
STRANGER: And probably weren't dangers but difficult necessities
   recorded as laws in the Eternal One's court. *(Silence)* Your love
   always felt like hate. And when you made me happy, you envied

me the happiness you gave me!—But when you saw me really
unhappy, you loved me!

LADY: Shall I leave you?

STRANGER: Then I'll die!

LADY: And if I stay, I'll die!

STRANGER: Let's die together and, in a higher life, live out our
love, *our* love which doesn't seem of this world, but on another
plane where there isn't distance or nearness, where two are one,
where numbers and time and space are different from here!

LADY: I wanted to die! But I don't want to . . . I think I'm already
dead!

STRANGER: The air is too strong up here!

LADY: You don't love me when you can talk like that!

STRANGER: Frankly—there are moments when you don't exist for
me. But there are times when I feel your hatred choking me
like smoke, literally.

LADY: And I sense when you're angry with me—it's as if my heart
were creeping out of my chest.

STRANGER: So we hate each other . . .

LADY: And love each other . . .

STRANGER: And hate each other because we love each other; we
hate each other because we are bound to each other; we hate
the bond, we hate love, we hate the most precious thing which
is the most bitter, the best this life can offer. We are finished!

LADY: Yes!

STRANGER: What a joke when one takes life seriously; and how
serious it is when one jokes!—You were going to lead me with
your little hand to the light; your gentler destiny was to make
mine gentler. I was going to raise you over the swamps and
the drifting sands . . . but you longed to go down there again
and you wanted to persuade me that down there was up there.
Is it possible, I ask myself, that you took up my evil when I
was freed from it, and that your goodness moved into me? If I
have made you evil, I ask your forgiveness, and I'll kiss your
little hand which caressed and clawed . . . the little hand that
led me in the darkness . . . led me through the long Damascus
journey . . .

LADY: Are you saying good bye? *(Silence)* So it is farewell? (*Silence.*
She leaves. The STRANGER *collapses into a chair by the table.*)

TEMPTER *(sticks his head through the window, rests his elbows on the
sill, smokes a cigarette):* Well, well!—*C'est l'amour!* The most secret
of all secrets, the most impossible to explain of everything that
can't be explained, the most uncertain of uncertainty.

STRANGER: Are you here?

TEMPTER: Always present where it smells of smash up! And in
love affairs there's always that!

STRANGER: Always?

TEMPTER: Always! I was at a silver wedding yesterday! Twenty-
five years aren't to be sneezed at———and there had been disas-
ters for twenty-five years . . . their whole love had been one
big disaster, with many small ones thrown in here and there!
And all the same, they loved each other, they thanked each other
for everything good; the bad was forgotten, wiped out—for one
moment's happiness makes up for ten days' pure hell with needles
and whips! Yes, the one who doesn't want to accept the bad
won't get the good! The shells are bitter, bitter, but the tiny
little kernel inside is sweet!

STRANGER: It's mighty little!

TEMPTER: *Mein lieber Freund,* it's little but good!———But tell me
why did the Madonna run away?—No answer, because you don't
know. Now we'll rent out the hotel, though!—Here's the sign!
I'll hang it up! "For rent." The one comes, the other goes! *C'est
la vie, quoi?* Rooms for travelers!

STRANGER: Have you been married?

TEMPTER: Yes, of course!

STRANGER: Why did it break up?

TEMPTER: Primarily—yes, it's probably a peculiarity of mine—primarily because—well, you know the man gets married to get a
home, into a home, the woman to get out. She wanted to get
out, and I wanted to get in! I was put together so that I couldn't
go out with her socially, because I felt other men's glances defiled
her. And among people my great wonderful woman became a
little grimacing ape that I couldn't stand looking at!

Oh well, I had to stay at home! And she went out! And when

I saw her, she was a different person; she, my clean white sheet of paper, was covered with scrawls; her beautiful distinct features were adjusted to the satyr expressions of strangers; I saw in her eyes in miniature the expressions of the bullfighter and the guardsman; I heard the unknown tones of unknown men in her voice; on our piano, on which only the harmonies of the great composers had been played, she now played only unknown men's junk; and on our table lay only unknown men's favorite reading material. In a word, my whole existence began to be perverted through spiritual intercourse with unknown men—which went against my nature which had always desired *Woman!* And—do I need to say it?—What these unknown men liked was always what I disliked. She developed a real genius for discovering what I despised! She called that "saving her personality." Can you understand that?

STRANGER: I understand it, but I don't want to try to explain it!

TEMPTER: And all the same she insisted she loved me; and that I didn't love her. And all the same I loved her so I didn't want to talk with another human being since I felt unfaithful to her if I enjoyed someone else's company, even masculine company. I had married to get feminine company, and to get it, I gave up my friends—I had married to get company but got absolute loneliness! And I supported a house and home to provide unknown men with a woman companion! *C'est l'amour, mein lieber Freund!*

STRANGER: One should never talk about his wife!

TEMPTER: No, because if one speaks well of her, people laugh; if one speaks unfavorably about her, she gets everybody's sympathy: and if one asks why they laugh in the first case, one doesn't get to know anything.

STRANGER: Yes! One never gets to know the one one is married to! You can never take hold of her—it's as if she weren't anyone!—What is woman?

TEMPTER: I don't know! Probably a larva, a chrysalis, out of whose sleep a man will someday develop. Resembles a child, but isn't; is a sort of child, but doesn't resemble it. Goes down when the man goes up! Goes up when the man goes down.

STRANGER: Always wants to have opinions opposite to her husband's; always has sympathy for what he can't stand; the coarsest under the finest exterior; the meanest under the kindest! And all the same! Every time I've loved one, I've always become finer . . .

TEMPTER: You, yes; but she?

STRANGER: She? She has always during the time our love has grown retrogressed! And become coarser and meaner!

TEMPTER: Can you explain that?

STRANGER: No. But once when I was looking for the solution to the riddles by assuming I was wrong, I assumed she sucked up my evil and I her goodness.

TEMPTER: Do you think woman is particularly false?

STRANGER: Yes and no.—That she tries to conceal her weaknesses means only that she has ambition and modesty; only the prostitute is frank, and that's why she's cynical.

TEMPTER: Say a little more in favor of woman!

STRANGER: I once had a woman friend. She soon noticed that when I was drinking I became uglier than usual . . . so she made me promise not to drink! . . . I remember one evening . . . we had been talking for many hours at a café. When it got close to ten, she asked me to go home to sleep and not drink any more. We parted after saying good night. Some days later I learned she had left me that evening to join a large crowd where she had caroused until morning—"Oh well!" I said—I was then looking for everything good in woman; "she wanted what was good for me, but had to sully herself that time because of her business!"

TEMPTER: That was nicely thought, and can be defended! She wanted you to be better than herself, higher and purer, so she could look up to you! Can you answer that just as nicely? A wife is always mean and dissatisfied toward her husband, and the husband is always good and grateful toward her; he does everything to suit her, and she does everything to torture him.

STRANGER: That isn't true!—It can look like that, of course, at times! . . . Yes, I once had a woman friend who ascribed every one of her faults to me. She was, for example, extremely fond of herself, so she called me the most self-satisfied of human beings. She drank, and called me a drunkard; she seldom changed her underclothes and called me filthy; she was jealous, even of my men friends, and she called me Othello; [36] she wanted power, and called me Nero; she was stingy and called me Harpagon.

TEMPTER: Why didn't you answer her?

STRANGER: You certainly know why! . . . The very minute I would have let her know what she was like, I would have lost her favor——and it was her favor I wanted to have, of course . . .

TEMPTER: *À tout prix!* At any price! Yes, there we have the source of degradation! You learned to keep still, and finally found yourself entangled in a web of lies . . .

STRANGER: Wait a minute! . . . Don't you think married people confuse their personalities so they can't tell mine from yours, can't tell each other's personalities apart, can't tell the one's faults from the other's? My jealous friend who called me Othello confused me with herself, identified me with herself . . .

TEMPTER: That sounds possible!

STRANGER: Yes, you see one usually comes closest to the explanations if one quits asking "Who's to blame?"—When husband and wife disagree it's a nation divided against itself, and is the greatest of disharmonies.

TEMPTER: There are times when I think a woman can't love a man!

STRANGER: Perhaps! For to love is an active verb and woman is a passive noun. He loves, she is loved; he asks, she merely answers!

TEMPTER: What is woman's love then?

STRANGER: The man's! . . .

TEMPTER: Fine!—And therefore when the man stops loving her, she is set free from him!

STRANGER: Yes, but even then . . .

TEMPTER: Sh-h! Someone's coming . . . A tenant!

STRANGER: A woman or a man?

TEMPTER: A woman! . . . and a man! . . . But . . . the man is stopping outside . . . he's turning around, and is going into the woods!—That was interesting!

STRANGER: Who is it?

TEMPTER: Well!—See for yourself!

STRANGER: *(looks out through the window):* It's she!———My first wife; my first love . . .

TEMPTER: Who now seems to have left her second husband . . . has come here with number three, who, to judge by certain movements of his back and legs, seems to be taking off after a somewhat stormy scene. . . . Yes, yes!———But she hasn't noticed his treacherous intention. That is extremely interesting! . . . Now I'll get over there to listen in!

(Disappears.)

(The WIFE *knocks.)*

STRANGER: Come in!

WIFE *(enters. Silence. Excited):* I came to rent an apartment . . .

STRANGER: Fine!

WIFE *(hesitates):* If I had known from whom, this wouldn't have happened!

STRANGER: What difference does that make?

WIFE: May I sit down for a minute? I'm tired.

STRANGER: Of course!

(They sit down on opposite sides of the table, in the same places where the STRANGER *and the* LADY *had sat in the preceding scene.)*

STRANGER: It's a long time since we sat like this!

WIFE: With flowers and candles on the table! . . . one evening . . .

STRANGER: When I was dressed as bridegroom and you as bride . . .

WIFE: And the candle flames stood still in reverence and the flowers were deep in thought . . .

STRANGER: Is your husband out there?

WIFE: No!

STRANGER: You're still looking———for what doesn't exist?

WIFE: Doesn't it exist?

STRANGER: No! And I always said so to you! But you didn't believe me but wanted to find out for yourself!———Have you found out?

WIFE: Not yet!

STRANGER: Why did you leave your husband? *(Silence)* Did he beat you?

WIFE: Yes!

STRANGER: How could he forget himself to that point?

WIFE: He was angry!

STRANGER: Why was he angry?

WIFE: For no reason.

STRANGER: Why was he angry for no reason?

WIFE *(gets up):* No, thanks; I'm not going to sit here getting scolded!—Where is your wife?

STRANGER: She just left!

WIFE: Why?

STRANGER: Why did you leave me?

WIFE: Because I felt how you wanted to leave me, so not to be deserted I left.

STRANGER: That's probably how it was! But how did you know what I was thinking?

WIFE *(sits down again):* How? Why, we didn't need to say anything to reveal our thoughts.

STRANGER: But we made one mistake in our life together when we accused each other before our evil thoughts had become acts; instead of living in reality, we lived in what was implicit . . . For example, I once saw you receive with pleasure the degrading glances of a stranger, and I accused you of unfaithfulness.

WIFE: You were wrong, but you were right, too; for I sinned in my thoughts.

STRANGER: Don't you think my habit of seeing what you did ahead of time actually kept your evil will from expressing itself?

WIFE: Let me think!———Yes, that's true! But in my annoyance about having someone spying on my innermost being, which was mine alone . . .

STRANGER: No, it wasn't yours—it was ours . . .

WIFE: Fine! But I considered it mine, that you didn't have the right to intrude; and when you did all the same, I hated you; and in self-defense I called you sick with suspicion!———Now I can tell you! Your suspicion was never wrong . . . your suspicion was pure sharpwittedness!

STRANGER: Ah-h!———You know, at night when we had said good night and fallen asleep as friends, I could wake up all the same and feel how your hatred sprayed poison over me so I almost got up in order not to be choked . . . One night I woke up and felt pressure on my head———I saw how you were lying awake keeping your hand close to my mouth . . . I thought you were having me breathe poison out of a bottle, and to make sure I grabbed your hand!

WIFE: I remember!———

STRANGER: And what did you do?

WIFE: Nothing! I just hated you!

STRANGER: Why did you hate me?

WIFE: Because you were my husband! Because I ate your bread!

STRANGER: Do you think it's always like that?

WIFE: I don't know, but I suspect it is!

STRANGER: But you despised me, too, on occasion!

WIFE: Yes, when you were ridiculous! A man in love is always ridiculous!———Do you know what being silly is?———That's what the man in love is! Like a rooster!

STRANGER: Since every man in love is ridiculous, how can you women love him?

WIFE: We don't! . . . We put up with—and look for somebody else who doesn't love us!

STRANGER: But when that fellow starts to love you, you look for a third?

WIFE: Perhaps that's how it is!

STRANGER: Strange! *(Silence)* I remember you always raved about someone you called the Toreador, and that I translated "the horse butcher!" You finally got your Toreador; he didn't give you any children and no bread, only beatings! . . . The Toreador always hits! *(Silence)* I let myself be fooled into competing with the Toreador: I began to cycle, take part in sports, fence and do things like that. But then you despised me! So: the husband may not but the lover may!———Then you raved about the young admirer!———The one who sat on the Brussels carpet reciting poor verse . . . my good poetry wasn't good enough for you! . . . Is it the young fellow you now have?

WIFE: Yes, but his verse isn't bad!

STRANGER: Yes, my friend, it is—I know him! And he has taken my rhythms and set them to a hand organ.

WIFE *(gets up and goes toward the door):* You ought to be ashamed of yourself!

TEMPTER *(enters with a letter in his hand):* A letter! For you, ma'am! *(Gives her the letter).*

  (The WIFE *reads it, then collapses on a chair.)*

TEMPTER: A little farewell note! Yes, yes!———All our beginning is difficult—in affairs of the heart!—And the one who doesn't have the patience to overcome the difficulties of the beginning—has to do without the golden fruit! Young admirers are always impatient!

  Unknown youngster! Have you had enough now?

STRANGER *(gets up; takes his hat):* Poor Anna!

WIFE: Don't leave me!

STRANGER: Yes, my dear! I have to!

WIFE: Don't go! You were the best all the same!

TEMPTER: Are you going to begin again perhaps? Well, that would be a sure way of putting an end to all this. Because all that's needed to lose each other is to get each other. What is love? Everyone, say something witty now before we part!

WIFE: I don't know what it is. The highest and most beautiful thing in life has to descend into the lowest and most ugly!

STRANGER: A caricature of divine love.

TEMPTER: A one-year plant which blooms during engagement, goes to seed in marriage and then bends over toward the earth to wither and die!

WIFE: The most beautiful flowers don't have any seed! The rose is the flower of love!

STRANGER: The lily the flower of innocence! It can produce seed but doesn't want to surrender its chalice for anything but kisses!

TEMPTER: But reproduces itself in bulbs, out of which new lilies spring as chaste Minerva sprang complete from Zeus' head,[37] not out of his loins!———Well, children, I've understood a lot, but not this: What the beloved of my soul has to do with . . . *(Hesitates)*

STRANGER: Say it!

TEMPTER: . . . What mighty love, which is the wedding of souls, has to do with reproduction!

STRANGER AND WIFE: Now you said it!

TEMPTER: I've never understood how a kiss, which is an unborn word, speech without sound, the silent speech of souls, can through a sacred act be exchanged for————a surgical operation! which always ends with weeping and gnashing of teeth. I've never grasped how the sacred night, the first one, when two souls should kiss each other in love, why that night should end with shedding of blood, quarreling, hatred, mutual contempt—and bandages. *(Covers his mouth with his hand)*

STRANGER: Imagine if that stuff about the fall of man were true? "With agony shalt thou bear children . . ." [38]

TEMPTER: Yes, then one could understand . . .

WIFE *(to the* TEMPTER*)*: Who are you?

TEMPTER: Only a wanderer on the shifting sands of the desert of life!

(The WIFE *gets up.)*

TEMPTER: Time to go!————Who's going first?

STRANGER: I?

TEMPTER: Where?

STRANGER: Upward! and you?

TEMPTER: I'll stay here, in between . . .

[CURTAIN]

[SCENE 7]

The chapter room in Gothic style. At the back open arcades toward the crosswalk and the cloister courtyard. In the middle of the yard a fountain with a statue of the Virgin Mary surrounded by long-stemmed white roses.

The walls of the room have oak chairs attached to them. The PRIOR'*s is to the right in the middle and is somewhat raised. In the middle of the room a huge crucifix. The sun is shining on the image of Mary*

(*The* STRANGER *enters from the back; he is clad in coarse black monk's garb with a rope around his waist and has sandals on his feet. He stops in the doorway and observes the room. Then he goes up to the crucifix and stops in front of it. The last stanza of a hymn can be heard from the other side of the yard.*)

CONFESSOR (*enters at the back; he is clad in black and white, has long hair and beard and a very slight tonsure that is hardly noticeable*): Peace be with you!———

STRANGER: And with you!

CONFESSOR: What do you think of the white house?

STRANGER: I see only black still . . .

CONFESSOR: You still are black, but you shall become white, very white!—Did you sleep peacefully last night?

STRANGER: Like a weary child without dreams . . . But tell me: why do I run into so many closed doors?

CONFESSOR: You'll learn to open them as time goes on.

STRANGER: It's a big building, isn't it?

CONFESSOR: It's endless: going back to the days of Charlemagne,[39] it has grown undisturbed with the help of pious foundations and untouched by the spiritual storms and changes of the various ages, it stands on its rock as a monument to western culture, that's to say: Christian faith with knowledge from Greece and Rome.

STRANGER: Not only religion then?

CONFESSOR: All the sciences and all the fine arts as well; libraries and museums, observatories and laboratories———that you'll get to see later on. They farm and run orchards here, too, and the cloister owns a hospital for laymen by our own sulphur springs . . .

STRANGER: A word before the chapter comes!—Who is the prior?

CONFESSOR (*smiles*): He's the prior!———Unique, without an equal, at the peak of human knowledge, and . . . well, you'll soon see him!

STRANGER: Is it true he's very old?

CONFESSOR: He has reached an unusually great age . . . he was born at the beginning of this century, the century that's about to end . . .[40]

STRANGER: And hasn't always been a monk?

CONFESSOR: Not always a monk, but always a member of the spiritual estate . . . He was a cabinet minister once, that was seventy years ago; a university chancellor twice, archbishop . . . sh-h, mass is over!

STRANGER: He surely isn't one of those unprejudiced priests who pretend to have vices they don't have?

CONFESSOR: Not at all! But he has seen life and people and is more human than priestly . . .

STRANGER: And the monks, the fathers?

CONFESSOR: Wise men, unusual destinies, the one not like the other . . .

STRANGER: Who have never lived life . . .

CONFESSOR: All of them have, several times over, have suffered shipwrecks, begun again, gone to the bottom, come up again . . . Just wait!

STRANGER: It's the prior who's to question me though . . . Don't think I intend to agree to everything . . .

CONFESSOR: On the contrary: be what you are and defend your ideas all the way!

STRANGER: They put up with contradictions here then?

CONFESSOR: Here? . . . You're a child who has been living in a childish world in which you've played with thoughts and words; and you've lived in the mistaken notion that language, something as material as that, could be a garment for anything as subtle as feelings and thoughts. We who have discovered the mistaken notion, we speak as little as possible, for we sense and see each other's innermost being; through "spiritual exercises" we have built our sensing so that we form a single chain and experience a feeling of pleasure and harmony when complete agreement takes place. The prior, who has trained himself longest, can sense when anyone's thoughts go astray; he resembles—note resembles, in a certain way, the telegraph engineer's galvanometer, which tells when and where breaks in the line occur. That's why we can't keep any secrets from each other, don't need confession either. Remember this carefully when you stand before the prior's searching eyes!

STRANGER: Am I to be cross-examined?

CONFESSOR: Oh no! They're only some customary questions without deeper significance which precede the practical tests . . . Sh-h, now they're here! *(Withdraws to the side)*

(The PRIOR *enters from the back; he is clad completely in white with a white hood thrown back; he is a large man with long white hair and a long white beard (Zeus head); his face is pale but full without wrinkles. His eyes are large, surrounded by shadows and huge eyebrows. A quiet, majestic calm rests over his whole person. He is accompanied by twelve fathers in black and white with black hoods. All of them bow as they pass the crucifix and then go to their places.)*

PRIOR *(after having observed the* STRANGER *for a while)*: What do you seek here?

(The STRANGER *confused, seeks an answer but does not come up with one.)*

PRIOR *(gently, with superiority, indulgently):* Peace! Isn't that right?

(The STRANGER *moves his head and mouth in agreement.)*

PRIOR: But when all life is struggle, how do you want to find peace among the living?

(The STRANGER *is unable to answer.)*

PRIOR: You want to turn your back on life since you felt deceived by it, perhaps unjustly treated?

STRANGER *(in a weak voice):* Yes!

PRIOR: Mistreated, unjustly treated! And these injustices began so early in your childhood that you as an innocent child couldn't imagine your having committed any sin that you deserved to be punished for! Oh well, you were once unjustly accused of stealing some fruit, tortured into admitting you had stolen it, forced to lie and to beg for forgiveness for a sin you hadn't committed. Is that right?

STRANGER *(firmly):* That's how it was!

PRIOR: Yes, that's how it was, and you've never been able to forget it! Never! . . . Listen to this—you who have such a good memory—do you remember *Swiss Family Robinson?*[41]

STRANGER *(collapsing): Swiss Family . . . Robinson?*

PRIOR: Yes! The date of your story of torture is 1857, but during

Christmas in 1856, a year earlier, you had torn a copy of *Swiss Family Robinson* to pieces and in fear of punishment you hid it under a cabinet in the kitchen . . .

(*The* STRANGER *is amazed and crushed.*)

PRIOR: The cabinet was painted as if it were oak, and clothes were hanging in the upper part, and there were shoes in the lower. It seemed extremely large to you, for you were a little child, and you couldn't imagine it could be disturbed . . . But the cabinet could be, and during the housecleaning for Easter what was hidden saw the light of day! Fear made you blame a friend; and he had to go through torture, for appearance was against him, and you had a reputation for being trustworthy . . . It was *after* that event that your torture came as a logical consequence. Do you admit the logic of it?

STRANGER: Yes! Punish me!

PRIOR: No, I'm no punisher, and as a child I myself . . . committed something like that . . . But will you now promise to forget your own story of torture and never tell it again?

STRANGER: I promise! If only the victim of that injustice could forgive me!

PRIOR: He already has! Isn't that right, Father Isidor?

FATHER ISIDORE (*the* DOCTOR *from the Damascus plays gets up*): With all my heart!

STRANGER: You're he?

ISIDOR: Yes!

PRIOR (*to* FATHER ISIDOR): Father Isidor, say one more word, just one!

ISIDOR: Fine! It was in 1856 I was tortured! But back in 1854 . . . one of my brothers had been tortured because of my false accusation . . . (*To the* STRANGER) So we're all guilty and not one of us is innocent; and I think I know my victim didn't have a clear conscience either! *(Sits down)*

PRIOR: Let's stop going to accounts with each other and above all with Eternal Justice! . . . for we are born guilty and inherit from Adam! [42] . . . Still—(*To the* STRANGER)—you wanted to know something? Isn't that right?

STRANGER: I want to know the very meaning of life?

PRIOR: The very essence of it? So you want to know what no
one may know! Father Uriel!

(FATHER URIEL, *who is blind, gets up.*)

PRIOR (*to the* STRANGER): Look at this blind father! We call him
Uriel in memory of Uriel Acosta,[43] whom you probably know
about?

(*The* STRANGER *makes a negative gesture.*)

PRIOR: Oh-h! All young people ought to know about him! Uriel
Acosta was a Portuguese of Jewish extraction, but was brought
up as a Christian. At a relatively early age he began to look
into things . . . you understand . . . look into whether Christ
really was God with the result that he went over to the Jewish
faith. Then he began to study the Mosaic scriptures and the im-
mortality of the soul with the result that the rabbis handed him
over to the Christian priesthood to be punished. After a period
of time he returned to the synagogue and the Jewish faith. But
his great desire for knowledge had no bounds and he kept up
his research until he stood before the silent nothingness, and
in despair over not having been allowed to know the essential
secret he took his life by means of a pistol . . . But here is
our good Father Uriel . . . At one time he was very young
and wanted to know; he always wanted to be at the head of
modern movements, and discovered new ways of looking at the
universe. By the way, he was my friend when I was young and
is almost as old as I . . . Oh well, about 1820 he began to
discover the so-called philosophy of the enlightenment,[44] which
had been buried twenty years before. By means of that philosophy, which was a universal skeleton key, one could open all
locks, solve all questions, and destroy all opponents. Everything
was very clear and very simple. He was then a dedicated opponent
of all religion and persecuted above all the mesmerists as the
hypnotists of that time were called. In 1830 our friend Uriel
became a Hegelian,[45] a little late to be sure, and now he got
God back, but God in nature and in man, and he discovered
he himself was a little god. But the bad luck was that there
were two Hegels just as there are two Voltaires; and the later

or rightest Hegel had evolved his pantheism into a compromise with Christianity, and so Father Uriel who never wanted to be behind a rationalistic Christian, got the thankless task of fighting against rationalism and himself. I'll cut the whole painful story short for Father Uriel's sake. In 1850 he became a materialist and an enemy of Christianity again. In 1870 he became a hypnotist, in 1880 a theosophist, and in 1890 he considered shooting himself! That was when I ran into him. He was sitting on a bench along Unter den Linden [46] and was blind. This Uriel was blind . . . Uriel means "God is my light" . . . Uriel who has gone in the vanguard of *all* modern movements for a century carrying the torch of enlightenment! (*To the* STRANGER) You see, he wanted to know, but wasn't allowed to! And that's why he now *believes!* . . . Is there anything else you want to know?

STRANGER: I want to put just one question!

PRIOR: Ask it!

STRANGER: If Father Uriel had kept his first faith from 1810, people would have called him conservative and old-fashioned, and now when he has kept up with developments in his time and consequently had given up the faith of his youth, people would say he was a traitor to the cause; that's to say, no matter how he would have behaved people would have criticized him.

PRIOR: Do you care about what people say? . . . Father Clemens, may I tell about you, how you cared about what people said?

(FATHER CLEMENS *gets up and nods permission.*)

PRIOR: Father Clemens is our greatest portrait painter . . . In the outside world he has another name, a very famous one! Well then: Father Clemens was young in 1830. He had talent for painting and devoted himself to it with his whole soul. At twenty he exhibited. The public, the critics, his teachers, and his parents agreed he had been mistaken about his calling; and young Clemens cared about what people said; so he gave up painting and went into business. He became a publisher. When he was fifty and life was behind him, an unknown person discovered the paintings of his youth; and now they were pronounced masterpieces by the public, the critics, the teachers, and his relatives. But it was too late. And when Father Clemens complained about the world's evil, the world answered with a heartless grin: "Why did you let yourself be fooled?" This disturbed Father Clemens so much that he came here to us. And now he isn't disturbed any more! Isn't that right, Father Clemens?

CLEMENS: Yes! But the story isn't finished yet. My paintings from 1830 were admired in a museum until 1880. Then taste changed suddenly, and one day a respected newspaper said my paintings were a disgrace to the museum. So they were put up in the attic!

PRIOR (*to the* STRANGER): That's a good story, isn't it?

CLEMENS: But it isn't finished yet! In 1890 taste had changed so that a professor in the Academy of Art wrote it was a disgrace for the nation that my masterpieces were hanging in the attic. So the paintings were brought down again and right now are considered classic. But for how long? . . . There, young man, you see what worldly honor amounts to! *Vanitas vanitatum vanitas!*

STRANGER: Is it worth living then?

PRIOR: Ask Father Melchior, who has been tested not only in the world of illusions but in that of mistakes, falsehoods, and contradictions. Go with him, he'll show you the art gallery and tell you stories!

STRANGER: I'll gladly go with anyone who can teach me something!

(FATHER MELCHIOR *leads the* STRANGER *by the hand out of the room.*)

[CURTAIN]

[SCENE 8]

An art gallery in the cloister; mainly portraits, all of them with two heads.

MELCHIOR: So: First of all, a little landscape painting by an unknown master . . . with the title The Two Towers. You've probably traveled in Switzerland and seen the originals?

STRANGER: I have traveled in Switzerland!

MELCHIOR: Well then! At the station Amsteg on the Gothard Line you've seen a tower called Zwing-Uri; Schiller celebrated it in *Wilhelm Tell.*[47] It stands there as a memorial to the horrible oppression of the people of Uri under the German emperors! Nice!

On the other side of St. Gothard toward Italy lies the station Bellinzona as you know. There are many towers there, but the most noteworthy is Castel d'Uri. That is a memorial to the horrible oppression of the Italian cantons under the people of Uri! Do you follow?

STRANGER: Freedom! The same as the freedom to oppress others! That's my latest discovery!

MELCHIOR: Then we'll go to the portrait gallery without further ado!

Number 1 in the catalog: Boccaccio [48] with two heads—all our portraits have two heads at least. His story is known! The great man began his career with pornographic godless stories dedicated to Queen Johanna of Naples, who seduced St. Birgitta's son. Boccaccio ended up as a monk in a cloister and had to lecture about Dante's hell and its devils, whom he had thought in his youth he could drive out in an extremely peculiar fashion!

You're surely noting how the two faces observe each other in confrontation.

STRANGER: Yes! But I miss the trace of humor I'd expect in a person who knew himself as well as Boccaccio!

MELCHIOR: Number 2 in the catalog: Well, that's the two-headed Dr. Luther.[49] The young champion of tolerance and the old champion of intolerance! Is that enough!

STRANGER: Quite enough!

MELCHIOR: Number 3 in the catalog: The great Gustav Adolf [50] receiving Cardinal Richelieu's Catholic money on behalf of Protestantism with the provision for the Catholic League's neutrality!

STRANGER: How do the Protestants explain this threefold contradiction?

MELCHIOR: They say it's a lie! . . . Number 4 in the catalog: Schiller, the author of *Die Räuber,* made an honorary citizen of Paris by the men of the French Revolution in 1792, but earlier than that—in 1790—a court councillor in Meiningen and the holder of a royal Danish fellowship in 1791. The picture presents the royal councillor—and His Excellency Goethe's friend—when he finally in 1798 actually received the French revolutionaries' diploma of honor. Imagine: the diploma from the reign of terror in 1798 during the Directory, when the revolution was over! I'd like to have seen the royal councillor and his friend His Excellency [Goethe] then! But that doesn't matter, for two years later in 1800 he paid for the honor by writing *Die Glocke,* in which he thanks for the honor and asks the revolutionists to take it easy.

Well, that's life! But it doesn't matter; we're enlightened human beings and love both *Die Räuber* and *Die Glocke,* both Schiller and Goethe!

STRANGER: The work endures, the master perishes!

MELCHIOR: Talking about Goethe! [51] Number 5 in the catalog. Began with *The Cathedral of Strassburg* and *Götz von Berlichingen,* two outcries for Gothic Germanic art against Greece and Rome. Fought the later part of his life against Germanism and championed Classicism. Goethe against Goethe! Note the traditional godlike, calm, harmonious, etc. person in the greatest disharmony with himself. But his distress becomes depression when the young romantic school pops up and with Goethe's *Götz von Berlichingen* theories attacks *Iphigenia's* Goethe. That "the great pagan" ends up by converting Faust in Part II and has him saved by the Virgin Mary and angels—that's generally disregarded by his admirers.

In the same way the fact the "crystal-clear" author toward the end began to find everything very "wonderful," very "exceptional," even the simplest matters he had seen through before. His last wish was to get more light on matters! Well,—well!

But it doesn't matter! We're enlightened and we still like our Goethe!

STRANGER: And rightly so!

MELCHIOR: Number 6 in the catalog: Voltaire! [52] That one has more than two heads! . . . The godless man who uses his whole life to defend God! The mocker who was mocked because he "believed in God as a child." The author of the cynical *Candide* who wrote:

"Sensual Joy, in my youthful lust
I sought your subtle pleasures;
soon amazed by your emptiness,
your sweetness turned to bitterness,
in the winter of my days,
I have discovered you are vanity."

Dr. Allknowing, who thought he had grasped everything between
heaven and earth through his reason and science, wrote like this
when he was writing his last verses:

"Led astray, pride in my genius
wandered through the realms of knowledge;
blind as a mole, I dared to question
the boundlessness of the heavens!—
What I know is my torture:
knowledge is vanity."

But that doesn't matter! Voltaire can be used for a lot; the Jews
use him against Christ, and the Christians use him against the
Jews because he was anti-Semitic—as Luther was! Chateaubriand [53] has used him for Catholicism and the Protestants use
him even today against Catholicism! Quite a man!

STRANGER: What is your opinion?

MELCHIOR: We don't have opinions here; we have faith as I said!
That's why we have only one head each and it sits right above
the heart! . . . However, number 7 in the catalog: Well, that's
Napoleon! . . .[54] The Revolution's own creature! The emperor
of the people, the Nero of liberty, the oppressor of Equality
and the "big brother" of Brotherhood. But he was the shrewdest
of all the two-headed people, because he could laugh at himself,
rise above his disharmonies, change skin, and in every change
be himself, a new incarnation, convinced, self-justified!

There's only one person who can be compared with him in
that way: that's the Dane Kierkegaard.[55] From the beginning
he was conscious of this parthenogenesis of the soul or its ability
in this existence to bear without procreating, to sprout offshoots.
For that reason and in order not to be fooled by life, he wrote
under a series of pseudonyms, each and every one representing
a stage on the pathway through life. But can you imagine? In

spite of all his efforts to be careful, the Lord of Life made him
a fool. Kierkegaard, who had fought against the pastors' control
of the state church and its self-serving preachers *had to* become
a self-serving preacher at last!
Yes, yes! That's how it can go!
STRANGER: The Powers are jesting with jest . . .
MELCHIOR: The Powers are playing in jest with jesters, and having
fun with the proud, especially with those who insist they alone
have the truth and the knowledge! . . .
Number 8 in the catalog: Victor Hugo.[56] Split himself end-
lessly. A peer of France, a grandee of Spain, a friend of kings,
the socialist author of *Les Miserables.* The peers naturally call him
a renegade and the Socialists, a reformer.
Number 9: Count Friedrich Leopold von Stolberg.[57] Wrote
a fanatical book for Protestantism, and immediately afterwards
was converted to Catholicism! . . . Can't be explained by a sane
person! A miracle, eh? A little journey to Damascus perhaps?
Number 10: La Fayette.[58] The hero of liberty, the revolutionary. Had to leave France as a recognized reactionary because
he wanted to help Louis XVI; was seized by the Austrians and
imprisoned in Ölmütz as a revolutionary! Which was he? . . .
STRANGER: Both the one and the other!
MELCHIOR: Ta! Both which make a whole, a whole man!
Number 11: Bismarck.[59] The paradox! The honest diplomat,
who said he had discovered speaking the truth was the biggest
trick. Was forced—by the Powers, eh?—to use the last six years
of his life to expose himself as a deliberate liar . . . You are
tired! We'll stop now!
STRANGER: Yes, my friend, if one has the same thoughts, keeps
the same views throughout life, one naturally becomes dated,
is called a conservative, old-fashioned, static; and if one follows
the law of development, one keeps up with one's time, renews
oneself through the always young impulses of the spirit of the
time, is called a vacillator and a renegade.
MELCHIOR: That's as old as the world! But does a sensible man
care about what he's called? What a person is, is becoming,
he is!

STRANGER: Who then revises the periodic, view-changing spirit of the time?

MELCHIOR: You should really answer that yourself and do it like this. The developing Powers promulgate the spirit of the time in *seeming* circles! . . . Hegel, the philosopher of his time, a dimorph, because they swear in the name of a Leftist Hegel and a Rightist Hegel, has solved the contradictions of life, history, and spirit best with his magic formula: thesis, affirmation; antithesis, denial; synthesis, summation! . . . Young man, relatively young man! You began life by affirming everything; then you denied everything by principle. Finish by summing up! So: Don't be exclusive any longer! Don't say: Either—or —but: Both— and! In a word or two: Humanity! and Resignation!

[CURTAIN]

[SCENE 9]

In the sanctuary of the chapel. An open coffin (with a bier-covering and two lighted candles) is standing there.

CONFESSOR (*enters leading the* STRANGER *by the hand. The* STRANGER *is dressed in white as a novice*): So you have considered carefully the step you intend to take?

STRANGER: Carefully!

CONFESSOR: You haven't anything more to ask?

STRANGER: Ask questions? No!

CONFESSOR: Stay here then while I fetch the chapter, the fathers and brothers, and the ceremony will begin.

STRANGER: Fine! Go ahead!

(*The* CONFESSOR *goes.*)

(*The* STRANGER, *alone, meditates.*)

TEMPTER (*comes forward*): Ready?

STRANGER: So ready I haven't an answer left, for you.

TEMPTER: At the edge of the grave, I see; you're to lie in that coffin and pretend to die; the old human being will get three shovels of dust and they'll sing *De Profundis*.[60] Then you'll rise

from the dead, have given up your old name, and then you'll
be baptized again like a little child!—What's your name going
to be?

(*The* STRANGER *does not answer.*)

TEMPTER: It's written there: John; Brother John, because he
preached in the wilderness and . . .

STRANGER: Don't disturb me!

TEMPTER: Talk a little with me before you go into the long silence;
why, you'll not be allowed to speak for a whole year!

STRANGER: All the better! Talking finally became a vice like drinking, and why talk when the words don't cover the thought?

TEMPTER: Now that you're at the edge of the grave, was life so
bitter?

STRANGER: Yes, *my* life!

TEMPTER: You never had any joy?

STRANGER: Yes, a lot of joy, but so fleeting, it seemed to exist
only to make the sorrow of missing it deeper.

TEMPTER: Can't you say in reverse: Sorrow existed to emphasize
joy!

STRANGER: One can say anything . . . *(A woman with a child ready
for christening crosses the stage).*

TEMPTER: A little mortal's story beginning . . .

STRANGER: Poor child!

TEMPTER *(A bridal couple crosses the stage):* And there . . . the most
delightful—the—most bitter! Adam and Eve in Paradise, which
in eight days will be a hell, and in fourteen days a paradise
again . . .

STRANGER: The most delightful! The most delightful! The first,
the only, the last, that which gave life worth; even I once sat
in the direct sunlight—one spring day on a porch—under the
first tree to burst into leaf, and a little crown on her head, and
a white veil lay like a light morning mist over a face that was
not human . . . Then the darkness came!

TEMPTER: From where?

STRANGER: From the light itself! . . . If it didn't, I don't know!

TEMPTER: It was only a shadow I suspect, for to have a shadow
there has to be light, but for darkness no light is needed!

STRANGER: Stop! Or there'll never be an end!
(*The* CONFESSOR *and the* CHAPTER *enter in procession.*)
TEMPTER *(disappears):* Farewell!
CONFESSOR *(with a large black bier covering):* The Lord grant him
  eternal rest!
CHORUS: May eternal light shine upon him!
CONFESSOR (*covers the* STRANGER *with the bier-covering*): May he
  rest in peace!
CHORUS: Amen!

[CURTAIN]

Notes on

'To Damascus, III'

1. Martin Luther's question in his *Catechism,* "Can we so keep the commandments of God as to become righteous before Him?" is followed by the answer, "No, our inherited sinfulness cannot be entirely overcome, and for this reason we sin in many ways." St. Paul says much the same, for example, in Romans 3:20: "Therefore by the deeds of the law there shall no flesh be justified in His sight" and in 3:23: "For all have sinned, and come short of the glory of God."

2. Corpus Christi (the Body of Christ) is the festival in honor of the Eucharist (the sacrament of the Lord's Supper or communion).

3. David, the brilliant king who succeeded in uniting the twelve tribes of Israel into one strong kingdom, was the author of the psalms, the hero of his people, and a thoroughly human being with flaws and imperfections, including family difficulties. See the Old Testament for detailed information about him.

4. See Genesis 3 ff. for the initial biblical references to the serpent that corrupted Eve and that serves as a symbol of wickedness, cruelty, and treachery. Satan or Lucifer is often called "the old serpent."

5. It is conceivable that such attacks as John Wilhelm Personne's *Strindbergs-litteraturen och osedligheten bland skolungdomen* (1897), (The Strindberg Literature and Immorality among Schoolboys and Schoolgirls) may have convinced Strindberg that he had corrupted young people through his writings of the 1870s and 1880s, particularly, of course, *Giftas* (1884, 1886). See, for example, the first story, "Asra" or "The Reward for Virtue," in the first volume, which deals quite frankly with the sexual problems of the young. The scene suggests treatment given victims of sexual disease in Strindberg's day.

6. The name of Venus, goddess of love, is reflected in *venery,* sexual love, and venereal disease, disease resulting directly or indirectly from sexual intercourse. Mercury in various forms was used in the treatment of venereal disease as a powerful disinfectant.

238

7. Aphrodite Urania-Venus "sprung from the foam of the sea" is the Venus of the highways when she becomes promiscuous. See any good volume on Greek mythology for further details.

8. See Shakespeare's *The Tempest.* Ariel is the charming spiritual being, while Caliban is the deformed savage, half-human and half-beast.

9. Ecclesiastes 7:26.

10. Ecclesiastes 8:16–17.

11. Proverbs 10:3.

12. Genesis 21:10.

13. Genesis 16:12.

14. Dogs terrified Strindberg.

15. See note 5.

16. St. George (Swedish Göran or Örjan) is generally portrayed as struggling with a dragon in order to rescue a princess. Bernt Notke's fifteenth-century statue of St. George and the dragon in the Great Church (or cathedral) of Stockholm is the most famous of Swedish representations of the saint whose struggle symbolizes the Christian's struggle against sin (evil). The devil has often been labeled a dragon.

17. See note 44, p. 93.

18. Dr. Faust (Johan or Georg Faust, ca. 1490-ca.1539) was the German practitioner of black magic whose adventures and miraculous cures became the initial matters of the legend of Faustus or Dr. Faust who sold his soul to the devil in order to have all his wishes granted. See Marlowe's and Goethe's plays for the most important literary treatments of the legend.

19. Strindberg's term is *amtmannen,* a title that has no American equivalent. Since the holder of the title has judicial as well as administrative roles and is acting here as judge, that title seems appropriate in the translation.

20. See Genesis 29–35 for the account of Rachel, the daughter of Laban for whom Jacob served for fourteen years before Laban would consent to her marriage to Jacob.

21. The Argives were natives of the Greek state of Argolis and its capital of Argos and is often used for Greeks in general. The implication here is that the citizens are sceptics who need persuasion through argument and evidence.

22. See Genesis 37:36, 39, and 40 for the account of Joseph's refusal to be seduced by his master's wife.

23. Hercules, *the* strong man in Greek mythology, as punishment for his stupid slaying of a friend was made a slave to Queen Omphale of Lydia, who humiliated him by having him dress as a woman and do woman's

work, particularly spinning and weaving. Strindberg was fond of the legend and used it most effectively in *The Father* (1887).

24. See Genesis 3.

25. The statue of *The Sharpener* or *The Slave* is in the Uffizi Gallery in Florence and represents an ugly, cruel-faced Scythian slave crouching as he sharpens a knife possibly to help slay Marsyas, the satyr who lost the flute-playing contest to Apollo.

26. Zeus Chronos or Jupiter (Latin Saturn), the chief god in Greek mythology.

27. See Joshua 8:30,33.

28. See Genesis 3:16–19.

29. Deuteronomy 28:3–13.

30. See Genesis 16 and 21 for the account of Hagar, Sarah's Egyptian bondswoman, who became the mother of Ishmael by Sarah's husband Abraham and who was driven into exile.

31. The riddle proposed by the Sphinx of Thebes in Greece to every passerby: What creature walks in the morning upon four feet, at noon upon two, at evening upon three? Oedipus' answer: Man. See Genesis for information about the Garden of Eden, the Hebraic-Christian paradise, and any book on Greek mythology for information about Olympus, the Macedonian mountain on which the Greek gods supposedly lived.

32. Psalm 34:21, for example.

33. Dante Alighiere (1265–1321), the Italian who wrote, among other things, *The Divine Comedy,* devoted a great part of his autobiographical work, *Vita nuova* to Beatrice Portinari (dead, 1290), his "ideal" woman, but *not* his wife. Beatrice and Dante are pictured as finally meeting at the top of Mt. Purgatory from where she guides him through Paradise to the ultimate revelation of divinity.

34. Strindberg's favorite composer, the German Ludwig von Beethoven (1770–1827), was betrothed to Theresa von Brunswick (d., 1861) in May 1806, but, for reasons not known for certain, they never married even though they continued to love each other as "her ideal man" and "his good angel."

35. When Orpheus, the greatest and most irresistable of human musicians, lost Eurydice, the woman he loved shortly after they were married, he went to the abode of the dead to bring her back. The gods permitted him to conduct her back provided he would not look back at her until they had reached the land of the living. Unfortunately, he could not resist his desire to look at her.

36. Othello is, of course, the central character in Shakespeare's *Othello*

who kills his wife Desdemona because of jealousy; Nero (37–68 A.D.), a power-mad profligate Roman emperor; and Harpagon, the repulsive miser in Molière's *L'Avare* (1668, *The Miser*).

37. Strindberg's use of Minerva's miraculous birth (she sprang "full grown and in full armor" from her father Zeus' head and had no mother) is one of many indications that he had been influenced by the teaching of his day that the body is evil and sex and reproduction animalistic and filthy.

38. Genesis 3:16: "Unto the woman he said, I will greatly multiply thy sorrow and thy conception; in sorrow thou shalt bring forth children . . ."

39. Charles the Great, king of the Franks (768–814) and emperor of the West (800–814).

40. The Damascus trilogy deals primarily with matters personal to Strindberg up to the turn of the century, primarily, of course, with his life before (1849–84) and during (1894–97) the Inferno crisis.

41. Johann Rudolf Wyss' *Der Schweizerische Robinson* (1813) was translated into English as *The Swiss Family Robinson* and into Swedish as *Den Schweiziske Robinson.*

42. Exodus 20:5: "I the Lord thy God *am* a jealous God, visiting the iniquity of the fathers upon the children unto the third and fourth *generation* of them that hate me . . ."

43. Gabriel Acosta (also called Uriel da Costa, ca. 1591 ca. 1647) was, as Strindberg says, a Portuguese Jew who changed faith from time to time.

44. The eighteenth century or the age of rationalism or enlightenment, during which the human power to reason was considered by many, as Strindberg says, "a universal skeleton key."

45. Georg Wilhelm Friedrich Hegel (1710–1831), the German philosopher.

46. Probably in Strindberg's day the best known street in Berlin.

47. Johann Christoph Friedrich von Schiller (1759–1805) was the German dramatist who in 1781 wrote the sentimental tragedy *Die Raüber,* a play about Karl Moor, a romantic rebel. Schiller's *Wilhelm Tell* (1804) glorifies the Swiss as liberty-loving opponents of oppression and presents the Swiss hero Tell as perfect in contrast to the evil Austrian tyrant Gessler.

48. Giovanni Boccaccio (1313–75) wrote the superb *Decameron,* which was published in 1353 and portions of which many have considered pornographic. At the royal court of Naples he met Maria, an illegitimate daughter of King Robert and the woman he has glorified in his writings as Fiammetta.

Birgitta, the Swedish founder of the Birgittine Order and canonized in 1391, was in Italy from 1349 on in company with her sons Birger and Carl and her daughter Katarina. In 1371 they visited Naples, where Queen Johanna I, according to one of Strindberg's favorite sources Starbäck's *Berättelser ur svenska historien* (I, 674 ff.), was smitten by Carl's physical and courtly charms. In his later years Boccaccio devoted his time to scholarly activities including the interpretation of Dante's *Divine Comedy* in a number of lectures as the first holder of the Dante professorship in Florence.

49. Martin Luther (1483–1546) did indeed start out his career as a reformer and as a champion of tolerance and did give significant indications of increasing conservatism toward the end of his life. See any of the numerous biographies.

50. See Strindberg's drama *Gustaf Adolf* (1900; my translation, 1957). In return for the "Catholic" subsidy from Cardinal Richelieu Gustaf Adolf did promise to observe neutrality toward the Catholic League and the elector of Bavaria so long as neither made any hostile move against him.

51. For an account of the changes in the thinking of Johann Wolfgang von Goethe (1749–1832), see any biography. Strindberg's nutshell summary is decidedly accurate: *Götz von Berlichingen* (1773) does express enthusiasm about liberty, Germanic culture, and Gothicism in general; "Über altdeutsche Baukunst" (1772) is a tribute to the builder of Strassburg's (Gothic) cathedral; *Iphigenie in Tauris* (1787) marks Goethe's turning to antiquity as the ideal in thought and form. Goethe paid tribute to Schiller in his *Epilog zu Schillers Glocke* (1805). Schiller's "Das Lied von der Glocke" (1799) has been called "a reflective lyric of wonderful beauty of form" and "a powerful series of typical scenes from life."

52. François Marie de Voltaire (1694–1778) did indeed change his thinking about deity, human beings and the world from time to time. His *Candide* (1759) satirizes Leibnitzian optimism ("This is the best possible of worlds") and recommends a philosophy of work and resignation. The two stanzas quoted by Strindberg are from the Swedish poet Johan Henrik Kellgren's "Mänskliga livet" (Human life), which is a translation of Voltaire's "Précis de l'Ecclésiaste."

53. François René de Chateaubriand (1768–1848), a French romantic.

54. See any account of Napoleon Bonaparte's remarkable ability to readjust and change his views.

55. Søren Kierkegaard (1813–55), the Danish philosopher, used such pseudonyms as Victor Eremita, Johannes, and Cordelia in considering the stages of human development (the esthetic, the ethical, and the religious). See Elias Bredsdorff's *Danish Literature in English Translation* (Copenhagen,

1950) for bibliographical information about Kierkegaard's *Either-Or* (1843), *Stages on Life's Way* (1845) and many other works.

56. Victor Hugo (1802–85), the French novelist and poet, was born a nobleman's son, was made a peer in 1845, was honored in Spain, associated with members of royalty, and wrote, for example, *Les Misérables* (1862), a novel in ten volumes narrating the lives of social unfortunates.

57. Count Friedrich Leopold Stolberg (1750–1819), poet and diplomat, was converted to Catholicism in 1800; he was the author of *Geschichte der Religion Jesu Christi* (1807–18).

58. In addition to what Strindberg says about Marquis de La Fayette (1757–1834), one should recall that he served in the American Revolution and was a friend of George Washington. He was imprisoned by the Austrians (1792–97).

59. Prince Otto Eduard Leopold von Bismarck (1815–98), the first chancellor of the German Empire. His *Gedanken und Erinnerungen* (1898) suggests what Strindberg applies.

60. Psalm 130: "Out of the depths have I cried unto thee, O Lord."

The Plays
as a Trilogy

THE DETAILED DIAGRAM shown on the following page may
be as effective a way as any to grasp Strindberg's broad linking
of the three plays and to permit one to discern their unity as a
trilogy. While the trilogy concerns a man who is a stranger even
to himself and who suffers the agony of disappointment and suffering
while struggling to come to terms with himself, his fellow human
beings, and with whatever higher powers there may be, it has a
timeless and universal application as well. That is, one may say
that the Stranger serves as a highly sensitive representative of human
beings, each of whom has his own Damascus experience, perceived
or not.

Strindberg's achievement in the Damascus trilogy is surely two-
fold: structural and substantial. He put it very happily in his brief
prefatory note to *A Dream Play*, part of which reads:

> In this dream play as in his earlier dream plays *To Damascus*, the
> author has tried to imitate the disconnected but apparently logical
> form of a dream. Everything can happen; everything is possible and
> likely. Time and space do not exist; on an insignificant basis of reality
> the imagination spins and weaves new patterns: a blending of memo-
> ries, experiences, free inventions, absurdities, and improvisations.

The "dream" experience that Strindberg has primarily exploited
in the trilogy stems, of course, directly from setting his imagination
free to play with his actual experiences as he "saw" them and with
his speculations about what had been, was, and might be. In other
words, Strindberg is not dealing primarily with the appearance of
actuality but with what he considered the most serious of all reality—

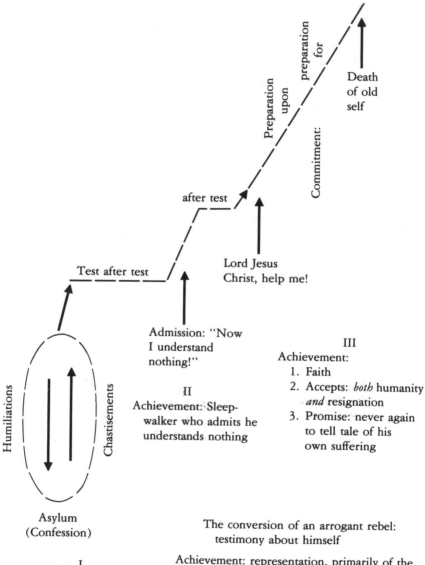

Preparation for

Preparation upon

Death
of old
self

Commitment:

after test

Preparation

Lord Jesus
Christ, help me!

Test after test

Admission: "Now
I understand
nothing!"

III
Achievement:
1. Faith
2. Accepts: *both* humanity *and* resignation
3. Promise: never again to tell tale of his own suffering

Humiliations

Chastisements

II
Achievement: Sleep-
walker who admits he
understands nothing

Asylum
(Confession)

The conversion of an arrogant rebel:
testimony about himself

I
Achievement: admits
1. He is a sinner
2. There are higher powers

Achievement: representation, primarily of the
inner life, secondarily of outer appearance of
reality

the inner reality. In so doing, he made an extremely important artistic contribution to the theater and the drama: he succeeded in representing on the stage the core of the human condition or, if you will, the matter that lyric poets had dealt with through the centuries.

Further clarification of his achievement can be gained through a comparison between a pre-Inferno play and the Damascus trilogy. Strindberg had written *The Father* (1887), for example, during a period dominated, among the intellectuals at least, by a naturalistic view of the world and man, a view that in Darwinian terms conceived of earth (Man's world) as a tiny part of the Universe, of man as the evolving product of natural forces rather than as a being created in the image of God, and of the God of Christian belief as probably nonexistant. Strindberg tried desperately during the 1880s to accept the naturalistic point of view: significantly, Captain Adolf (*the* father) is a scientist who believes only in the evidence presented to him by his senses and does not believe in the tenets of revealed religion. The Stranger in the Damascus trilogy, on the other hand, is driven to an acceptance of Christ, rejection of pride in his own individuality and personal abilities, and the conviction that supernatural powers control the destinies of human beings. The striking contrast is that between a materialistic world in which the individual can and should find self-expression in this life and a moral world in which the ideal is blind faith in the Eternal One and the Powers, self-control approaching a Christlike self-negation, and acceptance of the ideas that life on Earth is a Swedenborgian Hell (half-dream, half-reality) and that life after death is the *real* life.

Naturalism and realism had as their goal the presentation of observable actions and the presentation of an environment without visions; that is, they claimed the theoretical objectivity of the scientific or sociological case report. In his dream plays, Strindberg relied frankly on the subjectivity of his inner experiences, namely, his feelings and instincts and his inner moods (pressures on the ego such as anxiety, despair, bewilderment, disharmony). In his plays of the late 1880s key words are *the senses* and *the human mind;* in the dream plays key words are *the spirit* and *the soul.* What Strindberg was attempting in the Damascus plays was the revelation of the working of hidden forces within himself in their intricate and inseparable connections with external events in visible form. He was attempting then, as he thought, to give a truer and more accurate representation of life than naturalism-realism had done by synthesizing his own experience subjectively rather than analyzing it objectively. But Strindberg, who called himself a naturalistic occultist, never lost contact with outer reality, hence the wealth of realistic detail.

Both the substance and the structure of the Damascus plays reflect Strindberg's renewed interest in the Middle Ages, times supposedly of faith in an omnipotent, omnipresent, omniscient deity and His host of supporting powers. Just as *Everyman* and other medieval plays present life as a pilgrimage, the first Damascus play specifically and the trilogy as a whole are a dramatization of just that through the use of various dream experiences, primarily the free flight of the imagination and the speculative choice of material and its arrangement. The plays are *not* a naturalistic or realistic case report but an imaginative account of a religious or spiritual conversion. As Strindberg himself has more than suggested, the action takes place primarily within the Stranger's mind and imagination.

There is then obviously subjectivity rather than objectivity, emphasis on the violent inner conflicts that result from external as well as inner pressures on the individual, and almost constant shifts between such matters as defiance and humility, love of life and anguish about life, and doubt and faith. All of this happens to a human rebel who is a stranger to himself and whose entire external world seems to be crumbling. Captain Adolf in *The Father* may suffer as much as the Stranger, but the captain does believe that the individual can bring some order out of chaos through the use by his intellect of what his senses present.

But in the Damascus plays the ordinary criteria by means of which a still functioning Captain Adolf believes he can observe outer reality are not working. While the scientist must adjust his findings by taking into account the inevitable distortions caused by the limitations of the senses, the Stranger exploits the distortions stemming from unconscious rationalization, subconscious alterations, imperfect memories, and conscious changes in order to arrive at a measure of truth about himself and his world.

In the Damascus trilogy the "characters" are not sharply defined dynamic and complex characterless characters of the kind analyzed by Strindberg in his preface to *Lady Julie* (1888) and presented in that play, *The Father, Creditors* (1888), and *The Bond* (1892). The Damascus "characters" are not Adolfs, Lauras, Teklas, or Sprengels; they are the Stranger, the Tempter, the Lady, and so on. For want of a better term, one may say that they are types, not individuals, that they are synthesized rather than analyzed, and that they are all essentially alike in their human frailties. That they "split," as Strindberg says in his prefatory note to *A Dream Play,* must be noted. Even in his pre-Inferno plays, Strindberg had presented various aspects of the human individual and had discussed that fact in terms of secondary and minor characters in the famous preface.

The Damascus plays have fascinated both theater people and laymen—theater people certainly because of the tremendous challenge involved in presenting the plays on actual stages, and readers because of the universal and timeless applications of the content. No one has yet presented the plays in sequence on three evenings, but the great director Olof Molander did telescope the three parts into a memorable three and one half hour production in 1965. Usually, however, as Gunnar Ollén has noted in the editions of his *Strindbergs dramatik,* producers have chosen to present only one play, most often *To Damascus, I.* A production of the trilogy in telescoped form has not as yet won overwhelming critical or popular approval. Even Ingmar Bergman's highly personal production in the 1973–74 season failed to do so.

Bibliographic
and Biographic Notes

THE STANDARD SWEDISH edition of Strindberg's works is John Landquist's *Strindbergs samlade skrifter* (55 vols. Stockholm: Bonnier, 1912–20). The Damascus plays appear in volume 29.

For those who know Swedish the best bibliographies are in E. N. Tigerstedt's *Svensk litteraturhistoria* (Stockholm: Bonnier, 1948—) and in the Swedish journal *Samlaren*, which prints an annual bibliography.

For those who must rely on English sources, the basic bibliographies are: Esther H. Rapp's bibliography of Strindberg in England and America in *Scandinavian Studies* 23(1950):1–22, 49–59, 109–37; Alrik Gustafson's bibliography in his *History of Swedish Literature* (Minneapolis: University of Minnesota Press, 1961), pp. 601–10, which lists both Scandinavian and non-Scandinavian items; the annual American Scandinavian Bibliography in the May or August number of *Scandinavian Studies*, 1948 on; and the annual bibliography in *Publications of the Modern Language Association*. Since new articles, new books, and reviews of books about and productions of Strindberg plays appear frequently, it is rewarding to check these bibliographies, the annual ones regularly, and the others probably once.

Some of the Strindberg items basic to an understanding of the plays in this volume are available in English: *Inferno, Alone and Other Writings* (Anchor Books A492C; Garden City, N.Y.: Doubleday & Company, 1968); *From an Occult Diary* (New York: Hill and Wang, 1965); *Letters of Strindberg to Harriet Bosse* (New York: Thomas Nelson & Sons, 1959); and *Open Letters to the Intimate Theater* (Seattle: University of Washington Press, 1966).

Gunnar Brandell's *Strindberg in Inferno* (Cambridge: Harvard University Press, 1974), Barry Jacobs' translation of Brandell's *Strindbergs Infernokris* (Stockholm: Bonnier, 1948), is the standard study of Strindberg's experiences in the 1890s which affected all his literary works after 1897 and contains the finest Swedish interpretation of the Damascus plays. Equally important is Harry Carlson's translation of Martin Lamm's *August Strindberg* (Stockholm: Bonnier, 1948; New York: Blom, 1971). These two, supplemented by my *August Strindberg* (Boston: Twayne, 1976) will be useful.

PT
9812
T5   Strindberg, August.
E5   Plays of confession and
1979   therapy.

NORMANDALE
COMMUNITY COLLEGE
9700 France Avenue South
Bloomington, Minnesota 55431

DEMCO